The Origins and Early History of the English

Bryan Evans

Published 2019 by

Anglo-Saxon Books
www.asbooks.co.uk

Hereward, Black Bank Business Centre
Little Downham, Ely,
Cambridgeshire, England

© Bryan Evans

Design / Layout © Anglo-Saxon Books

Cover drawing Brian Partridge

PL

ISBN 978 1 898281 77 1

Other titles by Bryan Evans

The Life and Times of Hengest
Plain English: A Wealth of Words

Contents

Maps

Glossary

civitas, plural *civitates*

The *civitas* was originally the social body of the citizens, united by the law. Under the later Roman Empire the term came to be used of the largest unit of local government. In the case of Britain it was applied to the territory of a Romano-British tribe. Clearly the size of the *civitas* would depend on the size of the tribe. The leadership of a *civitas* was in the hands of a group of magistrates, supported by, and elected through, an *ordo* (council).

colonia

A *colonia* (the origin of the modern term colony) was originally a Roman outpost planted in conquered territory, to secure it. Later in Rome's history retired legionaries were given lands in a *colonia*. and the term came to signify a Roman city of the highest status.

damnatio memoriæ or 'condemnation of the memory'

The reference is to the removal from the historical records of the name of a man of notorious wickedness. This made the man an 'unperson', condemned to oblivion, even denied access to the afterlife. Pliny the Younger records the case of the emperor Domitian, assassinated, then subjected to an official *damnatio memoriæ* by the Senate. Something of the kind is seen in the cases of two short-lived Northumbrian kings, the apostates Osric of Deira and Eanfrith of Bernicia. After their early deaths it was agreed that the memory of them should be wiped from the historical record.

decuriones

The councillors who ran Roman local government. Membership of the town council was subject to property qualifications.

foedus

A treaty made by Rome with foreign states, client kingdoms, or barbarian tribes, under which Rome granted benefits such as land in exchange for military help. Those who entered into such arrangements with Rome were called *foederati* ('federates'). The term was later used of 'barbarian' mercenaries allowed to settle within the Empire.

grubenhäus

A pit-house, such as were built in many parts of northern Europe between the 5th and 12th centuries AD. In Germany such a building was called a *grubenhäus*, in Britain it was a 'sunken-featured building'. The house was built in a shallow sub-rectangular pit. Some archaeologists believe that a suspended wooden floor lay over the pit and that the space beneath was used for storage, or to control damp, but others have disputed this. These *grubenhäuser* may have been domestic dwellings, or perhaps workshops for activities such as weaving.

laeti

The word *laeti* seems to have Germanic roots, and it refers to people who were 'half free'. They were settled on empty lands within the empire, but were bound to contribute troops to the army.

Litus Saxonicum, 'The Saxon Shore'

The 'Saxon Shore' was probably so called because it was the Shore attacked by the Saxons. The Count of the Saxon Shore (a military office of the late Roman Empire) had command of a chain of fortified naval bases, sited at the mouths of rivers along the eastern and southern coasts of Britain.

Notitia Dignitatum, 'The List of Dignities (or Offices)'

The *Notitia* is a document of the late Roman Empire, setting out the administrative organisation. It lists thousands of offices from the imperial court to provincial governments, diplomatic missions, and army units. It is thought to be accurate for the Western Empire of the 420s and for the Eastern Empire for the 390s.

ordo

In Rome's local government arrangements the *ordo* was a town council.

pagus

The smallest unit of local government.

terp, plural *terpen*

As sea levels rose along the southern North Sea coast, AD 200-600, affected communities built large mounds with sods, for settlement and farming. The mounds are known as *terpen* (a German word akin to Old English 'thorp'), and they are found from the Elbe mouth in the east, as far as northern Holland in the west.

territorium

A rural area forming the hinterland of a town, and under its governance.

vicus

In Ancient Rome, the *vicus* was a neighbourhood or settlement. The word came to be used of the smallest administrative unit of a provincial town. It has also been applied to settlements that grew up haphazardly around military garrisons and state-owned mining operations.

Introduction

The poem *Widsith* is the oldest in the English language. R W Chambers thought that it was composed in Mercia in the time of king Offa (that is, the eighth-century).[1] The poem is set against the background of a journey made by Widsith, 'the wide-farer', as he accompanies the maiden Ealhhild. She is a Lombard princess, travelling 'eastward from Angel' (in modern Denmark) to the hall of Eormenric the Goth, there to become that king's bride. The geography is legendary, the chronology elastic. Some seventy tribes and their founders are named, nearly all of them from the coasts of the Baltic and North Seas. Sixty-nine heroes feature here, and many of these can be proved to have lived in the third, fourth and fifth centuries. The latest of them belong to the sixth century. The names are drawn from German heroic poetry, for at the time *Widsith* was composed there was still a deep awareness of belonging to the wider Germanic world, a world that stretched from southern Scandinavia to the Vistula and beyond.

The list begins with Attila, the feared king of the Huns who figures in a number of Germanic stories, such as *Waldere*. Next comes Eormenric, the fourth century king of the Ostrogoths, who built an empire said to have stretched from the Baltic to the Black Sea. He was remembered for his great open-handedness, rewarding Widsith, for example, with a ring that was 'six hundred shillings' worth of sheer gold', this for his escorting of Ealhhild. When Widsith reached home again he gave this ring (as the custom was) to his lord, Eadgils of the Myrgings. Ealhhild also gave Widsith a ring, one of less value, of course, but a ring he was to keep in memory of the service he had rendered her. He did keep it, and repaid her by singing the praise of her generosity, in every land where he went. Eormenric, by the way, 'the richest and most generous of tyrants'[2] was also remembered as a man of great cruelty, 'the ruthless troth-breaker' (*Widsith* line 9). In *Beowulf* he is a man of 'wily hatred', and in the poem *Deor*, he is one with a 'wolf's wit'.

The list goes on with Finn Folcwalding and Hnæf king of the Hocings, two who feature in the tale of the fight and slaughter at Finnsburg. We have Offa of Angeln, who fought single-handed against two champions, and overcame them. (We shall come back to him later.) *Widsith* refers to Hrothgar of the Danes, the king to whom the hero of the poem *Beowulf* came, when that king's great hall of Heorot was plagued, night after night, by the monster Grendel. Beowulf took on the creature and slew him. Another Hrothgar story concerns the ancient feud between his Danes and the Heathobards. Hrothgar gave his daughter, Freawaru, to Ingeld, the young leader of the Heathobards, in hope of healing the feud between their two peoples. It was not to be, the instinct for revenge was too strong (*Widsith*, lines 45-9).

---

[1] Chambers is cited in M Alexander, introduction to *The Earliest English Poems*, second edition, 1977, 32.

[2] R W Chambers, *Widsith: A study in Old English heroic legend*, 1912, 26.

Towards the end of his poem Widsith returns to the crimes of Eormenric, naming that king's murdered nephews, Emerca and Fridla. In this the king was egged on by the evil counsel of Sifeca (*Widsith* lines 113, 116). At the last Eormenric died by his own hand, despairing of holding back the Huns when they invaded his kingdom in the 370s. *Widsith* thus gives us some insights into the world-view of the Germanic peoples in their continental homeland. And it was very much the outlook of the Angles, Saxons, Jutes, Frisians, and Franks who settled in these islands in the so-called 'Dark ages'.

The winning of the English lands and, for the Britons, the loss of the same, was not something that happened over a few years, or even over one or two generations. The Conquest period lasted from roughly 350 to, say, 634. It was in the latter year that Oswald of Northumbria destroyed the great war-host of Cadwallon of Gwynedd on the battlefield of 'Denisesburn' near Hexham, and the Britons lost their last hopes of restoring their supremacy in Britain. The author of the Welsh *Brut* was moved to say: 'And from that time onwards the Britons lost the crown of the kingdom and the Saxons won it'. How did this come about? What led the Angles, Saxons and others to uproot from their old homelands and seek a new life in Britain?

'In time of "The breaking of nations" '[3]

One driver of migration from the coastal lowlands of north-west Germany was climate change, as the North Sea region became colder and wetter, and sea levels rose. Then there was the pressure brought by other peoples from further afield – the Huns pushing through central Europe, the Danes moving out from southern Scandinavia into the Jutland peninsula. And in these deeply unsettled times there was surely many an outlaw and adventurer fishing in troubled waters.

As the threat from across the North Sea grew the Romans put counter-measures in place. They built a string of fortified naval bases along the so-called 'Saxon Shore', that is, the coastline from the Humber round to the Portsmouth/Isle of Wight region. Kent, Surrey, Essex and the Thames estuary formed the centre and focus of the system. The authorities also recruited Germanic soldiers, *foederati* ('federates'), who held their land under a *foedus* or treaty, and *laeti*, who were settled on empty lands within the empire, but who were bound to contribute troops to the army.

Yet defence was undermined by the deep social problems of an Empire where there was a stark divide – wealth and power in the hands of the few, and poverty, servitude and oppression for the many. There were tensions between the army and the state, and between the army and civilians. The rich were at odds with the state, and the middle classes were caught in between, liable for government taxes which the rich would not pay. The bureaucracy was rigid and corrupt, and there was little justice to be had in the courts. This was, truly, a 'broken commonwealth'. There were also religious tensions between Catholics on the one hand and followers of the heretical Pelagius on the other. Both pagans and Christians were, in their differing

---

[3] The title of a First World War poem by Thomas Hardy.

ways, complacent. Pagans trusted that the glories of the past would return, while some Christians believed that the acceptance of Christianity had given Rome a whole new lease of life.

In Britain there was a kind of unstructured civil war, with the 'haves' against the 'have-nots', a 'Roman' party of the urban South-east, against a 'nationalist' party of the less-Romanised north and west, and Christians against Pelagians. It was probably the Roman party who, in 446, made an appeal to the Roman general, Aëtius. When it became clear that no help was forthcoming it was probably the nationalists who then sought to recruit German mercenaries.

The conquest: the first phase

It seems likely that gains in the early phase of the Anglo-Saxon conquest came about through the takeover of 'going concerns'. In other words, there were Anglo-Saxon leaders in positions of influence, as commanders of *laeti*, well-placed to take over the reins of power as the grip of the Romano-British leadership slackened. East Anglia and Lindsey were perhaps first settled by Germanic folk in the late fourth century, and taken over by Anglo-Saxon leaders in the early fifth. Deira (between the Humber and the Tees), and Essex probably came into Anglo-Saxon hands in the period 400-450, and Kent, Bernicia, Sussex, and the Isle of Wight/Hampshire coast area between about 450 and 500.

The second phase

In the second phase Anglo-Saxon settlers pressed inland. In fact there were Saxons in the Middle/Upper Thames region perhaps as early as the last days of official Roman rule or very soon after they left. These may have pushed boldly up such rivers as the Ouse and the Cam, which drain into the Wash (the Wash has been described as 'the great front door' of eastern England). But another possibility is that these Saxons were 'planted' here by the Romano-British authorities, a buffer of *laeti* along the border between the Catuvellauni and Dobunni peoples.

At this point the seemingly relentless Germanic advance may have stirred a British fight-back. There are indications from Gildas and other sources that at some time before the middle of the sixth century there was a check to the Anglo-Saxon advance, even a reverse migration, with English settlers moving out. As to what happened the answer may be that the Romano-Britons (who surely still had the advantage of numbers) sought to drive wedges between the various groups of Anglo-Saxon settlers. As Chester and Gloucester were key points on the western side of Britain, the Humber/Lincoln region, and the area around London may have been the key points on the eastern side. By holding the first of these regions the Britons could drive a wedge between the Angles of Deira and those of Lindsey and East Anglia. By holding the second they could separate the Saxons of Essex and Middlesex from those of Kent and Sussex. The tide of war probably ebbed and flowed over a number of years until the British triumph at the siege of Badon Hill (*Mons Badonicus*).

We do not know where Badon was, or when the siege took place. It is not even clear who was the besieged – Britons or Saxons – or who led the opposing forces. It is suggested here (and this is but guesswork) that mobile Romano-British forces (cavalry and light infantry) were led by the 'Arthur' of the *Historia Brittonum* – no king, but a war-leader who had won wide acceptance among the Britons. The Anglo-Saxon forces may have been led by Ælle of Sussex, the first of the 'Bretwaldas' named by Bede. Ælle might have tried to gather the Anglo-Saxon war-hosts of the south-east and East Anglia in the Wallingford area where the Icknield Way came down to the Thames crossing. The plan may have been to make a decisive thrust south-westwards to take the Wansdyke defensive line from behind, and to deny the Britons the cavalry country of the Wiltshire downs. But at Badon Hill (perhaps the Liddington Castle hill-fort) the Saxon forces were cornered and destroyed.

The third phase

The British ascendancy was not to last. They were surely weakened by their own infighting, and perhaps by the plague and within a generation Anglo-Saxon settlement was resumed.

The settlement of the Middle Anglian area, between the Mercians and the East Angles, probably began before the end of the fifth century. Much of this area was fenland, so that communities were isolated, and small people groups such as the Gyrwe long kept their own identity.

The first Mercian settlements were in the Trent valley, and it has been suggested that the settlers came not only by way of the Trent, but by rivers draining into the Wash. The incomers probably reached this area in the early 6th century. The Old English word *Mierce* means 'borderers, dwellers on the march', and the frontier area in question was probably the Welsh marches, rather than the border with Northumbria.

Fourth phase: the Western marches

The western kingdom of the Hwicce seems to have included Worcestershire, Gloucestershire, and part of Warwickshire, and it is likely that this kingdom closely followed the bounds of the earlier British kingdom of the Dobunni. The Anglo-Saxon penetration probably began in the late 5th century, and in the sixth.

The boundaries of the later diocese of Hereford are thought to have followed those of the kingdom of the Magonsætan. The most likely way for Anglo-Saxon settlers to establish themselves in Herefordshire was for them to have come from the Worcester/Warwickshire area, where there are pagan burials dating to about 500. It seems possible that the Magonsætan were also known as the Western Hecana or Hwicce, and that the Magonsæte and Hwicce were together known as the West Angles, distinguishing these folk from the East and Middle Angles.

The beginning of the Pecsætan settlement in the Peak District should probably be placed in the latter part of the sixth century. The Wreocensætan of the north Shropshire plain took their name from the Wrekin. This people are likely to have been as much British as Anglo-Saxon, and the Anglo-Saxon element appears to be no earlier than the second half of the seventh century. It could be that the Wreocensætan occupied all the land north of the Magonsætan, right up the Wirral.

Lords of war

In the decisive period from about 550 to 650 a number of redoubtable 'lords of war' held the stage in turn. Among them there were three formidable heathen warriors: Ceawlin of Wessex, Æthelfrith of Northumbria, and Penda of Mercia.

Ceawlin and his kin seem to have been based in the upper Thames. In his wars Ceawlin was sometimes partnered by his brother, Cutha or Cuthwulf, sometimes by his son Cutha or Cuthwine. The most important victories gained were at 'Bedcanford' (*Chronicle*, 571), and Dyrham (*Chronicle*, 577). The first resulted in the recovery of lands perhaps won earlier, but lost by the Anglo-Saxons after Badon Hill. With the victory at Dyrham, and the seizing of lands in Gloucestershire and north Somerset a wedge was driven between the Britons of the West Midlands and those of Dumnonia in the south-west.

Æthelfrith was king of Bernicia from 592, and of all Northumbria from 604. It was he who turned Bernicia from a small state clinging to a stretch of the Northumbrian coast into the leading power in the north. To the Britons he was Æthelfrith *Flesaur* ('The Twister' or 'The Artful'). He gained decisive victories over the Britons of Manau Goddodin, the Dalriada Scots, and the Welsh of Gwynedd. He was finally taken off-guard – the wily outwitted – and met his death at the battle of the River Idle, in 616/7, by the hand of Rædwald of East Anglia and his protégé, Edwin of Deira.

It has been said that the tale of Edwin would not be out of place in a treasury of Old English heroic verse. He lived through years of exile, knew what it was to face the danger of betrayal. Once his life was saved from an assassin's blow when a devoted thegn threw himself in front of him. After long heart-searchings and hesitations Edwin adopted the Christian faith. At the last he fell in battle against his people's enemies.

There followed a grievous time for Northumbria as Cadwallon of Gwynedd ravaged the land. Then in 634 Æthelfrith's sons, Oswald and Oswiu, came back from exile in Scotland. Cadwallon had with him a great host which he boasted was irresistible, but he was taken off-guard in a dawn attack at Denisesburn or Heavenfield, near Hexham. Some eight or nine years later Oswald was killed fighting against Penda at the battle of Maserfelth (long identified with Oswestry). Penda ordered that Oswald's head and hands be severed from his body and hung on stakes, an offering to the battle-god, Woden. A year later Oswiu came in a daring commando-style raid and retrieved his brother's remains.

After the three Christian 'lords of war' came the third and last of the great heathen warriors, the Mercian, Penda. In alliance with Gwynedd he had overthrown first

Edwin, then Oswald. About 654 or 655 he came with a great host, including, again, Welsh forces, thinking to destroy Oswiu of Northumbria. But at the battle of the Winwaed, perhaps in the narrow stretch of land between the Trent/Humber wetlands and the Pennines, Penda was defeated and killed. For the men of Gwynedd the defeats of 634 and 654/5 meant that they no longer had the power to campaign in England. The English conquest was irreversible.

There remained the British kingdoms of the South-west. The Saxons' westward advance is hard to track because most of the fighting happened in places which cannot now be identified. Dorset was most likely conquered in the seventh century rather than the sixth. Somerset was probably conquered following the victory of Cenwalh of Wessex over the Britons at the battle of *Peonnum*, on the Somerset/Wiltshire border, in 658. Exeter was in Saxon hands by 680-90, but the British kingdom of Dumnonia was still in existence in 710 when its king, Gereint, was attacked by the kings of Wessex and Sussex. The Saxon conquest of Devon was followed by a speedy and thorough settlement of the newly-won lands.

The Angles, Saxons, Jutes, and others who settled in these islands were sprung from the West Germanic group of peoples, and they in turn were come from the Indo-European group, whose first known homeland was in the southern steppe of what is now Russia. To these 'long-ago' roots of the English we now turn.

Chapter 1 The 'long-ago' roots of the English

The first homeland of the Indo-Europeans

Many of the languages of Europe and Asia have a common ancestor, for which the term 'Indo-European' has been coined. This language was current broadly within the period 4500 - 2500 BC. It is unlikely that it could be traced any further back.

In seeking the first-known homeland of the Indo-Europeans we get some help from mapping neighbour language groups, in particular the peoples of the Uralic language family. (Among the peoples of this group are the Hungarians, Mordvins, Estonians, Karelians, and Finns.) The languages of this group borrowed quite a lot of words from the Indo-European family, and this strongly suggests they were near neighbours. The Finno-Ugric homeland seems to have been in the northern forest zone stretching from the middle Volga, eastwards to the middle Ob. The Proto-Indo-European territory, then, probably lay to the south, in the lower Volga-Ural river region.

It was in this region that a culture known as the Kurgan (Russian for 'tumulus') emerged. The folk of this culture do not seem to have had permanent dwellings, and among their grave goods there are weapons and the remains of sheep, goats, cattle, and horses. It is thus reckoned that they must have been a warlike, pastoral society, moving from place to place in search of good grazing, using ox-drawn wagons and riding horses. During the fourth millennium BC some of these people moved eastwards into central Asia, others headed towards India, others again pressed through the Caucasus and down into Mesopotamia. And there were those who moved northwards and westwards into central and eastern Europe.

As the Indo-Europeans moved outwards from their heartlands the language diverged. Language, indeed, is always changing, though not at the same rate everywhere. The geographically more central Indo-European languages (Greek, Armenian, Iranian and Indic) seem to have shared changes that were made quite late in time. Language groups on the rim of the Indo-European world (Celtic, Italic and others) are marked by archaisms. This fits in with a well-known model of linguistic geography: 'peripheral languages conserve while central languages innovate'.

The movement of Indo-European folk into central and eastern Europe led to the emergence of the 'Corded Ware culture', named from the cord-like impressions or ornamentation characteristic of the pottery used. This was in the period 3200-2300 BC. The territory of this people stretched from the Netherlands in the west to the Upper Volga/Middle Dneiper in the east, and from Scandinavia in the north to Switzerland in the south. The Corded Ware culture may have spread both Proto-Germanic and Proto-Balto-Slavic. The sound changes which transformed what might be called 'late western Indo-European' into Proto-Germanic probably happened about 500 BC, and it was at about this time that the Bronze Age came to an end and the Iron Age began. The dominant Iron Age culture of Northern Europe was the Jastorf culture, and the Jastorf area, most likely with that of the neighbouring Harpstedt culture, may be taken as the Germanic homeland.[4]

In the second century BC some Germanic folk moved up the Elbe valley to Bohemia, and more followed in the first century BC. The Suebi, from the Elbe basin, pushed south-westwards towards the upper Rhine, also in the first century BC. And, probably late in that century, the Vandals, Burgundians, Goths and others (whose traditions, ethnic names, house-forms, philology and archaeology show their Scandinavian roots) moved down into continental Europe, perhaps driven by a worsening climate. Tacitus lists these groups as continental Germanic tribes, so their migration must have begun before the end of the first century BC. For Tacitus the Germani's southern boundary lay on the Danube, their western boundary on the Rhine, though in fact there were Germanic tribes west of the Rhine, perhaps as early as the middle of the last century BC.

Thus the Germania of the early centuries AD covered most of modern Germany, northern Holland, Denmark, southern Norway and Sweden, most of Poland, and most of Czechoslovakia. This territory falls into two natural physical divisions – the Northern Lowlands and the Central Uplands. The main river systems drain north and north-west from the Uplands through the Lowlands. The Lowlands fall into two broad zones, parted by the Elbe. To the west of the Elbe the land lies almost at sea-level and it is characterized by heath, moors, coastal marshland, and bog, but also by wide areas of fertile meadow. To the east there is a flat and fertile plain close to the shores of the Baltic, with undulating upland further south.

Tacitus

Publius Cornelius Tacitus (*c.* AD 56 - *c.* 120), was one of the greatest Roman historians. He was known for his thorough background work and careful, well-crafted prose. He wrote the *Annals* and the *Histories*, dealing with first-century Roman history, the *Agricola*, about the life of that Roman general (his father-in-law) and, in AD 98, the *Germania*. As a man who lived through the reign of terror of the emperor Domitian Tacitus shows understanding of those barbarians who stood against Rome's grasping and warmongering.

In the *Germania* Tacitus first described the lands, laws, and customs of the Germans (chapters 1-27) then went on (chapters 28-46) to give a name-list of the tribes. He began with the tribes who lived closest to the Roman empire, and ended with those who lived on the shores of the Baltic. Here and there he adds bits of information about the tribes.

---

[4] J P Mallory, *In Search of the Indo-Europeans*, 1989, 87.

Baltic
Sea

River
Volga

FINNO-UGRIC
PEOPLES

River Ob

INDO-EUROPEANS

River Ural

Caspian
Sea

**The first-known homeland of
the Indo-Europeans, *c.* 4000 BC**

Map 1

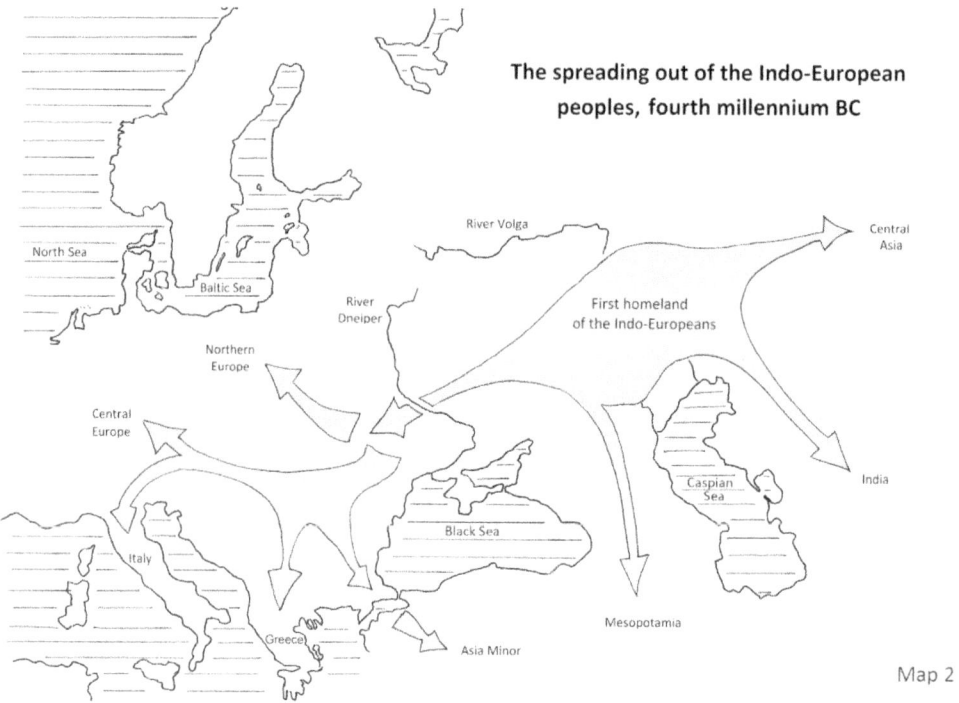

The spreading out of the Indo-European peoples, fourth millennium BC

River Volga

Central Asia

North Sea

Baltic Sea

River Dneiper

First homeland of the Indo-Europeans

Northern Europe

Central Europe

Caspian Sea

India

Italy

Black Sea

Greece

Mesopotamia

Asia Minor

Map 2

It is thought most unlikely that Tacitus was ever able to go to Germany, so where did he get his material? He probably picked up a fair bit by talking to those who *had* travelled: traders, soldiers who had campaigned in Germany, and members of barbarian embassies to Rome. There were also written sources Tacitus could have drawn on. He perhaps referred to the work of Pytheas who travelled northern waters in the fourth century BC, possibly reaching the Elbe and Heligoland. He might also have used the *Histories* of the Syrian philosopher, Posidonius of Rhodes (*c.* 135-51 BC). This writer, like Tacitus, tended to idealise the past, and the barbarian outlook of the present, as he understood it. He may have been a key source for the information Tacitus gives us on Germanic mythology, religion, festivals, and ritual. (Today only fragments of Posidonius's work survive, in brief quotations in other works.)

Tacitus may have used Caesar's *De bellico Gallico*. This work dealt with German affairs at some length, but it is thought that much of the material was second or third hand. Moreover Caesar had a strong political agenda – his writing was aimed at public opinion in Rome. It is likely that Tacitus used Livy's Book CIV (containing a description of Germany) and the Elder Pliny's *Bella Germaniae* (both these works now lost, sadly). Tacitus may have used Strabo's *Geography*, and he almost certainly made use of a map, such as that drawn by his contemporary, Marinus of Tyre, a geographer and map-maker to whom the Greek traveller Ptolemy owed much.

20

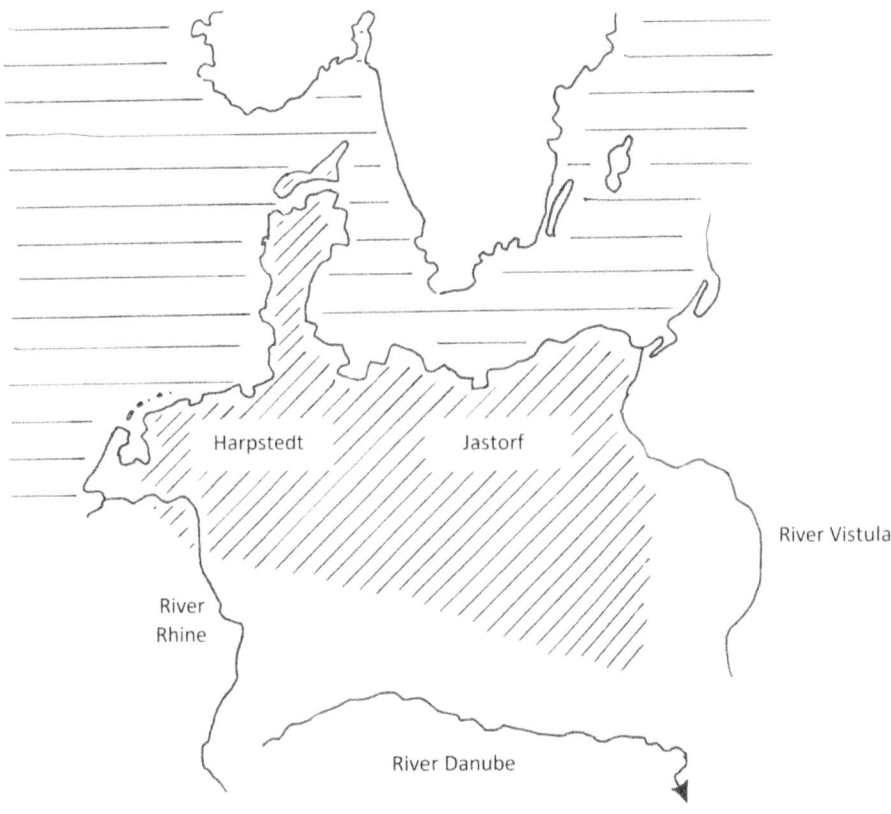

Harpstedt

Jastorf

River Vistula

River
Rhine

River Danube

The Harpstedt and Jastorf cultures, *c.* 100 BC

Map 3

Tacitus' sketch of the Germani [5]

Roots

Tacitus began his record of the Germani with an account of roots (*Germania* II).
German songs told of the god Tuisto who was born of the Earth. His son Mannus
('Man') was said to have had three sons, the forebears of three West Germanic
groups of tribes: the Ingævones of Scandinavia, Denmark, and the German coast to
the Ems; the Herminones of the 'midland country'; the Istævones, who lived near
the Rhine.

---

[5] All references to Tacitus are to his *Historical Works: The History, Germania, Agricola*, Volume 2,
translated by Arthur Murphy, edited by E H Blakeney, 1908, 1939.

The war-song

On the day of battle the Germani would give forth their long swelling war-cry.[6] By this they stirred up their minds for the fight, and they believed the outcome of the battle was foretold. This, says Tacitus, came about 'from the impression which it happens to make on the minds of the soldiers, who grow terrible to the enemy, or despair of success, as the war-song produces an animated or a feeble sound' (*Germania* III). The chanting was a 'furious uproar', 'uncouth and harsh'. It was sometimes broken off for a moment when the warriors set their shields before their mouths. They then took the shields away again so that the song burst forth once more with twice the force.

Weapons, protective wear, the 'wedge'

Tacitus commented (*Germania* VI) that the Germani had very little iron. Their neighbours, the Celts, had the edge in metalworking and the making of weapons. It was the technology of iron-working, and geographical access to supplies, that underlay Celtic military and political expansion in the La Tène period. The beginnings of iron-making in Germania cannot be earlier than the fourth/third century BC. Traces of the earliest furnaces for this purpose have been found in the north-east of the area then occupied by the Celts, that is, Bohemia, Moravia, south-western Poland. It is likely that the Germani derived from the Celts not only iron technology, but the word 'iron' itself.[7] The Germanic word for breastplate (Old High German *brunna*) is also of Celtic origin, so it seems likely the Germani also learned this form of body protection from their more advanced neighbours. Yet learning was rarely followed by practice. The Germani went on using spears with fire-hardened tips, and went into battle with no body protection other than shields of wood. When facing the armoured Romans they simply sought to keep them at bay for as long as they could. Swords and helmets were rare prestige items used only by the leaders. The weapon's name ('tester', 'charger', 'attacker', and such) might be inscribed with letters in the runic script, then widely used in northern Europe.

The Germani made good horse-warriors, though because few could afford to keep a horse, there were not many of them. (The East Germanic tribes, who were in touch with steppe nomads, made more use of the horse.) To break the Roman ranks the Germani made use of the wedge (*Germania* VI), otherwise known as the 'wildboar formation' or 'snout'.

Kings, generals, and priests

Tacitus begins *Germania* VII with a passing reference to kings and generals. The former were chosen from within the royal kindred, but their power was not arbitrary, nor was it unlimited. It seems that the root words for 'king', **kuniz* and *kuning*, denoted someone from a (royal) kindred, though his authority was more like that of a chieftain. Generals were chosen for their valour, their authority depending on their

---

[6] Ammian xxxi, 7, 11, cited in Murphy, *Tacitus* 313n.
[7] D H Green, *Language and history in the Early Germanic world*, 1998, 155.

22

warlike example. The power to judge and punish offenders was vested in the priests, and it was believed that the sentences they handed down had the sanction of the gods.

The Germani further believed that the gods oversaw battle, guiding and helping their worshippers, and the war-host carried to the field certain images and banners. These were brought from woodland groves, the sacred sites of the Germani, places which they regarded with awe. The sites were probably fenced enclosures around rough altars. Tacitus' statement that the Germans did not have temples (*Germania* IX) is confirmed by later Christian writings dealing with pagan worship, and by the finds of archaeology, as far as these go.

Discipline in battle, in the sense of some overall control of the war-host, was lacking. In the field each kindred group tended to act on its own, and the emphasis was on keeping faith with one's lord rather than on mere obedience. Tacitus said that in the battle the Germanic leader achieved more by his example (being in the van) than by the exercise of authority. Wives and children stayed near the battle, to spur their men on, to dress wounds, to give out refreshments (*Germania* VII). An army put to flight might, in truth, turn and fight again, goaded by wives and daughters, for the German mind dreaded the thought of womenfolk being led into captivity (*Germania* VIII). Tacitus went on to explain the German attitude to their womenfolk: 'There is, in their opinion, something sacred in the female sex, and even the power of foreseeing future events. Their advice is, therefore, always heard; they are frequently consulted, and their responses are deemed oracular.'

The aftermath of battle sometimes saw the ritual slaughter of prisoners and the destruction of horses and equipment. Perhaps these were offerings to the war-gods, or it may be that the weapons of defeated foes were seen as worthless as they had failed those who wielded them. Yet destruction did not always happen and it is not clear why equipment was sometimes seized, sometimes destroyed.

Religion
Tacitus speaks of human sacrifices being offered to Mercury, and animal sacrifices to Hercules and Mars (*Germania* IX). These three are taken to be Woden the chief god, Thor, and Tiu, a god of war. The name '*Wôdan*' is formed from a Common Germanic suffix *-an-* referring to someone who has authority over whatever is expressed by the stem. The Wôdan name, then, indicates someone who is a 'leader or lord of the *wôd*', and the latter seems to refer to rage or fury. *Wôd* could have meant both 'ecstatic warrior frenzy' and also 'a body of warriors incorporating this warlike fury.'[8] (Kindred words in Latin, Gaulish and Old Irish suggest also the sense 'divinely inspired poet or prophet'.) Woden, then, was a god who gave superhuman warrior virtues to military bands that devoted themselves to his worship.

In *Germania* XL Tacitus tells of seven tribes known together as the Suebi, who shared in the worship of the Earth Mother, Nerthus. The sanctuary of Nerthus was on an

---

[8] Green, 1998, 66.

island in 'the Northern Ocean', and since Tacitus called the Baltic 'Mare Suebicum' the Northern Ocean must have been the North Sea. Tacitus writes: 'There stands her sacred chariot, covered with a vestment, to be touched by the priest only. When she takes her seat in this holy vehicle, he becomes immediately conscious of her presence, and in his fit of enthusiasm pursues her progress. The chariot is drawn by cows yoked together. A general festival takes place, and public rejoicings are heard, wherever the goddess directs her way. No war is thought of; arms are laid aside, and the sword is sheathed. The sweets of peace are known, and then only relished. At length the same priest declares the goddess satisfied with her visitation, and re-conducts her to her sanctuary.' Tacitus goes on, 'The chariot with the sacred mantle, and, if we may believe reports, the goddess herself, are purified in a secret lake. In this ablution certain slaves officiate, and instantly perish in the water'. (Nerthus resembles the goddess Freya of the sagas, and even more Frey, her brother, the god of Uppsala. Frey was drawn through the land in a wagon, to spread fertility.[9])

Augury was a weighty matter with the Germani (*Germania* X). One method was to cut the branch of a fruit-tree into pieces, mark those pieces, then throw them at random onto a white garment. They were then 'read' by the priest, or by the head of the family if it was only a household matter. The Germani also heeded the flight and notes of birds, and they put much faith in horses. For this purpose a number of milk-white steeds, 'unprofaned by mortal labour' were kept at public expense, pastured in the religious groves. When the need arose they were harnessed to a sacred chariot, and the priest (the king or chief being with him), followed, to watch the goings and the neighings of the horses. No other mode of augury was received with such wholehearted belief by the people, nobility, and priesthood. The horses, upon these solemn occasions, were taken to be the organs of the gods, and the priests their chosen interpreters. Another mode of foretelling, used to discern the outcome of a war, was to take a captive from among the enemy, and pit him against one of their own champions in single combat, 'and the victory, wherever it fell, was deemed a sure prognostic of the event' (*Germania* X).

The Assembly

When it came to making decisions lesser matters were settled by the chiefs, but more weighty questions had to go to the whole community. The general gathering was held at fixed times, either at the new or the full moon, for, 'This is thought the season most propitious to public affairs' (*Germania* XI). (Tacitus here notes that the Germans reckoned time by so many nights, rather than days.) At the assembly each man took his seat fully armed. The king or chief opened the debate, then 'the rest are heard in their turn, according to age, nobility of descent, renown in war, or fame for eloquence'. A man could seek to sway the outcome by his words, but he might not lay down the law. A matter would be thrown out by a general murmur, but if a proposition found favour it was greeted with a shaking and beating of weapons.

---

[9] *Germania* 337n.

It was in these assemblies that charges of wrong-doing were brought, and penalties handed down according to the nature of the crime. For treason or desertion a man would be hanged. Those guilty of 'unnatural practices' would be thrust down into bog or fen. Other offences were punished by fines of livestock (*Germania* XII).

A youth attained to manhood when he was presented to the assembly and provided with shield and spear, either by one of the chiefs, or by his father or some other near kinsman. Until that time he was looked upon as part of a household, but thereafter he was regarded as a member of the commonwealth, having the right to attend the tribal assembly (*Germania* XIII).

The truly weighty matters were such things as the bringing together of former enemies, the forging of alliances between kindreds, the choosing of chiefs, the making of peace or war. These were most often talked through at feasts. Says Tacitus, 'The convivial moment, according to their notion, is the true season for business, when the mind opens itself in plain simplicity, or grows warm with bold and noble ideas' (*Germania* XXII). The matter was then settled on the following day, so that 'when warm, they debate; when cool, they decide.'

The lord and his followers

To work the soil, and wait for a crop, was not to the taste of young aristocrats. 'In a word, to earn by the sweat of your brow, what you might gain by the price of your blood, is, in the opinion of a German, a sluggish principle, unworthy of a soldier' (*Germania* XIV). Young well-born men would therefore attach themselves to the household of a chief. And a chief's glory was weighed by the number and boldness of his warrior-band, his *comitatus* (*Germania* XIII). A successful lord might draw men from far and wide, so that the war-band cut across kindred groups. However, the members of the band could be seen as tied to their lord and to each other by the same kind of bonds as those between kinsmen. Indeed, the lord/follower bond was seen as being stronger than kinship.[10] In the field it would be a matter of shame for the chief to be outshone by one of his followers. Likewise the follower would think himself shamed if he did not strive to match his chief in warlike deeds. 'The chief fights for victory; the followers for their chief' (*Germania* XIV).

Settlements and trade

Tacitus noted that the Germans had no cities as such, and in their villages houses were not built in rows, but each dwelling had some land around it (*Germania* XVI). In *Germania* V Tacitus tells us that as payment for traded goods the Germans much preferred Rome's older coins, the *bigati* (with two-horsed chariots on the reverse), and the *serrati* (with notched edges). These were heavy denarii of the late Republic, minted before the days of devaluation, so they were prized for their weight and familiarity. Archaeological evidence supports Tacitus on this point.

---

[10] Green, 1998, 80.

Family ties

'Marriage is considered as a strict and sacred institution' (*Germania* XVIII). One man, one wife was the general rule, though there were a few instances of polygamy. These were not the outcome of 'loose desire', however, but were wrought for the sake of advantageous alliances. The bride brought no portion to the marriage. Rather, she received a dowry from her husband, and there were no 'frivolous trinkets', but instead 'oxen, a caparisoned horse, a shield, a spear, and a sword' – for she was to share with her husband in toil and danger. She in turn would give her husband a gift of weaponry. It was by this exchange of gifts that the marriage was made.

Tacitus assured his readers that among the Germans only virgins married, and adultery was rare (*Germania* XIX). When it was found it was at once punished. The adulterous wife was shorn by the husband, then whipped naked from the house and through the village. Thereafter the woman had no prospect of marriage. Tacitus stressed that, 'Vice is not treated by the Germans as a subject of raillery' nor is it 'called the fashion of the age'. (He says nothing, however, about the man, the other half of the adulterous act.)

Tacitus noted the strong ties of children to their mother's brother (*Germania* XX). The man who inherited the homestead of his mother's father took on the duty of protecting his sister and his sister's son. Protection was owed to the lad not as nephew, but as kin of the grandfather.

Hospitality was a duty. The master of the house received a stranger and entertained him to the best of his ability. 'To refuse admittance to a guest were an outrage against humanity' (*Germania* XXI).

Kinship and feuding

The Old English word *frith*, 'peace', described the relations one had with those seen as kindred. The contrast was not so much between peace and war as between peace and feuding. Before the days of kingly power and Church influence justice was an affair of the kindred and, in the last resort, it was dealt with by means of the feud. If the kindred was 'shamed' in some way a feud followed, and all those of the kindred were bound to take part. Tacitus also noted that, 'To adopt the quarrels as well as the friendships of your parents and relations is held to be an indispensable duty' (*Germania* XXI). Paradoxically it was by the feud that law and order were upheld, because as long as the kindred held together the threat of their answering violence might check other kinship groups who thought to do them harm. The weight and standing of the kindred could be strengthened through a wise marriage policy, so long as the wife's kindred was willing to help the husband against his foes as if he were their own kinsman. The word 'friend' was used in the contexts of both kinship and friendship. The man who had no kinsmen to stand with him before the law was truly 'friendless'.

The Church had a hard battle against the culture of revenge. In German eyes the Christian virtue of *humilitas*, 'humility', was rather the 'humiliation' of wrong unavenged. Bede tells us that Sigbert, the Christian king of Essex, was killed by his kinsmen because he was 'too ready to forgive his enemies'.[11] The Church fostered efforts to hammer out an agreement, and encouraged the acceptance of *wergeld*, 'man-price', rather than the taking of another life. It also introduced the idea that vengeance was a matter for God and the Last Judgment.

Farming, slavery and gambling

The greater part of the German farmer's activity was spent in raising flocks and herds, using the village community's common pasture. The land for tillage underwent a rough rotation, the land cultivated one year being left fallow the next. Ordinary tribesmen did not own land, but allotments were made by the headman.[12] Agrarian slaves worked the land. They had their own households (rather than being part of their master's household), a system more akin to medieval villeinage than slavery.[13] A man might end up a slave through gambling. Tacitus said that the Germani were addicted to dice, and a man would even hazard his own person, so that, losing, he must yield himself to slavery (*Germania* XXIV).

The Germani in war

In his sketch of the Germani Tacitus has much to say about their warlikeness, but we should not overlook the fact that this was not the whole story. To have divisions between, and within, the Germanic tribes fitted well with Rome's political and military objectives, and so they fostered pro-Roman *and* anti-Roman factions. The outcome was the militarised Germanic society pictured by Tacitus.

We have already seen that the Germani fought in clan-groups, though a successful chief might draw men from far and wide. If a man was to keep his warrior-band he must needs be open-handed in giving gifts. Kings such as Eormenric the Goth were famed as much for their open-handedness in hall as for their hardihood in war. But for this a chief needed plunder, and to gain plunder he must make war. If a long time should pass with no war a-foot, then young well-born warriors would often seek fighting-work elsewhere.

It was young men of this background who might be given names of the 'theriophoric' type, that is, names built round an animal-name. *Ebur* 'wild boar' is an example. To this might be added a second element such as *hard* ('strong, brave'), so making *eburhard*. The name expressed the wish that the bearer would grow up to share the hall-marks of the animal, its strength and speed, its thirst for fighting. The oneness of man and animal was seen as being even stronger when the animal name was placed second (as in Old English *Heathulf* 'battle-wolf'), for linguistically this equated the warrior with the animal.[14] (Note that in Germanic society name-giving was a matter that concerned the kindred as a whole.)

---

[11] Bede, *Historia Ecclesiastica* III. 22; see also Green, 1998, 51.
[12] *Germania* XXVI, and 328n.
[13] *Germania* XXV, and 327n.
[14] Green, 1998, 81.

Much of the wealth won by the follower was given to his lord. Widsith gave Eadgils, lord of the Myrgings, the gold ring bestowed on him by Eormenric (*Widsith*, lines 88-96). When Beowulf reached home after his triumphs over the monster Grendel, and Grendel's mother, the gifts he had from King Hrothgar he gave to Hygelac, his own lord, and to Hygelac's queen, Hygd (*Beowulf*, lines 2142-9). The lord in turn was expected to give treasure to his men.

If the lord was driven into exile his men must follow him (or be shamed). Thus, when Æthelfrith's sons, Oswald and Oswiu, fled before Edwin (Bede *HE* III. 1), many young thegns went with them. On the field of battle the follower was bound to fight to the death on behalf of his lord, and to fight on even after his lord had fallen. According to Tacitus (*Germania* XIV) the man who fled the field of battle brought on himself everlasting shame, for it was thought utterly wrong that a man should come to terms with those who had slain his lord. This is the background to the *Anglo-Saxon Chronicle*'s entry for 755. Here we read how king Cynewulf of Wessex went to see his mistress at Merton, and was slain there in a surprise attack by the usurper Cyneheard. The latter then offered terms to the king's followers, but they, as one man, turned a deaf ear. They fought on until all were killed, save only a British hostage who was badly wounded. The same scene was repeated when Earl Osric, the king's man, arrived with a greater body of warriors. Cyneheard and his men fought to the death, with only one among them surviving – a godson of the earl, and he was severely wounded. There is, on the other hand, one tale that seems to be an exception. This is found in the so-called *Finnsburg Fragment*, and also in an episode recounted in the *Beowulf* poem. The tale concerns Hnæf Half-Dane, a guest at the hall of Finn Folcwalding of the Frisians. A treacherous night attack is made on him and his men, and the fighting goes on through five days and nights of slaughter. Finn's son, and the Danish leader, are among those killed, and they should be avenged. But the two sides have fought themselves to a standstill, and when Finn (who had no part in the treachery) offers honourable terms to the survivors, their new leader, Hengest, accepts and becomes Finn's man. Such a pact should have been unthinkable, and yet there seemed to be nothing else to be done. The following spring, however, fresh warriors came from Dane-land. In the renewed fighting Finn was slain, Finnsburg overthrown, Hnæf avenged.

In warring against Rome the Germani came up against a foe with better discipline and better equipment. Yet the Romans were worsted in the end. Various reasons for this have been offered. Several Germanic leaders served for a time in the Roman army, and there gained a good military education. They learned something of the worth of discipline, and they afterwards sought to instil such Roman ways in their own war-hosts back home. We thus see, on the one hand, the barbarisation of the Roman army, and, on the other, the 'Romanization' of Germanic war-bands. Other factors were: the wide front the Romans needed to hold, the land-hunger of the Germani, their sheer numbers, pressure from other tribes behind them, and perhaps the irrational features of the German's fighting mind-set. The 'technical inferiority (of the Germani) was counterbalanced, among other things, by the élan and wild impetus with which the Germani eventually swept aside the defences of the Empire.'[15]

Germanic people groups

Tacitus located most of the Germanic tribes of about AD 100 in a region bounded by the Rhine in the west, the Main to the south, and the Oder to the east.[16]

Chadwick says that the course which Tacitus adopts in his *Germania* is as follows. He begins with the upper Rhine and follows that river to its mouth. Then he traverses north-western Germany from the Rhine apparently to the Elbe. After one chapter (XXXVII) relating to the Cimbri, he goes on to speak of the various tribes included under the name Suebi. Among them were the Semnones and the Langobardi, and a sub-group of seven tribes also known as Suebi. Unfortunately he gives no indication in any of these cases as to the geographical position of the tribes.

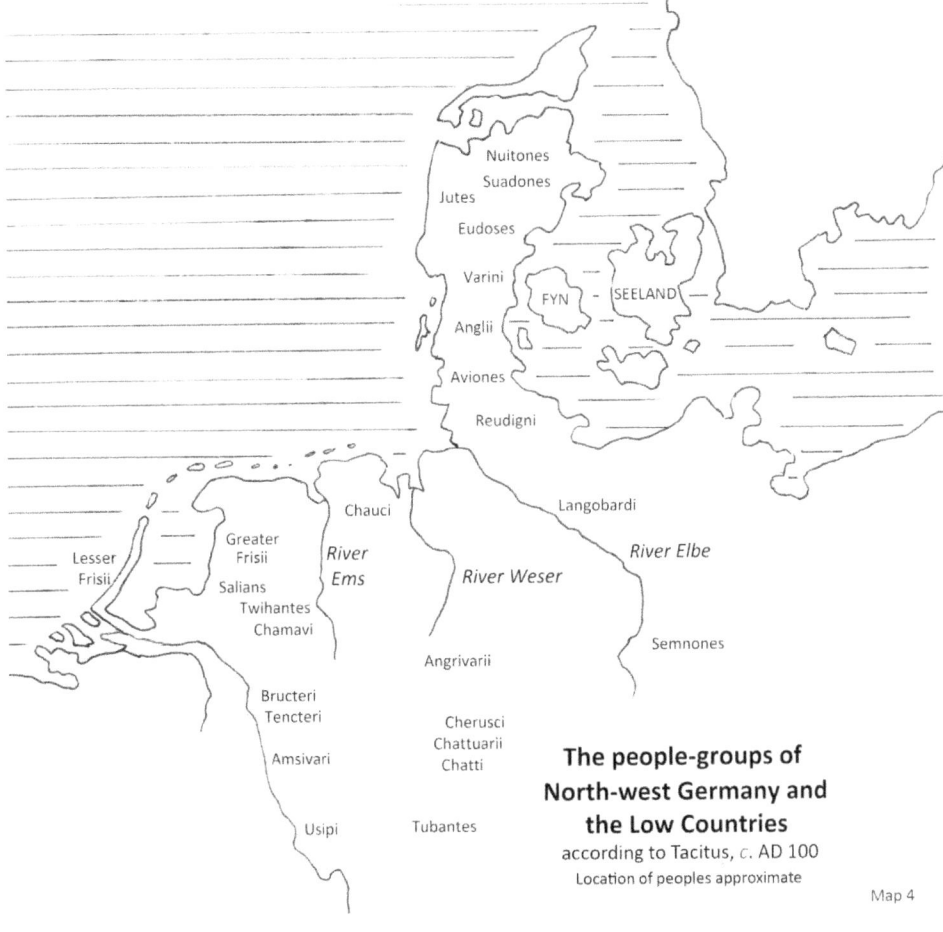

The people-groups of
North-west Germany and
the Low Countries
according to Tacitus, *c.* AD 100
Location of peoples approximate

Map 4

---

[15] Green, 1998, 83.
[16] Mallory, 85.

The Chatti lived by the Hercynian forest. They were a folk who bridled their inbred rashness. They trusted in their hardihood, yet did not rely on mere strength but on their commanding general. From the time when the young Chatti warrior came to manhood he let his hair and beard grow, and he only shaved them off when he had slain a foe ('the true end of his being') and so shown himself worthy of his father and mother and his country. A Chatti man would also wear an iron ring, a badge of slavery, until by slaying a foe he redeemed his freedom (*Germania* XXX, XXXI).

Beyond the Chatti were some groups that were part of the Frankish confederation. This confederation most likely began to come together somewhere about AD 230. The main folk-groups among them were the Chamavi, Bructeri, Chattuari (the Hetware of the *Beowulf* saga), Salians, Amsivari, Twihantes, Usipi, and Tubantes. The name 'Frank' (perhaps meaning 'bold') must have been one they gave themselves. These tribes were settled between the Zuyder Zee and the river Lahn, and eastwards as far as the Weser. They were settled most thickly around the Ijssel, and between the Lippe and the Sieg.[17]

Northwards of the Franks were the Frisians. Tacitus refers to Lesser Frisians, west of the lakes of the Low Countries (later the Zuyder Zee) and the Greater Frisians who dwelt east of those lakes, beyond the reach of Rome. Finds of Roman pottery and metalware at the sites of *terpen* (man-made mounds) show that the Frisians traded with the Roman provinces (*Germania* XXXIV).

Eastwards of the Frisians, in Tacitus' portrayal, were the Chauci, and beyond them the group of seven tribes (noted above) who were together known as the Suebi or Suevi (later the 'Swæfe'). These seven were: the Reudigni, Aviones, Anglii, Varini, Eudoses, Nuitones, Suarines. They were 'all defended by rivers, or embosomed in forests' (*Germania* XL). (These tribes occupied the well-watered and forested land of Schleswig-Holstein and Jutland.)

Tacitus says nothing of the Saxons, but Ptolemy in his *Geography* (written about AD 150) placed the Saxons next to the Chauci, on the North Sea shore between the Elbe and the neck of the Cimbric peninsula (modern Holstein), and also in the North Frisian islands. It seems these Saxons were there by the first/second centuries AD, and that they were likely a confederation of Reudigni and Aviones (the first two of the seven Suebic tribes) and perhaps others. In the third century the Saxons spread south-westwards across the lower Elbe to the Ems, and either drove out the Chauci or made them part of their own folk-group. They may also have overrun some Frisian land. The historian and Christian apologist, Orosius (who lived from *c.* 375 until sometime after 418) wrote of the Saxons 'as a people of the Ocean settled in pathless swamps and on the sea shore.'[18]

---

[17] A S Esmonde Cleary, *The Ending of Roman Britain*, 1989, 144; J Haywood, *Dark Age Naval Power*, 1991, 81.

[18] Orosius, *Historiæ adversus Paganos* VII, quoted in Myres, 51.

In Bede's passage about 'three very powerful Germanic tribes' (*HE* I.15) he placed the Anglii in Angulus, between the Saxons and the Iutae. According to the *Historia Brittonum*, 17 (which seems to have used the same traditions as Bede), Hengist and Hors came from an island called Oghgul, which can hardly be anything else than Bede's Angulus. This land of the Anglii lay in the southern third of the Cimbric, or Jutland, peninsula, and it stretched as far north as the earthwork known as the 'Olgerdiget'. (This north-facing earthwork was perhaps first built about AD 50, and was then further developed in the third century.) Anglii territory also seems to have included most of the island of Fyn.

The Varini of Tacitus (the Werns of the Old English poem *Widsith*) lived to the north of the Anglii. Where were the Jutes? Myres thinks that Bede implies they dwelt 'beyond' the Angles, which could mean either that they were settled north of Schleswig, or to the east, in modern Holstein, where there is a suggestive district name, Eutin.[19] It is perhaps more likely that their first known homeland lay beyond the Varini, in the north of the Cimbric peninsula. Ealdorman Æthelweard, a kinsman of Alfred the Great, wrote a Latin version of the *Anglo-Saxon Chronicle* (*c*. 990). He stated (under the year 449), 'Now the ancient Anglia is situated between the Saxons and the Gioti, having a chief town which is called Slesuuic in the Saxon language, but Haithaby by the Danes.' There can be little doubt that Æthelweard identified Bede's Iutae with the inhabitants of Jutland, for the form which he uses (Gioti) seems to be an attempt to represent the Scandinavian form Iótar.

In the northernmost part of Jutland there lived the Cimbri (*Germania* XXXVII). These would be a remnant, whose forebears stayed behind after the main body of the tribe, with the Teutoni, moved south. These folk terrorised Celts and Romans, 113-105 BC, before being destroyed by the Roman general Marius – the Teutoni in 102 BC, the Cimbri in 101 BC.

Tacitus says of the Langobardi (later Lombards) that they were not many in number, but they maintained their independence by their warlike spirit (*Germania* XL). (They lived on the lower Elbe in Roman times, but their traditions told how, earlier, they had dwelt on a Scandinavian island, which archaeology shows to have been Gotland.)

Another folk-group known to have been in what is now Denmark was the Heruli, who were settled there in the late third century. As for the Danes, they had long lived in the southern part of Sweden and in Seeland, with the Geats to the north of them and the Swedes further north still, beyond the lakes. The Danes moved from Skåne to Sillende and other islands in the late fourth/early fifth century, and into Jutland in the late 400s, though Seeland remained their main centre.

---

[19] Myres, *The English Settlements*,1989, 46-7.

Chapter 2 Offa of Angeln

For the most part we know little or nothing about those named in early kinship lists. However, there is one name with a story attached, and that is Offa, who was among the forefathers of the kings of Mercia. (His better-known namesake, the man behind the building of Offa's Dyke, was king of Mercia, 757-796.) The first Offa, the son of Wærmund, figures in two Old English poems, *Widsith* and *Beowulf*. The poem *Widsith* lists nations or dynasties and the most famous of their chiefs. We saw earlier that it does not regard chronology, but lists rulers from different centuries, side by side. We have, for example, Eormenric for the Goths (fourth century), and Aetla/Attila for the Huns (fifth century). We hear about Offa in lines 35-44 of the poem, and the fact that he is here must mean that he was the most famous of the kings of Angel. The passage reads:

> Offa ruled Angel, Alewih the Danes;
> he (Alewih) was of all these men the most courageous,
> yet he did not outdo Offa in valour:
> before all men Offa stands,
> having in boyhood won the broadest of kingdoms;
> no youngster did work worthier of an earl.
> With single sword he struck the boundary
> against the Myrgings where it marches now,
> fixed it at Fifeldor. Thenceforward it has stood
> between Angles and Swaefe where Offa set it.

In *Beowulf*, 1931-62. the poet tells of the virtues of Queen Hygd, the wife of Hygelac, king of the Götar. He goes on to say how different was the haughty Modthryth, a princess fair, but fraught, who would demand the death of any man in hall who dared to glance at her!

> Unqueenly ways
> for a woman to follow, that one who weaves peace,
> though of matchless looks, should demand the life
> of a well-loved man for an imagined wrong! (lines 1940-43)

Then one day her father gave her in marriage to Offa, and she was:

> strong in her love for that leader of heroes,
> the outstanding man, as I have heard tell,
> of all mankind's mighty race
> from sea to sea (lines 1954-57)

Modthryth now mended her ways, won a name for virtue, and became a gracious and well-loved queen.

The *Widsith* poet, as is often the way of the Anglo-Saxon word-shaper, draws on the old tales of his folk, taking it for granted that his hearers will know what he is talking about. Today, without that store of knowledge, we are rather in the dark when we read how Offa with single sword 'struck the boundary against the Myrgings.' However, in this case there are some clues in the works of two Danish historians of the twelfth century, in the *Gesta Danorum* of Saxo Grammaticus (*c.* 1150 - *c.* 1220) and in the *Brevis Historia Regum Dacie* written by Svend Aagesen (*c.* 1140/50 -?). This is the story as they tell it:

The king of the Danes, Wermundus son of Vigletus, had an only son, Uffo. The son was tall and strong, but he did not speak, and so was thought to be dull-witted. However, his father found him a wife, the daughter of one of his leading men, Frowinus, the governor of Slesvig. This province suffered raids led by of a warlike king of Sweden named Athislus, and in one such raid Frowinus was slain. After some time the sons of Frowinus, Keto and Wigo, went to Sweden in disguise, seeking a reckoning for their father's death. Coming upon Athislus when he was alone Keto fought with him, but was thrown down. Wigo came to his brother's help, and at last Athislus fell before this onset. When the brothers reached home Wermundus welcomed them warmly, but when it became known that they had fought two-against-one it was widely felt that they had shamed their people. (According to the historian, Svend Aagesen, it was this feeling of shame which led to Uffo losing his power of speech.)

As Wermundus grew old the king of Saxony sent an embassy calling on him to hand over his kingdom. Should he be unwilling, then let the matter be settled by a fight between the sons of the two kings. (The Saxon king knew well enough that Uffo was dumb, and was taken to be dull-witted.) The situation seemed hopeless, but at this point Uffo spoke, and said he would fight not only with the son of the king of Saxony, but with another warrior chosen as that king's helper. By this he hoped to wipe out the shame which had been brought upon the Danish kingdom by the trothless deed of Keto and Wigo. At first, Wermundus (who was by now blind) could not believe that this was truly his son, and he was not convinced until he had passed his hands over him.

The problem now was to find war-gear and weapons for Uffo. His broad chest split every mail-shirt. Wermundus therefore said a mail-shirt should be cleft down the left side (where the shield would give some protection) and fastened with a clasp. Likewise, several swords were offered to Uffo, but each shattered upon his first wielding it. At last the old king told his men where they might find his own great sword, 'Skrep '. He had buried this sword in sorrow, thinking that his son would never be worthy of it. (The name *Skrep* is Anglian, and is the same as West Frisian *schrep*, Low German *schrap*, meaning firm, steadfast.[20]) The sword, when found, seemed to be so frail from age that Uffo did not test it. (Wermundus told him that, if he broke it, there could be no other strong enough for him.)

---

[20] R W Chambers: *A study in Old English Heroic Legend*, 1912, 91n.

In Sweyn's account Uffo entered the lists with his father's sword, but also holding another in his hand. This other sword broke, so that the Saxons exulted, while the Danes quaked with fear. But Uffo then drew 'Skrep', and he went on to slay both Saxon warriors.

The Uffo and Wermundus of the Danish chronicles can hardly be other than the Offa and Wærmund of English tale. Moreover, the name of Wermundus' father, Vigletus, is not Danish. It is, in fact, not so very different from Wihtlaeg, the name borne by Wærmund's father in the Mercian genealogy. Vigletus might be a corruption of Vitleg, and, as with the name Wermundus, it looks as if the Danes took over a name which did not conform to the sound-laws of their own language.

The presence of the Swedish king, Athislus, is a puzzle. Apart from Saxo, Scandinavian tradition knows of only one Swedish king of this name, the Aðils (Eadgils) who had dealings with Hrólfr Kraki (Hrothwulf) and Biarki (Beowulf). It seems that this Aðils lived in the early part of the sixth century, long after the time of the first Offa. The only other prince in English and Scandinavian tradition to bear this name is Eadgils 'lord of the Myrgings' in the poem *Widsith*, lines 93-4, who seems to have lived in the mid-fourth century. It seems likely that he is the one who figures in the Wermundus/Uffo story.

Chadwick notes that there are two other names of interest in Saxo's story, those of Frowinus, the governor of Slesvig in the time of Wermundus, and of his son Wigo. In West Saxon kinlore we find a father and son with the same two names in English form, namely Freawine and Wig. Like Wærmund and Offa in the Mercian genealogy they are found in the fourth and fifth generations from Woden. Both these names are uncommon, and it seems unlikely that the coincidence is accidental. Therefore, though no traditions have been preserved in England with reference to these reputed forebears of the West Saxon house, we may reasonably identify them with the two governors of Slesvig whose deeds are recorded by Saxo.[21]

There are thus some noteworthy likenesses between the Danish and English tales, but also some marked differences. Whereas to the Danish historians the heroes are Danes, the Old English poem *Widsith* clearly refers to Offa of *Angel*. The foe, in the Danish record, is a warlike king of Sweden, whereas in *Widsith* it is the Myrgings.

In weighing up these things one point to bear in mind is that the material of the two Old English poems is centuries older than that in the other sources. The latest person named in *Widsith* (line 70) is Aelfwine/Alboin, king of the Langobardi, who died in 572-3, while the folk named in *Beowulf* belong to an even earlier period. Chadwick notes, 'I do not see how the substance of these poems can date from later than the end of the sixth century.'[22]

It seems clear that the two traditions, English and Danish, have been handed down independently since the sixth century. It seems, further, that as Angel was brought into the Danish kingdom, so its stories became part of the stock of Danish national

---

[21] Chadwick, *The Origin of the English Nation*. 1907, 133.
[22] Chadwick, 1907, 129n.

legend. Offa came to be regarded as a Danish king, and his enemies were first, a king of Sweden, then the Saxons.

The English tale

The English tale, in outline, seems to be as follows: Freawine was lord of the Waernas, and under-king to Wærmund of Angeln, Offa's father. This Freawine was slain by Eadgils, the war-like king of the neighbouring Myrgings. His sons Cedd and Wiga, bent on revenge, set off for the Myrging land and came upon Eadgils alone in the forest. Cedd fought with him while Wiga looked on, but when Cedd was hard pressed and like to be slain, Wiga stepped in and slew Eadgils. The brothers were welcomed as heroes when they first came home, but then tales began to be heard of how, trothless, their onset had been two-against-one. Offa was linked to the brothers in some way, either as brother-in-law or as foster brother (or he might have been both), and he felt himself to be caught up in their shame. Time went by and king Wærmund grew old and blind. He was then challenged by the king of the Myrgings, a folk who seem to have been part of the Swæfe (Suebi) confederation. He demanded that Wærmund hand over his kingdom, and if he was unwilling, then, since he could hardly take the field himself, let the matter be settled by their sons. The situation seemed hopeless, but to Wærmund's amazement his son Offa stepped forward and said he would fight both the Myrging lord and a Myrging champion together. So would he undo the shame of Cedd and Wiga.

The place chosen for the fight was at 'Fifeldor', which is thought to be a poetic name for the river Eider. Here, with his makeshift mail-shirt and the sword 'Screp' Offa first cut down the Myrging champion (who he judged to be the more dangerous of his foes), then the king's son. And so was the Angle-Myrging boundary fixed at Fifeldor.

Can we put a date to these events?

When might the first Offa have lived? One way to seek an answer is to count back from the seventh century Mercian king, Penda, whose dates are more or less known. He comes eight generations after Offa, and if thirty years are allowed for each generation, then Offa's birth would be placed about 360. If we apply the same process to the West Saxon genealogy and suppose that Cerdic was born about the year 470 (making him twenty-five or so years old when he came to Britain, see *Chronicle*, 495), then the birth of Wig, four generations back would be dated about 350.

Another approach to the dating is to look at Saxo's Athislus, king of Sweden, who in fact (as we have seen) is probably Eadgils of the Myrgings. The time at which Eadgils lived is clear from several passages in *Widsith*. The poet states in line 94 that he (the poet) was in Eadgils' service and that he accompanied 'the peace-weaver, the fair Ealhhild' (lines 5 ff.), a Lombard princess who was to become the wife of Eormenric the Goth. We know from the fourth century Roman historian, Ammianus Marcellinus (*Res Gestae*, XXXI 3.1), that Eormenric died about the year 370. It seems we may conclude that Eadgils lived about the middle of the fourth century, and that Offa's deeds took place in the latter half of that century. This agrees well with the dates surmised from the kinship lists.

Legendary forebears

The entry for 855 in the *Anglo-Saxon Chronicle* gives a lengthy genealogy for Æthelwulf of Wessex, the father of Alfred the Great. The line is traced back to Cerdic, the traditional founder of the house of Wessex, then on to Woden. Beyond Woden sundry shadowy figures are included, as the line goes on all the way back to Sceaf, and so links the Wessex kinship 'tree' with the old heartlands of northern Europe. The last gap to bridge was that between the northern world and the Great Flood and the early patriarchs of Genesis, for the Anglo-Saxons wished to belong, to know where they fitted in the great drama of world history. The book of Genesis told nothing of the origins of the Germanic peoples. But in the works of the Fathers of the Church Japheth son of Noah was taken to be the ancestor of the Europeans. Sceaf then became the son of Noah, 'born in Noah's Ark'.[23]

The line beyond Cerdic is as follows: Elesa – Esla – Gewis – Wig – Freawine – Frithugar – Brand – Bældæg – Woden – Frithuwald – Freawine – Frealaf – Frithuwulf – Finn – Godwulf – Geat – Tætwa – Beow – Sceldwea – Heremod – Itermon – Hathra – Hwala – Bedwig – Sceaf – Noah.

Is anything known of the ones named in this list? In seeking answers we will start with the first, Sceaf, and work from there.

Sceaf/Sheaf

Ealdorman Æthelweard in his edition of the *Anglo-Saxon Chronicle* (*c*. 990) and William of Malmesbury in *Gesta regum Anglorum* ('Deeds of the English kings') tell us something of the tale of Sceaf. According to the former, Sceaf appeared, a very young child in a light boat, and came to land on an island in the Ocean called Scani (the southern tip of Sweden, and the ancient home of the Danes). He was surrounded with weapons and was not known to the dwellers of that land. But they watched over him as one of their own, and in due time chose him as their king. William of Malmesbury wrote of a child who came in a ship without oars, and made landfall in Scandza 'a certain island in Germany'. He was asleep, with a sheaf of corn beside his head, and was on this account called Sceaf (that is, 'Sheaf'). The people received him as a wonder-child. They cared for him, and when he came to manhood they made him king in the town of Slaswic, later Haithebi/Hedeby.

The poem *Beowulf* (a much older work) opens (lines 4-53) with the tale of Scyld Scefing, the foundling who came from oversea (though from whence no one knew). In manhood he was a doughty warlord, and neighbour clans had to yield to him and pay him tribute. He in turn fathered a famous son, Beow, known throughout the northern lands. When Scyld's time was come his body was borne down to the sea-shore and, in accordance with his word, laid in a ship, with treasure, weapons, coats of mail piled all around, a golden standard over his head. He was then sent 'on his far faring into the flood's sway', and no one knew what became of his ship (lines 41-2). In the poem it is

---

[23] See D Anlezark, 'Sceaf, Japheth and the origins of the Anglo-Saxons', *Anglo-Saxon England*, Volume 31, December 2002, 13-46.

clear that no one knew anything of Scyld's father or mother, so the term Scefing cannot be taken as a patronymic in the strict sense. Rather it must mean 'child of the sheaf'. It would seem that at some point the foundling story was transferred from Scyld to Sceaf, with Scyld being the father of Beo (as in Æthelweard).[24]

It does seem clear that agricultural lore lies behind these tales. Copley thought Sceaf/Sheaf and Beow ('barley') were perhaps vestiges of a vegetation cult.[25] Kathleen Herbert asks, did Sceaf bring the secrets and gifts of Mother Earth?[26] Chadwick thought that the story of the child Sceaf was drawn from the ritual of a cult connected with agriculture, and that it was not improbable that the story was blended with another – that of a hero who came from over the sea and eventually returned the same way, whether in life or death.[27]

Hwala, Heremod

Two generations on from Sceaf we come to Hwala. The *Widsith* poet tells us (line 14) that among master-rulers Hwala 'was for a while the best'. The name of Heremod comes in *Beowulf*, lines 901ff., 1709ff., but he is not of Anglo-Saxon stock. He is a former king of the Danes.

Geat

In the Anglo-Saxon poem *Deor*, lines 14-16, there are some cryptic lines. L J Rodrigues translates:

> Of Maethhild many of us have heard tell:
> the Geat's love for her was limitless,
> their hapless devotion deprived them of sleep.

And Chadwick, has 'Many of us have heard that Geat's desire for Maethhild was beyond measure, so that his anxious love robbed him entirely of sleep'.[28] M Alexander's rendering is somewhat different:

> All have heard of Hild's ravishing:
> the Geat's lust was ungovernable,
> their bitter love banished sleep.

Maethhild was not a part of Germanic legend and the name itself was not a common English name. As for her lover, translators have varied between taking 'Geat' as the name of his tribe, or as his own name. Then came a breakthrough: Kemp Malone discovered two Scandinavian ballads, one Norwegian ('Gaute og Magnild'), the other Icelandic ('Kvæði af Gauta of Magnhildi'). He believed the stories might have

---

[24] Chadwick, 1907, 282.
[25] G J Copley, *The Conquest of Wessex in the 6th century*, 1954, 130.
[26] K. Herbert, *Looking for the Lost Gods of England*, 1994, 15-18.
[27] Chadwick, 1907, 285, 288.
[28] Chadwick, 1907, 271.

been brought from Scandinavia to England, and that the *Deor* poet might have heard of them and related one of them to his poem. Malone published the two stories in his 1936 article, 'Mæðhilde'.

The lover – Gaute in the Norwegian version, Gauti in the Icelandic – finds his lady, Magnhild, weeping. When he asks the cause she answers that she is lamenting her approaching death in the river. Gaute/Gauti tells her that he will build a bridge, to which she answers that no one can escape their fate. At the bridge Magnhild falls in and is drowned (in the Icelandic version the bridge collapses). Gauti, like a Germanic Orpheus, calls for his harp, and by the magic power of the harp his wife's body rises from the water. In the Norwegian version she is alive again, and the water demon is confounded. But in the Icelandic version she remains dead. Geat kisses his dead wife, buries her body, and makes new strings for his harp out of her hair.

Godwulf, Finn, Frithuwulf, Frealaf

After Geat comes Godwulf in the Wessex genealogy, Folcwald (meaning Folk-wielder/ruler) in the Kent genealogy (*Historia Brittonum*, 31). It looks as if Godwulf is the man's name, Folcwald the title he gained (compare 'Bretwalda', ruler of Britain). His son Finn would seem to be the Frisian ruler who figures in *Beowulf* and the *Finnsburg Fragment*. After Finn come Frithuwulf, then Frealaf. Alan Bliss[29] thought these two were actually brothers, and that Frithuwulf was the elder (he is always next to Finn in the sources). He was then the one who fell in the Fight at Finnsburg, and it was the younger brother, Frealaf, who carried on the kingly line. He has, however, been listed as the son of his brother (something which is found in other genealogies).

Freawine and Wig

We have already come upon Freawine and Wig in the tale of Offa of Angeln. Copley thought that it was at this point that we emerge from legend into 'the dim light of ancient Germanic history.'[30]

Giwis, Esla and Elesa

Chadwick thought Giwis obviously fictitious, his name derived from the early name, Gewisse, used by the West Saxons of themselves in the southern parts of their territory. (This name is mentioned by Bede, and it is thought to come from an Old English adjective meaning 'sure' or 'reliable'.) Copley is not so sure that this is fiction, and he even dates Giwis, *c.* 396-426. Esla and Elesa are unidentified, though they occur in place-names.[31]

The interest in the hero stories of other Germanic peoples, seen in Anglo-Saxon poetry, reflects a sense of common origin. Further, the names seem to be very old. Many of them (and even the single elements of which the names are compounded)

---

[29] A Bliss, Ed, J R R Tolkien, *Finn and Hengest: The Fragment and the Episode*, 1982, 45-50.
[30] Copley, 1954, 135.
[31] Copley, 1954, 136, 137, 139.

do not seem to have been used in England within historical times, though we meet with them in the history or traditions of other Teutonic nations.

Two closing comments: from Woden back to Geat the Wessex genealogy is almost the same as the Bernician (see *Anglo-Saxon Chronicle* 547); from Cynric back to Woden the genealogy preserves perfect alliteration.[32] (See further under 'The West Saxon royal genealogy'.)

---

[32] Copley, 1954, 134.

Chapter 3 The stage set

The North Sea region in the late Roman period saw folk-groups on the move, adventurers on the loose, coastal homelands lost to rising sea-levels, 'barbarians' tempted by Roman wealth and Roman weakness. Though the Empire took measures to defend itself, it was hampered by its deep social divisions and by ambitious pretenders to the imperial throne. Into this melting-pot stepped Angles, Saxons, Jutes, Frisians, Franks, and a host of smaller people-groups (see, for example, Bede, *HE* V.9).

Why were folk-groups on the move?

One factor was climate change, as the North Sea region became colder and wetter. And then from AD 200-600 the tribes on the rim of the North Sea began to feel the effects of the Dunkirk II marine transgression. By the fourth century the sea was some 3-8 feet above modern levels, while in the south of the area the sinking of the land meant that there was an effective sea level rise of 12-14 feet around the Rhine mouths.[33] Seaboard dwellers saw their fields flooded, their cattle drowned, their wells salted, while they themselves had to move to mounds built with sods. These mounds are known by the German word *terpen*, which is akin to Old English 'thorp', meaning a farm or hamlet. These *terpen* are found from the Elbe mouth in the east, as far as northern Holland in the west. To take one example, at Feddersen Wierde on the Weser estuary, north of Bremerhaven, several small mounds were linked together in the first century to form one large *Terp*. The settlement grew and in the second century there were some fifty houses round a large hall, with workshops and granaries. Then occupation ended about the middle of the fifth century, suggesting, perhaps, migration to Britain.[34] Migration to richer lands like Britain would have been a tempting thought to folk holding out on the *terpen* – though there was also a sinking of the land on the east coast of Britain.

Another factor was pressure on the North Sea peoples from others further afield. In the first half of the fifth century the Huns were thrusting through central Europe. Further north the Danes and others from southern Scandinavia were beginning to press southwards. This must have unsettled the Angles, and their neighbours the Jutes, in the Jutland peninsula. The Saxons, too, were forced from their earlier home in Holstein, and they crossed the Elbe into the lands of the Chauci. The Lombards had left their homes in the lower Elbe valley in the second half of the 4th century, probably following bad harvests, and they were now driven further up the valley towards the Alpine passes. Their long migration at last took them down into northern Italy in AD 568.

---

[33] J Haywood, 1999, 46.
[34] Myres, 1989, 51-2.

And this time of 'the breaking of nations' would surely have spawned many a foot-loose adventurer, men driven from their homelands in the fall-out from feuds or through their own wild deeds, men now seeking wealth, war-fame, vengeance. Hengest was surely one such.

Roman counter-measures

So there were folkgroups seeking new homes, and adventurers-turned-pirates hoping to fish in troubled waters. To counter these threats the Romans established three military commands in Britain. The Count of the Britains (plural because Britain had been divided into four or five provinces) headed a small mobile field army. The Duke of the Britons commanded the army of the north and had his headquarters at York. (Note that the office of Duke was below that of Count.) The Count of the Saxon Shore[35] had command of a chain of fortified naval bases. Why the name 'Saxon Shore'? Was it 'the Shore where Saxons dwell', or 'the Shore attacked by Saxons'? It was not the Roman way to guard a frontier with troops raised from among the enemy who threatened it, so this was most likely 'the Shore attacked by Saxons'. The forts were sited at the mouths of rivers along the eastern and southern coasts of Britain. From such bases warships could quickly set out in response to a threat.

The forts are listed in a late Roman document called the *Notitia Dignitatum*, 'The List of Dignities (or Offices)' dated *c*. 400-430. There were standard forts at Reculver and Brancaster, built early in the third century. Late in that century the Roman authorities began building more specialist forts, ones that could withstand a siege if need be – it would seem the threat had become more than that of small-scale piracy. These forts had half-circle bastion towers at each end of a stretch of wall, and from these towers the defenders could fire on their foes along the whole line of the wall. The towers may also have mounted catapult weapons such as the ballista.

New fortifications were established at the Roman fleet bases of Boulogne, Lympne and Dover, and a new fort was added at Richborough. The Thames estuary could be policed from the harbours of Colchester and Rochester, and new forts were now built at Walton and Bradwell on the northern shore. There was a defended port at Caister-by-Yarmouth, and a Roman site at Skegness, on a stretch of eroded Lincolnshire coast, may have been a fort. There may also have been one near Dunwich, also eroded away. At Brough-on-Humber the earlier earthworks were replaced by stone walls shortly after 270. However, Brough seems to have played little part in coastal defence after the middle of the fourth century. Perhaps the harbour silted up. Further north a chain of signal-stations lined the Yorkshire coast. These consisted of enclosures with stone walls, a single gate, and semi-circular projecting towers at each of the rounded corners. The towers probably stood several storeys high. Warnings of raiders could have been signalled inland, perhaps to Malton, which was probably the base from

---

[35] Or the 'Count of the Maritime tract' in the work of the fourth-century Roman soldier-historian, Ammianus Marcellinus.

which they were supplied. From here the alert might be passed to the Duke of the Britains in York, and/or to a naval squadron in the Humber. It is likely that each tower housed thirty to forty troops, enough to deal with small groups of intruders.[36] The signal stations may have fallen out of use by the early 5th century.

At the other end of the Saxon Shore Carisbrooke on the Isle of Wight overlies a late Roman military structure which could well have been a Saxon Shore fort. The fort at Portchester was probably a late addition to the network, built in the period 285-93. Pevensey was built sometime after 335, to plug the gap between the Dover Straits and Portchester, but Lympne was abandoned about 340. Bitterne may not have been fortified until *c.* 370.

Kent, Surrey, Essex and the Thames estuary formed the centre and focus of the Saxon Shore, and Roman control must have been maintained here longer and more thoroughly than on any other part of the coastline.[37] It has been suggested that in the late Roman period the Saxon Shore may have been divided into a number of administrative sections, which then came to be controlled by Saxon or Saxon-British families.[38]

To complete the defensive picture we may note that on the west side of Britain there were forts at Lancaster and Cardiff (the only ones similar to the Saxon Shore forts), and perhaps at Caer Gybi (Holyhead). These may have been part of a defensive system against the Scotti from Ireland, and the Picts. Carmarthen, Caerwent, Chester, Caernarfon and, to a lesser extent, Gloucester, assumed a new importance as points of defence. Carmarthen was linked to the sea by a series of signal stations along its river. Loughor and Pembroke, and possibly Neath, seem to have been late Roman bases.

Late Roman naval warfare

For the Saxon pirates the richest pickings lay beyond Dover, in southern Britain and western Gaul, where there were large villas and landed estates. But to get there they had to pass through the Straits of Dover, and this was a natural bottleneck. If the Straits were strongly held there was no real need for complete cover further west. And it was only in the Straits that regular patrolling was possible. If a few raiders did slip through, at night or in misty conditions, Pevensey and Portchester had their own small fleets, and they could send ships to chase the intruders. If raiders did manage to land their presence would quickly become known, and mounted troops stationed at the bases could be sent to head them off. There would be a further chance of catching the reavers as they sought to sail back through the Straits. In the late third century Mausaeus Carausius, a Menapian from the lower Rhine, was given the task of fighting Saxon and Frankish piracy. After a while he was accused of only

---

[36] P Bidwell, *Roman Forts in Britain*, 2007, 106-7; J Haywood, *Dark Age Naval Power*, 1999, 69.
[37] Myres, 1989, 113.
[38] Myres, 1989, 141.

intercepting pirates when they were on their way home. It was said that he seized the booty, but did not give it back to the owners. Carausius responded to these charges by breaking away from Rome in 286/7, and he ruled until his assassination in 293. Allectus, his supplanter, was not overcome by Rome until 296.[39]

How would this cat-and-mouse naval warfare have been waged? A late Roman warship found at Mainz in 1981-82 was long and sleek, with a shallow draught, drawing only about 18 inches of water. It would have been stable, seaworthy, manoeuvrable and, with a full crew of thirty oarsmen, capable of going at seven knots, or reaching ten knots over short distances. It may also have carried a mast and a light, possibly lateen, sail. There was a fighting platform in the bows, and an unusual protruding forefoot, possibly a short ram. Another such ship provided evidence of a shield rail around the sides, and this would have given some protection for the oarsmen.[40]

Vegetius, a 4th/early 5th century military writer, refers to light craft used for scouting. These had twenty rowers a side, and they were camouflaged with bluish-green wax daubed on hulls, sails and ropes, and on the men's clothes and faces. Action at sea may have involved the use of bows and arrows and slings, very likely followed by boarding, and hand-to-hand fighting.

Laeti, foederati

Germanic troops had been stationed in Britain from the time of the Roman conquest onwards. For example, we know of Frisian cavalry units at Burgh by Sands near the Solway Firth, and at Housesteads fort on Hadrian's Wall. In the late Roman period, at Housesteads, we hear of a *numerus* ('army unit') designated 'Nottfried's troop' and closely associated with the Frisians. We do not hear of Angles, Saxons and Jutes being recruited into Roman auxiliary forces at this time. Either they were all lumped together as Germani, or they were simply too far away from the Roman frontiers.

In the later Roman period (fourth century onwards) the authorities recruited *foederati* ('federates'), who held their land under a *foedus* or treaty, and *laeti*. The word *laeti* seems to have Germanic roots, and it refers to people who were 'half free', settled on empty lands within the empire, but bound to contribute troops to the army. It has been suggested that when Vortigern and his council brought in Hengest and his warband as *foederati*, they were not launching into a new and dangerous experiment, but following an example set by the late Roman government in Britain.

What archaeological evidence is there for the presence of Anglo-Saxon *foederati*, or *laeti*, or both? Anglo-Saxon cremation urns, held to go back to the early 5th century at least, have been found at two burial grounds near Caistor-by-Norwich. Other early Anglo-Saxon burials have been identified near the walled towns of Cambridge,

---

[39] Bidwell, 2007, 43, thinks that most of the Saxon Shore forts were built by Carausius and Allectus, AD 286-96, as a defence against the emperor Maximian.
[40] J Haywood, 1999, 71-3.

Great Chesterford, Leicester, Great Casterton, Ancaster, Lincoln, York, and Dorchester-on-Thames. Two classes of pottery, and the art-style of certain belt-buckles and other fittings, have been seen as Germanic, perhaps issued to Germanic *foederati*. These have been found in Germanic graves on the Continent, and at four Roman cities in Britain: Canterbury, Colchester, London, and Winchester, and near strategic points, such as along Roman roads and at some of the Saxon Shore forts. A Germanic cremation cemetery outside Malton, probably the supply base for the Yorkshire coastal signal stations, could be a connecting link between the late Roman scene and early Anglo-Saxon Deira.[41] At Portchester archaeologists have found timber buildings dated to the late 3rd/4th centuries. A *grubenhäus*, 'sunken-featured building', has been found there, with a sherd of Anglo-Saxon pottery from the period 400-450, and a brooch of 450-500. Cunliffe concluded that the site was 'Germanised' in the first half of the 5th century.[42] But around the Thames estuary – the focus of the Saxon Shore defensive network, where the settlement of *laeti* is likely to have been dense – there is little archaeological trace. Myres thinks this is because the newcomers quickly adapted to the Roman culture.[43] (Some archaeologists now question these conclusions, see under Appendices, 'Limitations of archaeology'.)

Upheavals and pretenders

The Roman army permanently stationed in Britain had been made up of three whole legions, and this gave local commanders a head-start in any bid for the imperial throne. A certain Clodius Albinus made such a bid in 193-7. Then at York, in AD 306, Constantine the Great began his rise to overlordship of the whole Roman world. A certain Crocus, 'king of the Alemanni', apparently took a leading part in the proclamation of Constantine. In AD 350-53 one Magnentius rebelled against Rome, and only a few years after this the land was plunged into great upheaval by the so-called 'barbarian conspiracy' (AD 364-7), when Picts, Scots and Attacotti all attacked at the same time. The breaching of Hadrian's Wall was helped by the treachery of the frontier scouts, and both Fullofaudes, Duke of the Britains, and Nectaridus, Count of the Saxon Shore (Germans, judging from their names) were killed. Troops deserted and joined in the plundering. The emperor Valentinian had to send Count Theodosius the Elder to retake the island. Fraomar, an Alemannic king, was sent to Britain in 372, perhaps to take charge of Alemanni already here (as *laeti* or as otherwise unrecorded *numeri*, that is, army units).

The next pretender was Magnus Maximus, who set out from Britain and made a bid for the imperial throne, 383-88. He possibly withdrew the 20th legion and at least part of the 2nd, though this may have been the work of Stilicho in 401, in the face of the Gothic threat to Italy. At this time greater emphasis may have been placed on a

---

[41] Myres, 1989, 187, 189.
[42] B Cunliffe, *Wessex to AD 1000*, 1993, 285.
[43] Myres, 1989, 131.

mobile field army, led by the 'Count of the Britains'. This force of infantry and cavalry was probably no more than about 6,000 strong.

On 31 December 406 Suebi, Vandals and Alans crossed the frozen Rhine and poured into Gaul. Shortly afterwards a soldier named Marcus who had been made emperor in Britain earlier that year was assassinated by the army. His successor, Gratianus, suffered the same fate after just a few months. The army then proclaimed another soldier, Flavius Claudius Constantinus, a man of low birth, making him emperor Constantine III. He quickly crossed the Channel and succeeded in bringing much of the western empire under his rule, before being defeated and executed in 411.

Divisions in Romano-British society

Late Roman Britain (and, indeed, the empire) was a house divided.[44] First, the army was at times at odds with the state. The problem was that the army had to be strong enough to defend the frontiers, but if it was strong enough to do that, then it was strong enough to overthrow the government. And this army became less and less 'Roman', as landlords made money payments rather than see their workers drafted into military service. The money was then used to hire Germans. Corruption was another factor. There were stories of officers deliberately allowing units to fall below strength so that they could pocket the pay of non-existent soldiers.

There were tensions between the army and civilians. Synesius of Cyrene remarked that if the army was not terrible to its enemies it was terrible enough to the common people. And there were tensions between government and people. The former drew more than 90 per cent of its revenue from the agricultural population, but taxation was not progressive, so it hit the poor hardest. After paying their taxes the poor did not have enough left with which to raise children, so they had to sell them into slavery. At the same time the rich made a fine art out of delaying payments and ducking out of taxation. Destitute civilians joined army deserters in robber gangs, and there was scarcely any viable commonwealth left.

The rich were also at odds with the state. The latter became less and less able to defend life and property, and so the rich took the law into their own hands. They made their landholdings into little kingdoms, forcibly throwing out tax collectors, and harbouring deserters and brigands. They seemed blind to impending doom.

The middle classes were caught between the state and the rich. Those with landholdings of 25 Roman acres (15 modern acres) within a city's territorial boundaries, were eligible to sit on town councils, and were forced to do so. They thus became responsible for the taxes which the rich would not pay. They were virtually squeezed out of existence.

---

[44] See M Grant, *The Fall of the Roman Empire*, 1975.

The Provinces of
Late Roman Britain

The provincial
boundaries are conjectural

• sites of *Saxon Shore* forts

Hadrian's Wall

BRITANNIA
SECUNDA

York •

Lincoln •

FLAVIA
CAESARIENSIS

BRITANNIA PRIMA

MAXIMA
CAESARIENSIS

Cirencester •

London •

Map 5

The *Civitates* of
Roman Britain

The *Civitates*
boundaries are conjectural

Carvetii

Brigantes

Parisi

Corieltauvi

Deceangli

Cornovii

Iceni

Ordovices

Dobunni

Catuvellauni

Trinovantes

Demetae

Silures

Atrebates

Cantiaci

Belgae

Regni

Durotriges

Dumnonii

Map 6

48

The bureaucracy was rigid and conservative, and desperately corrupt. The Western Empire, being unable to pay its staff decently, left them to plunder whatever they could. Lawyers used their skills on behalf of criminal frauds. They created hopeless legal tangles to delay and thwart justice. There was not even a pretence of equality before the law. And there were whole armies of spies, particularly in the imperial postal service.

Emperors became isolated among their advisers and courtiers, separated from the people and from the hard realities of the waning empire. The Eastern and Western empires looked askance at one another. Racism was another element in the story, with a kind of *apartheid* practised against Germans in the empire. People of Roman stock who might have given valuable service to the state instead opted out and became monks.

Religious persecution reappeared in a new form. The state sought to force Christian 'nonconformists' back into the fold (misusing Luke 14:23, 'compel people to come in'). Theodosius I forbade pagan worship, and even forbade visits to temples. Pagans were excluded from the army. In AD 407-8 heresy was declared a public crime, an injury to the whole community.

For their part the pagans relied too complacently on the glories of the past. When Ammianus compared the Visigoths to the Germanic invaders of 500 years before, his point was that those Germans, terrible though they were, were driven out in the end – and their modern-day counterparts would likewise be thrown out. Some Christians, in their own way, were just as complacent. Prudentius believed that the acceptance of Christianity had given Rome a whole new lease of life.

These dreams faded after the sack of Rome in AD 410. In pagan eyes the world was now steadily declining from the 'golden age' of the past to the 'iron age' of the present, and on to future catastrophe. Augustine (AD 354-430), bishop of Hippo in north Africa, taught that providence, not human endeavour, would decide whether the Roman world collapsed or not. Salvian (a presbyter or church elder) made two realistic comments. First, the empire was already dead, or breathing its last. Second, most Romans lacked the imagination to see the great peril they were in – or, if they did see, the will to do anything about it. He wrote of the public games: 'The Roman people are dying and laughing'.

What of Britain? It is likely that in 409 there were revolts of peasants and slaves in parts of Britain, inspired partly by a popular uprising in Armorica (Brittany). According to the Greek historian Zosimus the British leadership expelled the Roman administration. (This most likely means the civil servants put in place by the usurper Constantine III.) These leaders were men who saw themselves as the rightful heirs of legitimate Roman government, and now in the face of popular unrest they felt under siege. They appealed to the emperor Honorius in Rome for help. This was not so much a national plea for aid against the Saxons, but a cry from the ruling class that Rome might send troops once again and impose law and order. Perhaps the plea was issued by a council of the diocese made up of representatives of the *civitates*, and of leading soldiers and businessmen.[45] The emperor answered, in his 'Rescript', that the Britons would have to look to their own defence. The country was now on its own! (It has been said, however, that it is doubtful whether the Roman state ever *de facto* or *de jure* ceded control over Britain.[46])

If this understanding of the events of 409/10 is right then it can help us understand the next half-century when there seems to have been 'a long straggle of unstructured civil war'[47] between a 'Roman' party drawing support from urban settlements in the South-east, and a nationalist party which saw a chance for Britain to carve out a path of its own. The latter perhaps felt that Britain had had its fill of Roman bureaucracy, Roman taxes, and would-be Roman emperor-adventurers robbing the country of its manpower. There was also an economic dimension to this divide – the 'haves' set against the 'have-nots' – and a religious dimension, that is, the breach between Pelagians and orthodox Christians. Pelagius (*fl.* 390-418), a Briton who had settled in Rome, held that a Christian believer was cleansed from sin in baptism, and thereafter God's enlightening enabled him or her to do what was right by their own freewill and strength. Augustine, however, knew what it was to struggle against human weakness, and he felt that no one could turn to God, or do anything good and right, apart from the grace of God. He strongly opposed what he saw as a destructive heresy. Myres writes, 'This conflict seems to have bedevilled civilized thought among the Britons just at the time when unity was above all things essential'.[48] Because of the strength of Pelagius' heresy in his native Britain the Catholic party sought help from the bishops of Gaul, who, with the blessing of pope Celestine, sent two of their number, Germanus of Auxerre and Lupus of Troyes. These two routed the Pelagians in theological debate, healed a blind girl, and then in the face of a threat from Picts and Saxons, they gathered an army of raw recruits, baptised them, and led them to a victory in which a great shout of 'Alleluia' overawed their foes and made them flee. This was in AD 429.

In sum we seem to have here rivalry between a pro-Roman/Catholic party upholding *Romanitas*, and a 'nationalist'/Pelagian party asserting 'Britishness'. (It was probably the Roman party who sought help from Aëtius in 446, and, after the failure of that appeal, the nationalists who invited in German mercenaries a few years later.) In Thomas's view the divisions in the fifth century were so sharp that, had the Anglo-Saxon settlements never taken place, the sixth century might well have seen a major split in British society.[49]

Division among the Britons was, in fact, nothing new. In his *Agricola*, written about AD 98, Tacitus said of the Britons: 'they are divided into factions under various chieftains; and this disunion, which prevents their acting in concert for a public

---

[45] A Roman diocese was a province of the Empire under the rule of a governor.
[46] Esmonde Cleary, 1989, 42.
[47] Thomas, *Celtic Britain*, 1997, 41.
[48] Myres, 1989, 20.
[49] C Thomas, *Britain and Ireland in Early Christian Times*, 1971, 22-23.

interest, is a circumstance highly favourable to the Roman arms ... A confederation of two or more states to repel the common danger is seldom known' (*Agricola* XII). Writing perhaps about 540 Gildas said of his countrymen, 'It was always true of this people (as it is now) that it was weak in beating off the weapons of the enemy but strong in putting up with civil war' (Gildas, *De Excidio*, 21.1). About 580-590 an alliance of four British kings headed by the famous Urien of Rheged hemmed in the Angles on Lindisfarne Island. A great victory seemed to be within their grasp, but during a three-day blockade Urien was murdered by a man sent by a rival king, and the British alliance broke up..

A new political landscape

At the end of the third century the administration of the diocese of Britannia was reorganised. The province of Britannia Superior (so-called because it was nearer to Rome) was divided into Britannia Prima (Wales and the South-west), with its capital perhaps at Cirencester, and Maxima Caesariensis, with its capital at London. Britannia Inferior became Britannia Secunda, with its capital at York, while Lincoln probably became the capital of the new province of Flavia Caesariensis.

Within the provinces the largest unit of local government was the *civitas*, this being the territory of a Romano-British tribe. Clearly the size of the *civitas* would depend on the size of the tribe, and it might vary from modern county-size to something perhaps about two-thirds the size of Wales. The leadership of a *civitas* was in the hands of a group of magistrates, supported by and elected through an *ordo* (council). The *ordo* was made up of *decuriones*, the choice of whom was subject to rules of property qualifications. The Romans also introduced *territoria* into the political geography of Britain. A *territorium* was a rural area forming the hinterland of a town, and under its governance. The smallest unit of local government was the *pagus*.

In Kenneth Dark's portrayal of events a change from bureaucratic government to kingly rule began while Constantine III was in Gaul.[50] He suggests, further, that the post-Roman states of fifth- and sixth-century Britain may have been the Roman *civitates* reborn, and that these, in turn, may have been based on the Iron Age kingdoms that were here before the Romans came. Dark sees a close likeness between the pattern of the early Anglo-Saxon kingdoms of eastern England and the pattern of the Roman *civitates* of eastern Britain. As to the West, Dark adds, 'It may be significant that, in the West Country, polities of the fifth to seventh centuries more closely resembled, in extent, those of the pre-Roman period than those of Roman Britain.'[51] The one polity to disappear was the *civitas* of the Belgae, centred on Venta Belgarum (Winchester). This was a somewhat artificial creation of the Romans in which three tribal groups were thrown together: the Belgae of the Winchester area, the Belgae of northern Hampshire and part of Berkshire, and the Regni of Sussex.

---

[50] Dark, *Civitas to Kingdom*, 1994, 94.
[51] Dark, 1994, 135.

Dark suggests that the new kingly households of lowland Britain employed Anglo-Saxon and Irish mercenary forces to defend their kingdoms, and also moved their political centres from the towns to neighbouring hill-forts. He also makes the interesting suggestion that, paradoxically, the decentralization and divisions of Roman Britain may have helped it to hold out longer. He makes the point that it must have been difficult to militarily 'knock out' a Roman diocese with no 'core'.[52]

Areas of friction between the Romano-British *Civitates* First half of the fifth century

The boundaries are conjectural

Map 7

---

[52] Dark, 1994, 253-4.

The *Historia Brittonum* hints at one specific example of strife among the Romano-Britons. There we read that in a year which has been taken to be 437 there took place 'the discord (dissension) between Vitalinus and Ambrosius ... that is *Gwoloph*, the battle of *Gwoloph*' (*HB* 66). Who were these two men, and where was 'Gwoloph'? The place has been identified with Wallop in Hampshire, though Gelling is very doubtful. She writes, 'It is surely an Old English compound, with *hop* ('secluded place') as its final element'.[53] We have, then, to acknowledge that we do not know where Gwoloph was.

As regards Vitalinus one suggestion made is that this was the personal name of the man better known as Vortigern. This name may be roughly translated 'overlord', and some think it was a title adopted by Vitalinus, rather than a name. Charles Thomas, however, sees it as a bombastic personal name, but not as a title. Nor does he think it is a translation of the phrase *superbus tyrannus* found in Gildas.[54] As for Ambrosius the name implies an origin in the upper levels of the Romano-British nobility, someone of senatorial or magisterial rank.[55] He may have been a distant relative of one of the imperial families, such as the House of Theodosius (the Late Roman aristocracy had long memories for illustrious forebears). To Gildas Ambrosius was a *vir modestus*, the son of parents who had 'worn the purple' but who had died in the storm.[56] His 'Roman-ness' linked him to the God-derived authority and military virtues which Gildas consistently ascribed to the Romans. The Amesbury area of central Wiltshire may have been his power base.[57]

Areas of friction

In two works Stuart Laycock quotes the Tacitus and Gildas passages cited above, underlining the inability of the Britons to come together against a common foe. Laycock goes on to suggest that the Britons thought of themselves as Dobunnic, Catuvellaunian, Durotrigan, and so on, rather than British.[58] He further argues that the evidence points to a number of potential areas of friction, or 'hotspots', where there could well have been tribal conflict at the end of the Roman period.

One place where there was potential for conflict was the border area in East Anglia between the Iceni on the one hand and the Catuvellauni/Trinovantes on the other.

Then there was the Upper Thames area, where the territory of the Catuvellauni bordered that of the Dobunni. This fact might throw light on the puzzle why some of

---

[53] Margaret Gelling, 'Towards a Chronology for English Place-Names' in D Hooke, *Anglo-Saxon Settlements*, 1988, 61. Ekwall explains Wallop as *wiell-hop*, *wæll-hop* 'valley of the stream' (*The Concise Oxford Dictionary of English Place-names*, 1960, 493).

[54] C Thomas, *Celtic Britain*, 1997, 42.

[55] Alcock, *Arthur's Britain*, 1975, 358.

[56] Gildas's, *De Excidio Brittaniae* XXV 3; if the grandchildren of Ambrosius were alive in Gildas's day then he could have gained family information from them.

[57] Myres, 1989, 160.

[58] See Laycock, *Warlords, The Struggle for Power in Post-Roman Britain*, 2009, and *Britannia – The Failed State: Tribal Conflict and the End of Roman Britain*, 2008.

the earliest Anglo-Saxon settlements should be so far inland, in the area around Dorchester-on-Thames. Might this have been an ideal place for the Catuvellauni, say, to locate a band of Anglo-Saxon mercenaries to guard against Dobunnic ambitions?

Third, there was the Salisbury Plain area where the *civitas* of the Atrebates met the *civitas* of the Dobunni. The Wansdyke, a north-facing linear earthwork, may have been built here to check Dobunnic expansion.

The Salisbury area was a fourth possible area of friction, and thus a good place, perhaps, to station Anglo-Saxon mercenaries. Here the lands of the Atrebates bordered the territory of the Durotriges of Dorset. The presence of the late Roman or post-Roman Bokerly Dyke on the border suggests conflict.

A fifth possible conflict zone was in the northern part of Corieltauvi territory, where it bordered the lands of the Parisi and the Brigantes. Early Anglo-Saxon settlement was clustered here.

A 'Heptarchy'?

Before looking at the beginning of the Anglo-Saxon settlements it may be helpful to consider the traditional view that England began as a 'heptarchy'. This is the view that there were once seven independent kingdoms which were eventually forged into one kingdom of England. The seven were: Northumbria, Mercia, East Anglia, Wessex, Essex, Sussex and Kent. But this picture is over simple. The political map was forever changing as some kingdoms grew stronger and took over weaker neighbours, only to wane in their turn and become subject to a new rising power. Thus a larger kingdom might be formed through bringing together two or three smaller kingdoms, but after some while it might split up again. Northumbria came into being through the joining of Bernicia and Deira. East Anglia was probably originally two kingdoms, those of the 'north folk' and the 'south folk'. Kent also began as two kingdoms, the Jutish kingdom of East Kent, and the Saxon lands of West Kent. Likewise Wessex was a union of Saxon folk with the Jutes of the Isle of Wight and their sister Jutish state of the Meonware on the Hampshire coast. Other small people groups/states included the Hwicce, the Lindiswara, the Magonsaete, and a string of small 'Middle Anglian' kingdoms in the south-east Midlands. We seek here to tell the story of the beginnings of these kingdoms, their rivalries, and their growth at the expense of each other and of the Britons.

Chapter 4 The eastern seaboard:
the takeover of 'going concerns'?

(c.400 - c.480)

Who led the Germanic incomers?

F M Stenton says that, unlike Gaul, Spain and Italy, Britain was invaded not by tribes under tribal kings, but by adventurers.[59] Such were Hengest, Ælle, and Cerdic. And Chadwick argues that the invaders could hardly have been drawn entirely from the continental territories of the Angles, Saxons and Jutes. They must have attracted warriors from a wider area – as did William of Normandy in 1066, when he was accompanied by knights from Brittany, Flanders and elsewhere.[60]

It may well be that some of these adventurers had in fact been in place since late Roman and early post-Roman times, as commanders of *laeti*. They would thus have been in positions of influence, well-placed to take over the reins of power as Roman structures broke down, and the grip of the Romano-British leadership slackened. East Anglia, Lindsey, Deira, Essex, Kent, and Bernicia, on the eastern seaboard may have been originally based on former Romano-British *civitates*, now taken over as 'going concerns'. This is also true of Sussex, and perhaps of early south Wessex.

East Anglia

East Anglia was the homeland of the Iceni tribe in Iron Age and Roman times. In the later fourth century it seems that the Romans settled various Germanic groups here, as *foederati* or *laeti*. The situation then took a new turn in the early fifth century. The brooches buried with the Anglo-Saxon dead were now of types known from the lower Elbe (the traditional Saxon region) and Schleswig-Holstein (perhaps Anglian). These were the so-called 'equal-arm', 'supporting-arm', and early 'cruciform' brooches. H W Böhme sees here evidence of the settlement not of *laeti* but of free Germans with their families. This would mean that although the Roman administration was still functioning elsewhere in Britain the early settlers in East Anglia had worked loose from its control and set up a territory of their own. This was fifty and more years before the settlement of Kent, Sussex and Wessex, the kingdoms which feature in the early annals of the conquest in the *Anglo-Saxon Chronicle*. It may be that the Chronicler began his record of the English settlements with the landing in Kent, not because it was the earliest known, but because it was the earliest to which reasonably firm dates could be attached.[61] It would seem, then, that the East Angles were the first Germanic settlers (as distinct from garrison troops liable to transfer). Around their borders other kingdoms, thoroughly British in nature

---

[59] F M Stenton, *Anglo-Saxon England*, 1967, 37.
[60] H M Chadwick, 1907, 184.
[61] Myres, 1989, 11.

and origin, may have formed.[62] (We should perhaps speak of 'New' Anglia, or some such, at this time. The territory could not truly be called 'East' Anglia until there were other Angles further west.)

F M Stenton notes that the place-name evidence backs up the story in the archaeology. There are names found in East Anglia which contain words not recorded elsewhere in England, and they give the definite impression of a self-contained people.[63]

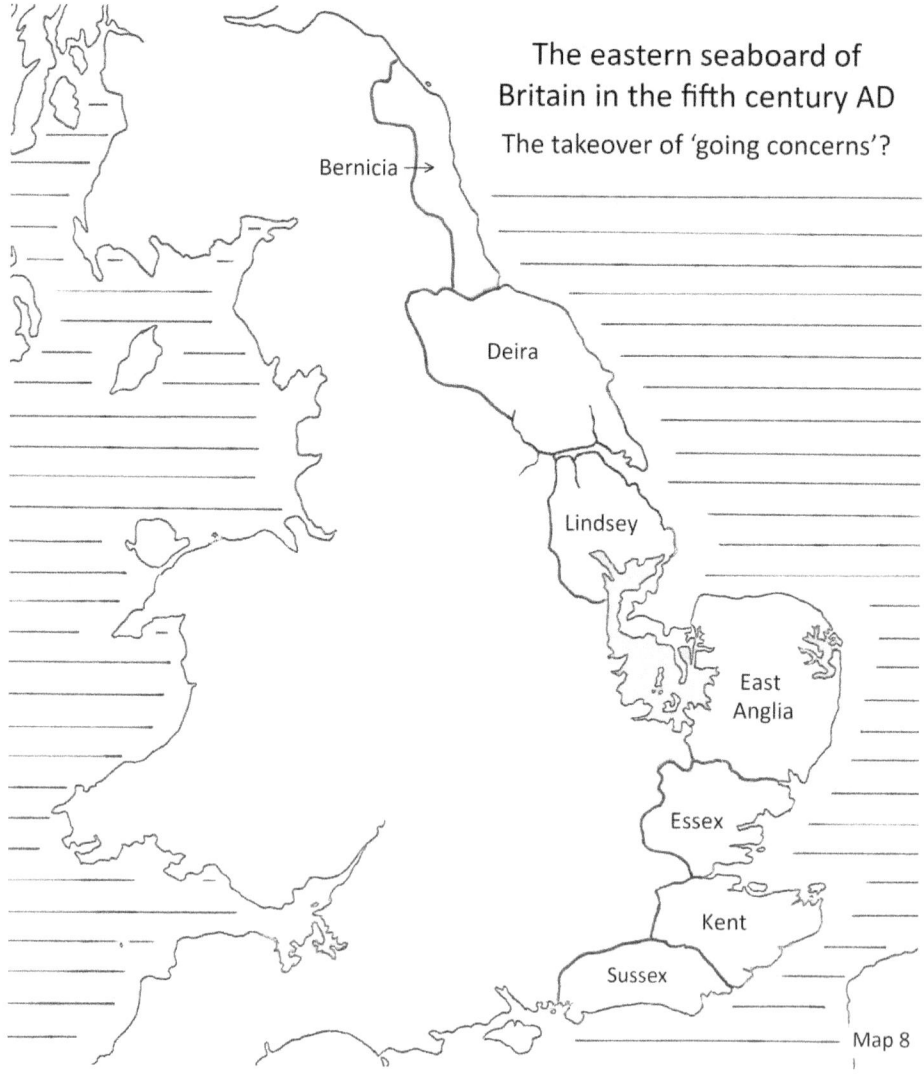

The eastern seaboard of
Britain in the fifth century AD

The takeover of 'going concerns'?

Bernicia

Deira

Lindsey

East
Anglia

Essex

Kent

Sussex

Map 8

[62] M Carver in Bassett, ed, *Origins*, 1989, 148; B Yorke, *Kings and Kingdoms of early Anglo-Saxon England*, 1990, 61.
[63] Stenton, 1967, 52.

Then in the second half of the fifth century new cemeteries indicate the arrival of fresh groups from Saxony and south Denmark. These Anglo-Saxons, like the later Danes, almost certainly used rivers as highways, and settled along the Lark, Waveney and Sandlings river systems. But the Wash was 'the great front door', and from it incomers could make their way north into Lincolnshire, south into Norfolk, or west into the Midlands and on to the upper Thames and upper Avon.

In the Sandlings area of south-east Suffolk early settlements grew markedly in the late fifth century and in the sixth. And in the sixth and seventh centuries there was (so John Hines has argued) continuing contact with Scandinavia, and especially south-west Norway. This contact took the form of exchange, migration, or ideology. Hines agrees that Swedish influence is clearly seen in the Sutton Hoo finds, but he says that ship burial has a more likely origin in Norway. 'The link with Swedish Uppland appears strong because that is where the principal and most affluent power centre had emerged at the time of East Anglia's own period of demonstrative wealth'.[64]

A reasonable hypothesis would be as follows:

East Anglia was settled in the early fifth century by immigrants from north Germany, particularly from the Saxon and, possibly, some Anglian areas.

Later immigrants included folk from the Anglian areas of what became south Denmark, many of whom passed through East Anglia to the Midlands and Northumbria. Both East Anglia and the Humberside area experienced further immigration in the sixth century, from south-west Norway. Ideological contact was strong at this time between East Anglia, Norway, Denmark and the Uppland area of Sweden.

The famous Sutton Hoo site, the burial place of the early kings of East Anglia, is right in the south-east corner of the land. This suggests that a central location was less important than having access to the cultural wealth of the North Sea rim. The Sutton Hoo hoard shows links with Sweden, and it is possible that Snape (where there was another high-status ship burial), the 'royal village' of Rendlesham (Bede, *HE* III. 22) and Sutton Hoo are to be linked with a group of Swedish incomers.[65]

Oars or sail?

How did settlers from Jutland and the lower Elbe/Weser reach eastern England? Did they come in the large open rowing boats of the Germanic peoples? It could have been done this way, but with a rowing speed of, say, three knots an hour for twelve hours, the crew could only cover about 36 nautical miles in a day. They would have had to make landfall regularly, for supplies, and this on a hostile, defended coast. Hugging the German and Dutch coastlines, with rests on the way in deserted coves and inlets, would have taken about eleven days, followed by a short sea-crossing of, say, twenty-four hours.[66] On the plus side, the lack of a sail would make it less likely that the ship would be spotted.

---

[64] Carver in Bassett, ed, *Origins*, 148-9, summarising Hines.
[65] Carver in Bassett, *Origins*, 152; A C Evans, *The Sutton Hoo Ship Burial*, 1986, 107.
[66] Bidwell, 2007, 43.

What of sail? Might Anglo-Saxon settlers have come straight across the North Sea, seeing it as a thoroughfare rather than a forbidding barrier? With a following wind even a primitive sailing ship could have covered two to three times the distance made by a rowing boat, and a crossing under sail from north Germany to East Anglia would have taken a few days only. Haywood notes that the archaeological evidence points clearly to a massive population movement out of the area between the Weser and the Jutland peninsula in the second half of the fifth century. This must have been part of a great folk migration to eastern England, not simply an aristocratic or political takeover of Romano-British lands and population. It is much easier to assume that the settlers came in sailing ships with small professional crews who could make several return journeys in a season. How many folk could a ship of this period take? A seventh-century ship referred to by Eddius (c. 664) had 120 men on board.[67]

So were the Anglo-Saxons familiar with the use of the sail? Sidonius Apollinaris, the fifth-century Gallo-Roman bishop and diplomat, refers, in a letter of c. 473, to the Saxons' use of sailing ships in their raids on the Gallic coast. Sidonius had a close friend in the Visigothic fleet on the Garonne, and he had seen Saxon and Herul seamen at Bordeaux and elsewhere. And a century earlier Ammianus had spoken of the Saxons going wherever the wind drove them, which suggests sailing ships.[68]

Experiments have been made with replica ships. Martin Carver tells how a replica of the Oseberg ship (given the name *Edda*) was sailed on the Heroy fjord in 1988. It ran beautifully before the wind, but when the crew tried to tack this narrow boat with its single square sail and no keel, it capsized and quickly sank.[69] He concludes that this does not mean the Anglo-Saxons could not have made the direct crossing under sail, but they would have needed seacraft of a high order.

Edwin and Joyce Gifford gathered a lot of evidence that suggests the Sutton Hoo ship was designed and built as a sailing ship. They believe its waterline shape would have made the ship fast and generated lateral resistance to leeway in a side or head wind. The leaf-shaped plan of the ship is one generally associated with sailing ships (rowing galleys have nearly parallel sides to maximise the output of the oarsmen). Additional frames in the stern area were probably needed to strengthen the hull against the heavy rudder loads of sailing.

---

[67] J. Haywood, 1999, 108-9.
[68] Haywood, 1999, 106.
[69] Carver, *The Sutton Hoo Story*, 2017, 61.

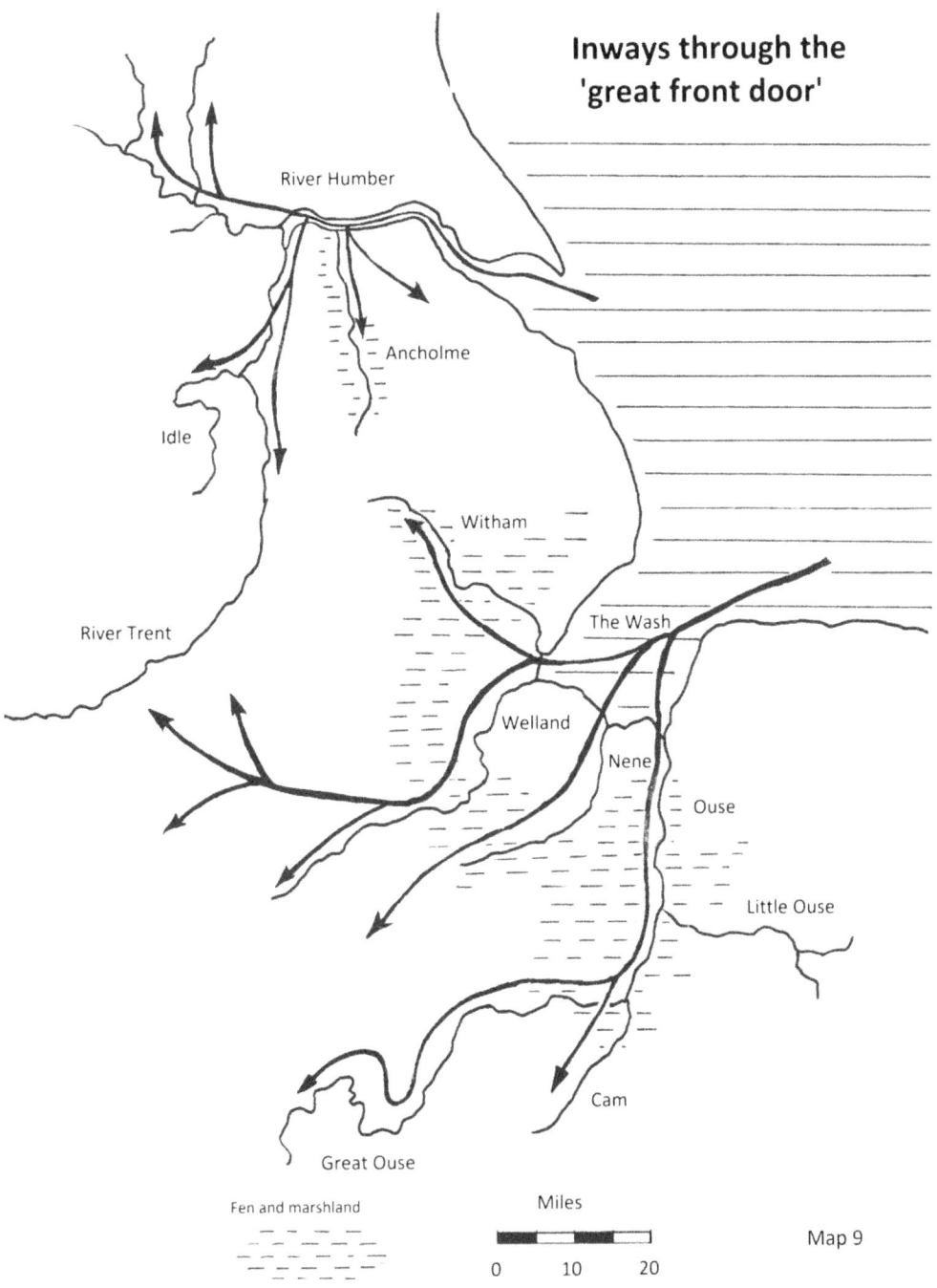

Inways through the 'great front door'

River Humber

Ancholme

Idle

Witham

River Trent

The Wash

Welland

Nene

Ouse

Little Ouse

Cam

Great Ouse

Fen and marshland

Miles

0   10   20

Map 9

59

The Giffords tested their observations with *Sæ Wylfing*, a half-size replica of the Sutton Hoo ship. The boat was found to be fast and manoeuvrable, and able to sail directly to windward, albeit slowly (about 1.5 knots). The hull of *Sæ Wylfing* proved more than strong enough to bear the modest stresses of carrying a light mast and square sail. The shallow draught and flat bottom made it easy to beach the boat. In a moderate wind the Sutton Hoo ship could have reached 10 knots, and it had a theoretical maximum speed of 12 knots. The ship was well adapted to the shallow shoaly seas of the southern North Sea. It could have sailed close inshore and far up rivers.[70]

Expansion of the East Anglian kingdom

With the sea to the north and east of them, and the East Saxon kingdom to the south, beyond the Stour, the only scope for East Anglian expansion was to be found in the west. Here lay the Fenlands, home to the small people-groups known by the general name of 'Middle Angles'. The East Anglian leaders certainly extended their rule as far as the Isle of Ely. And Cambridgeshire as far as the Devil's Dyke (the boundary of the medieval diocese of Norwich) may also have been incorporated. Mercia and East Anglia may have striven with one another for influence over the Middle Anglian groups. The Fens would have thwarted East Anglian expansion to the west, but then in the seventh century they would have hindered any Mercian attempts at making East Anglia a province of their kingdom.

Spong Hill, Coddenham and Snape

Spong Hill in Norfolk is one of the few Anglo-Saxon cemeteries to have been excavated in its entirety. It was much used for cremation burials throughout the fifth century, then in the first part of the sixth century the rate of burial slowed down. Inhumations now appeared along the north-east flank of the site, among them four richly furnished mound burials. Altogether 2,323 cremations and 57 inhumations were recorded, together with seven sunken-featured buildings and four post-hole structures. The cemetery served a community of around 850 people during its first seventy years, and around 150 for the next 60 years.

Another rich seventh century burial ground has been investigated at Coddenham, upriver from Ipswich.

The Snape Anglo-Saxon cemetery stands in the Sandlings area of east Suffolk, a few miles north-east of Sutton Hoo. The first recorded excavations on the site were carried out in 1862–3 by the landowner, Septimus Davidson and some friends. The work revealed a large number of Anglo-Saxon cremation burials, and in trenching the largest barrow they came upon the impression of a clinker-built ship about fifty feet long with rows of iron rivets almost the same size as the ones found at Sutton Hoo. The burial had been ransacked and no traces of an amidships burial chamber were recorded. This was the first Anglo-Saxon ship burial to be found in England. Although it had already been robbed, the explorers did recover a gold Germanic

---

[70] Haywood, 1999, 101-3.

finger-ring, now in the British Museum, which showed that the burial had been of the highest status.[71]

Afterwards the site was almost forgotten until in 1970 a dowser found an Anglo-Saxon urn in the field to the north of the nearby road, and in 1972 a sewer trench excavated along the road yielded a further nine cremations, one in a bronze bowl. Then in 1985 a research project was begun under the Snape Historical Trust. Excavations showed that the site was a mixed cremation and inhumation cemetery. Amongst the inhumations were two, possibly three, where dugout log boats had been used to hold bodies. And there were a few more exotic finds, among them a lyre (grave 32) and a horse's head with tack (grave 47). The cremation burials were dated to the late 5th to 7th centuries, and the inhumations to the mid-6th to 7th centuries.[72]

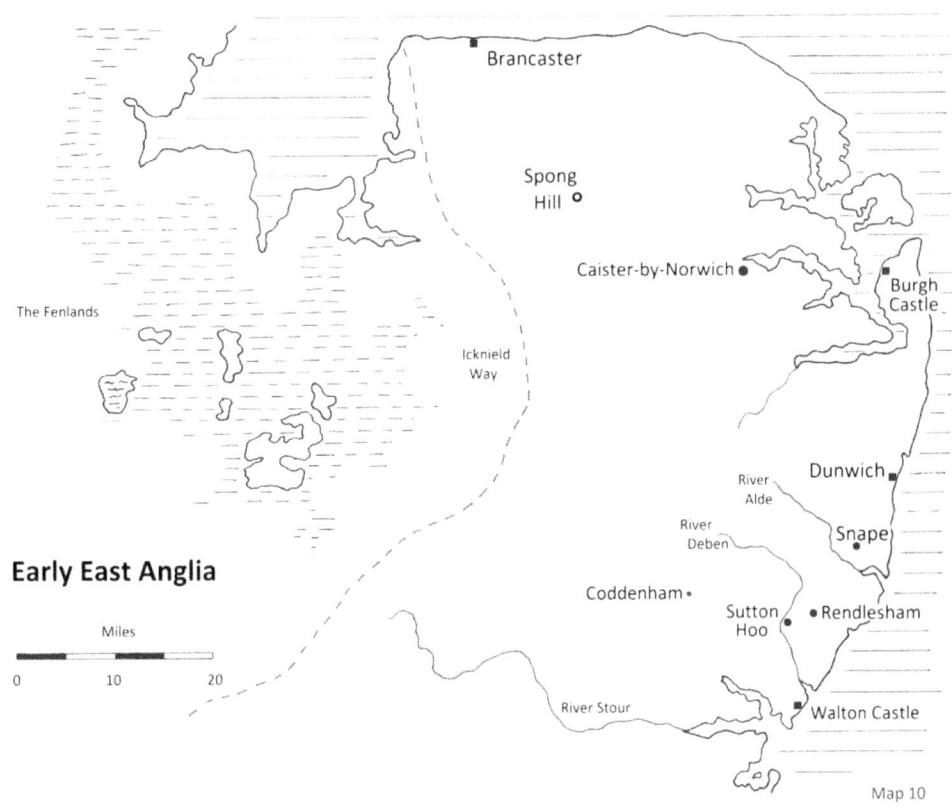

Map 10

---

[71] Carver, 2017, 179; Evans, 1986, 23.
[72] William Filmer-Sankey, Tim Pestell, 2001, 'Snape Anglo-Saxon Cemetery: Excavations and Surveys 1824–1992', *East Anglian Archaeology* 95.

Sutton Hoo

The Sutton Hoo estate beside the River Deben was owned by Mrs Edith Pretty, a widow. As a child she had seen the pyramids, and her father had once been allowed to excavate the site of a Cistercian monastery adjoining the family home at Vale Royal, Cheshire. Mrs Pretty had a 'keen eye and an educated curiosity', and in 1938 she made up her mind to explore some of the burial mounds on her estate. She took on a local, self-taught archaeologist named Basil Brown, who was recommended to her by the curator of Ipswich Museum. After starting work on the largest of the mounds, Mound 1, it was decided to leave it for the time being, and try some of the smaller mounds. Three were explored that first year, and all were found to have been robbed. However, ship rivets were found in Mound 2, then a boat-shaped pit – clear evidence that there had been a ship-burial here. As a second season of excavation began in May, 1939 (with war looming in Europe) it was decided that Mound 1 should be tackled again. Basil Brown and his helpers soon began to find more ship rivets, then the outlines of a ship. Rumours of the finds spread around the archaeological world and soon the British Museum and the Office of Works had become involved. They asked an archaeologist named Charles Phillips to take responsibility for completing the excavation. Other archaeologists joined him and over the next few weeks an astonishing hoard of Dark Age treasure was unearthed. Here were found all the gear of a warrior: a helmet, sword, shield and spears, a coat of mail. But the bearer of these weapons had been much more than a warrior of the shield-wall, for here, too, were a sceptre and some kind of standard, a great silver dish and other silverware from the Eastern Mediterranean, jewelled shoulder-clasps, a great gold buckle, a purse and coins (also some blanks and two ingots), an otter-trimmed cap in a deep fluted silver bowl, drinking vessels of aurochs horns and a maplewood lyre wrapped in a beaverskin bag. Here, too, were iron-bound wooden buckets, an axe, an iron lamp, and a great cauldron, with the chain to hold it over a cooking fire. The archaeologists just managed to complete the dig before war broke out. The emptied outline of the ship was hastily covered over with bracken, and all the finds were placed underground again, in a disused arm of the London Underground (tube).

Narrow escapes

The burial has since been dated to the early seventh century. In the long years since then the Sutton Hoo mounds were ploughed nearly flat, but they still proved to be a draw for treasure-hunters. The first known excavation of Mound 1 took place in the sixteenth-century. Thankfully the seekers did not find the hoard: they did not go deep enough, and they were off centre – perhaps because ploughing had changed the shape of the mound.

One of the mounds (most likely Mound 2) had been opened in 1860, in an 'afternoon spree',[73] and a lot of 'iron screw bolts' were found. These must have been rivets from the ship burial already noted, but they were sent to a blacksmith to be turned into horse shoes!

---

[73] Evans, 1986, 12.

There were further narrow escapes for the Sutton Hoo site in 1940-41, when war again threatened the old maritime frontier of East Anglia, with its Saxon Shore forts, and Martello towers of the Napoleonic period. A grid of deep ditches was cut all over the heath of Sutton Walks, to hinder the landing of gliders, and these ditches came right up to the burial mounds. Then in 1942 the site was taken over by the army as a training ground. The mounds were used as backgrounds for rifle practice, while two-man slit-trenches were dug on the flanks of four of the mounds, and the drivers of Bren-gun carriers used them to practice going up gradients. Fortunately, Ted Wright, an archaeologist then in the army, managed to get this activity stopped.

'Chance' played a further part in the story as the records made of the ship by the Science Museum were destroyed during the war, leaving only two published plans – provisional and not wholly accurate. However, in 1939 two holidaying schoolmistresses, Miss Mercie Lack and Miss Barbara Wagstaff, both keen amateur photographers, had asked if they could make a photographic record of the ship. They took over a thousand black-and-white photographs, as well as a small number of colour transparencies, and a short length of 8 mm film. '(T)hey captured the most astonishing details of the ship's original structure. It was a record that was to prove vital in the later work of reconstructing the detail of the ship'.[74]

The site was excavated again, 1965-71, when the lack of finds is testimony to the very great care taken in 1939 to recover every fragment. Another archaeological campaign took place, 1986-92, followed by thirteen years of post-excavation work, 1992-2005 (the story is told in Martin Carver, *The Sutton Hoo Story*).

Chance played a further part during this latest campaign. One year, in the quiet period before a new season began, some of the archaeologists who were keeping an eye on the site took to practising golf shots, trying to chip a ball from the top of Mound 1 to the top of Mound 12. It was found that balls which landed short did not roll on, but rolled back. Then as the sun was going down the reason could be seen, as faint shadows showed the presence of two more mounds, now numbered 17 & 18.

The Sutton Hoo cemetery was placed over a prehistoric settlement (mainly Neolithic and Beaker) which should have been evident as earthworks when the first Anglo-Saxon barrows were built. We have to wonder whether Sutton Hoo was an attempt by the Anglo-Saxons to stake a claim as the true heirs of the past.

---

[74] Evans, 1986, 25.

The ship

The Sutton Hoo ship was buried *c.* 625. It was not new at the time – it had been repaired in several places, showing that it had seen life as a working ship. R L S Bruce-Mitford suggested a building date of *c.* 600-610.

It was a very large vessel, some 80 feet long as traced in the ground, and its original length may be estimated at 89 feet. (At the time it was the longest ship of the pre-Viking era to have been found in Europe.) Its greatest beam was 14 feet, and its depth amidships was 4 feet, 6 inches. The prow rose to a height of at least 12 feet, six inches above the level of the keel-plank. It drew two feet of water unladen.[75] It was clinker-built, probably of oak. The keel was formed by a flat, heavy plank reaching about 2 inches below the hull. It is often claimed that the ship's flat keel would have been too weak to support a mast and sail.[76] The ship had fourteen pairs of rowlocks, with space for a further six pairs amidships. Were the latter removed to accommodate the burial chamber? Haywood does not think they were ever there, as there were no rust traces from the iron of such rowlocks. Others think there were a full twenty pairs of oars. No evidence of a mast and mast-step were found, but then they would have had to be removed to make space for the burial chamber.

For dating the finds there were three main methods available: the evidence of archaeology, the evidence of art history, and the documentary record. Radiocarbon dates were taken from a piece of oak from the bottom of the ship, and from beeswax in the iron lamp. The first gave a date of AD 694, plus or minus 45 years, and the second a date of AD 523, plus or minus 45years.[77] The 37 coins were from the time when the Merovingian dynasty ruled France, and they were at first dated by French coin experts to AD 650-60. Then in 1960 the French numismatist Lafaurie revised the end date of the coin parcel to around AD 625. Five of the coins bear the names of identifiable rulers, and all 37 may have been minted before AD 613. John Kent of the British Museum carried out an analysis of the specific gravity of the coins, proposing that the gold content would have reduced through time, as the metal was progressively recycled. By comparing the specific gravity of gold coins from dated hoards he arrived at a date for the Sutton Hoo coins in the early seventh century. The historian Philip Grierson put forward the imaginative hypothesis that the 37 coins, three blanks and two ingots represented the payment of 40 oarsmen, a pilot and a steersman.[78]

The cremations can be dated 530-585, the inhumations 510-610. There is a noteworthy lack of finds from the early migration period and from the period of the conversion to Christianity. There are, however, signs of earlier graves, not yet excavated. They seem to have been rich ones and they are thought to date from the mid-fifth to the mid-sixth centuries.

---

[75] R L S Bruce-Mitford, *The Sutton Hoo ship Burial, A handbook*, 1968, 40-41.
[76] Haywood, 1999, 100.
[77] Carver, 2017, 153.
[78] Carver, 2017, 41.

Was Sutton Hoo a protest against Christianity?

The site has been described as 'arrogantly pagan', a protest against the advance of Christianity, a statement of solidarity with the Germanic North.[79] The left bank of the Deben opposite Woodbridge is still notable for its lack of churches (the only one is at Sutton). Was the area around Sutton 'a pagan enclave'? The seventeenth green of Woodbridge Golf Course, situated on a hillock, was once called Harrow Pightle, a name indicating a pagan temple site. Moreover the use of bronze bowls for cremated remains (as at Sutton Hoo), seems to have been a throw-back to a practice of people of the second century AD living in Germany beyond the Roman frontier.[80]

Carver sees the young men buried under Mounds 3-7, and 18, as the new aristocracy of the seventh century, young men who rejoiced in their riches, in the beauty of their weapons, their horses, their clothes, their prizes – things won by daring deeds. They were the spiritual forebears of young aristocratic cavalry officers down the ages.[81] The young man in Mound 3 was buried with his horse, and with a Frankish iron axe-head. Also in the grave there were burnt fragments of a bone casket with Christian chi-rho inscription, a bronze ewer from Nubia, and a limestone plaque with a winged victory or angel from Alexandria.

Mound 17 housed the intact burial of a young man with a long sword, and what turned out to be horse harness, and there was a horse buried in an adjacent pit. This was the burial of a 'young Siegfried',[82] using a rite that was known in continental Europe in the Iron Age. By the later sixth century horse burial was practised in the upper Rhine, and along the Weser and Elbe rivers, and it spread from there to Scandinavia. At first the horse would be buried in the same grave as the rider, but, after AD 600, horse and man were placed in separate pits, the bridle being placed with the rider. (The early kings claimed to have the blood of horses in their veins.[83])

And so to Mound 1: At one time it was thought that the monument was a cenotaph, in other words there never was a body in the burial-chamber. But in the central area of the ship the finds carried corrosion products that were slightly phosphate-enriched, and the most likely explanation of this is that there had been a body, rendered invisible by the seeping rainwater that had been acidified by its passage through the sand.[84] Two rows of iron clamps suggested there may have been a tree-trunk coffin.

When it became possible to make a more detailed study of the finds a ladybird was uncovered in a goose-down pillow, and there were two pairs of indoor shoes, one measurable at size 7. Was the buried man short and stocky? There was a little bell,

---

[79] Evans, 1986, 109; Carver, 2017, 57, 158.
[80] Carver, 2017, 63, 65, 180.
[81] Carver, 2017, 125, 181.
[82] Carver, 2017, 88-94, 126-9.
[83] Carver, 2017, 182, and endnote 22, citing Chris J Fern, 'Horses in mind' 2011, 150-1, in Carver and others, 2010, 128-57.
[84] Carver, 2017, 36.

perhaps from a favourite falcon. The hanging bowls have their most probable place of origin among the Britons of the north-west – for example, at Mote of Mark, Dunadd – suggesting 'an island-wide equestrian class'. An axe-hammer was found. Its purpose may have been the killing of sacrificial animals (one of the tasks of a pagan king).

Mound 14 was the only rich burial that could be readily identified as that of a woman. The burial was high status, of the mid-seventh century.

The two gallows cemeteries

In the last phase in the use of the burial site, between the eighth and tenth centuries, bodies were buried in odd positions – the excavators spoke of 'ritual trauma' or 'deviance'.[85] It was later established that these were not sacrificial victims but executions. The victims (who have survived as 'sand bodies') were mostly male, and mature, though still young. In Burial 42 two women had been laid face down on top of a beheaded middle-aged man. These were people who had sinned against God and against man (in the person of the ruler), and a pagan cemetery was a proper place to dispose of them.

Wider contacts

The ship-burials in Mounds 1 and 2 find their best parallels in the Mälaren district of Sweden, the cradle of the Svear, the people whose kingdom gave Sweden its name (Sverige). Here there are early medieval cemeteries at Vendel, Valsgärde, Tune in Badelunda and Tune in Alsike. Most of the Valsgärde graves date from the sixth to eighth centuries. There are 15 boat graves, and they show many similarities to those at Sutton Hoo. In fact 'archaeology suggests that the practice of high-status boat-burial in the sixth and early seventh century is restricted to just one small area of Sweden and an equally small area of East Anglia.'[86]

It has been suggested on the strength of these parallels that the Wuffingas, the royal house of East Anglia, were descendants of an eastern Swedish dynasty. An alternative theory sees them as descendants of the royal house of the Geats, who fled to England with their treasures, in the sixth century, after the conquest by the Swedes.[87] But now some of the objects thought to be heirlooms from Sweden have been shown to have been made in England.

The Sutton Hoo helmet has its roots in the parade helmets of the late Roman Empire, but its immediate ancestry lies in a group of helmets buried in the chieftains' graves at Vendel and Valsgärde, where face and neck guards of mail of similar manufacture to the Sutton Hoo mail coat are known. The design of one of the helmet plates (depicting dancing warriors) is found in eastern England and in Sweden. It seems the

---

[85] Carver, 2017, 79.
[86] Evans, 1986, 114.
[87] J L N O'Loughlin,1964: 'Sutton Hoo – the evidence of the documents', *Medieval Archaeology* 8, 1-19

helmet is the product of an English smithing tradition but decorated in a Swedish style. As regards the Sutton Hoo shield there are three possibilities: first, that it was made in Sweden; second, that it was made in England by Swedish craftsmen who had come from the Vendel area;[88] third, it was imported from Frankish workshops that produced fine metalwork for the aristocracies of both Sweden and England. (The early trading links with the Franks of the Rhineland may have been direct, rather than through Kent or London.[89])

The Wuffinga dynasty

The Wuffingas of East Anglia were much more strongly associated with Suffolk than with Norfolk. They took their name from Wuffa, though it seems he was not the first king. A gloss in the *Historia Brittonum*, written by Geoffrey of Monmouth, states that Wehha, the father of Wuffa, was the first ruler of East Anglia. Sam Newton sees the family as relating to the Wulfingas of Sweden. He maintains that they came to the Deben area in the sixth century, and that their successors were responsible for writing down the *Beowulf* poem in the eighth century. The Helmingas, the kin of Hrothgar's first lady in *Beowulf*, have been glimpsed in the place-name Helmingham in Suffolk. The Mound objects feature a number of wolf images. Thus the Wuffingas, Sweden, Sutton Hoo, and Beowulf can be seen as connected. It has been suggested that the carved faces on the Sutton Hoo whetstone are ancestral portraits of the Wuffinga tribe.[90]

Who was buried here?

The relevant part of the East Anglian kinship list reads: Wehha – Wuffa – Tyttla – Rædwald – Rægenhere. Of these kings Rædwald was the most noteworthy, the fourth in Bede's list of 'Bretwaldas' or Britain-wielders (rulers).

Martin Carver[91] has put forward the following suggestions (listed in order of construction):

The one buried in Mound 5 had died violently, the skull cut at least nine times by a sword or similar blade. The body was cremated, then buried with grave goods that suggest this was a man. It was around Mound 5 that the later series of traumatic inhumations were found. It seems that the Mound 5 man was remembered as notable or notorious, and Carver suggests that this was Wuffa.

Carver identifies Mounds 6 and 7 with unnamed warriors who died at the same time as Wuffa – two of the new aristocracy of the seventh century.

Carver suggests that the 'young Siegfried' of Mound 17 was Tyttla, Wuffa's son (who was the right sort of age and date to have been buried with his horse).

---

[88] Evans, 1986, 55, 114, 115.
[89] Hodges, cited by Carver in Bassett, *Origins*, 146.
[90] Evans, 1986, 85.
[91] Carver, 2017, 195.

Mound 2 had been robbed, but the quantity and shape of the rivets indicated that there had originally been a full-sized early medieval ship here. It had been placed above the hole for the burial, not in it. Though no body was now visible there was enough evidence to identify this as the burial of a high-ranking male, and Carver suggests this was Rædwald's son, Raegenhere, killed at the River Idle in 616.

Mound 1 must surely be Rædwald.

Mound 14 may be Rædwald's wife and queen (this would assume that she died aged 60-70). It may well have been Rædwald's wife who organised the great Mound 1 funeral.

Lindsey

'Lindsey' is *Lindesege*, with the 'ege' or 'ey' likely to be the Old English word for 'island', hence 'Lindes island'. Certainly Lindsey is island-like, bounded by the Humber estuary to the north, the sea to the east, and the marshes of the Trent and Witham valleys to the west and south. The Witham valley marshes reached almost as far as Lincoln. Around AD 400 there was a fall in mean temperature, with marked changes in relative sea level, and widespread flooding. This would have reduced the relative gradient of the Humber, and the water backing up would have caused flooding inland. Two north-south ridges are key to the geography of Lindsey: the limestone escarpment of Lincoln Cliff or Edge, and, further east, the chalk of the Lincolnshire Wolds.

In the Roman period Lincoln was in the northern part of the *civitas* of the Corieltauvi tribe, the *civitas* capital being at Leicester. As part of the late third century reorganisation Lincoln probably became the capital of the new province of Flavia Caesariensis. This province likely included the territories of the Corieltauvi and the Iceni.[92]

Roman villas – eight on Lincoln Cliff and six on the Wolds – testify to the prosperity of fourth century Lindsey. This was based on agriculture, salt extraction, iron-smelting, pottery manufacture, and resources from rivers and the sea.

The region also had good communications. Lincoln was a focus for the Roman road system. Ermine Street, the direct route from London to York, passed through Lincoln, but then avoided the Humber crossing by turning north-westwards a few miles north of the city, to cross the Trent at Littleborough. Lindsey was also served by a network of minor roads and ancient trackways. An important ridgeway track followed the western escarpment of the Wolds. It is now known as Caistor High Street between Horncastle and Caistor, while further north, it becomes Middlegate Lane. The Trent and Ancholme rivers gave access to the Humber, the gateway both to coastal trade and overseas trade across the North Sea. The Trent also gave access to the Midlands, while from the Humber the Ouse led into the heart of Yorkshire. Coming from the south the routes into Lindsey were by the Steeping Valley, and the

---

[92] B Eagles, in Bassett, *Origins*, 1989, 202-3.

Witham and its tributaries. East-west travel was much more problematic. There were few crossing places in the broad, marshy valley of the River Ancholme, Brigg probably being one of them. (The valley was, however, perfect beaver habitat, and among amulets found in Anglo-Saxon graves in Lindsey are silver-mounted beavers' teeth in a woman's grave at Worlaby, near the Ancholme.)

Clearly the Lindsey area would have been worth defending. There may have been Saxon Shore forts at Skegness and Grainthorpe, since lost to the sea, and perhaps another at Brough-on-Humber. Forts inland at Horncastle and Caistor, closely resembling those of the Saxon Shore, offered defence in depth.[93] The Roman walls and projecting towers of Horncastle date from the late third century, or perhaps a little later. It is probable that there was an inlet of the sea only 5½ miles south of Horncastle. Caistor dominated the Ancholme valley, and the main north-south route along the Wolds passed through it, so it, too, was of strategic importance.

Chip-carved belt equipment of the second half of the fourth century is fairly widespread in north Lincolnshire, and it is not clear whether this had belonged to soldiers or civilians. It may have been the equipment of some kind of civilian militia recruited by the *Vicarius* (governor) of Roman Britain in the fourth century, to farm, and to guard lines of communication in the Kirmington area.[94] On the other hand units of the Roman field army may have been billeted in Lincoln from time to time.

Kirmington has yielded the earliest object of certain Germanic origin to have been found in Lindsey, a *tutulus* brooch, probably of the second half of the fourth century. This brooch type was worn by women, and it originates in the Elbe/Weser area of north Germany. A supporting-arm brooch, of *c.* 400, has been found at Hibaldstow, and another at the Elsham cremation cemetery. Thus at two late Roman sites there is evidence suggesting the presence of Germanic women in the population *c.* 400. Perhaps these were the wives of Germanic soldiers, recruited as *laeti* and given unused land in return for military service. At Hibaldstow they would have been well-placed to protect settlements on the Cliff, and at Kirmington, with its strategic cross-roads, they could have guarded the important route through Brigg and the Kirmington Gap. The enigmatic Yarborough Camp at Croxton, overlooking Kirmington, has mounds at its corners which might be explained as earthen versions of the bastions of a Saxon Shore fort. It seems to have been fortified or refortified in the fourth or fifth century, clumsily based on Roman military architecture. Another important route used the Ancaster Gap, and there is some evidence that from the first half of the fifth century Germanic soldiers were stationed here to defend it.[95]

[93] Eagles, in Bassett, *Origins*, 1989, 205-6, citing Field and Hurst, *Roman Horncastle*, 85-7; K Leahy, *The Anglo-Saxon kingdom of Lindsey*, 2010, 26.
[94] Leahy, 2010, 30-1.
[95] P Stafford, *The East Midlands in the Early Middle Ages*, 1985, 81.

Early Lindsey

Winteringham

Humber

Winterton

Middlegate
Lane

Elsham

Kirmington

Brigg

Caistor

Cleatham

Hibaldstow

South Elkington

Caistor High Street

Lincoln

River
Trent

Horncastle

River
Steeping

West Keal

Loveden

River
Witham

Miles

| 0 | 10 | 20 |

Map 11

As for Lincoln itself, the 'dark earth' is late Roman, not post-Roman. ('Dark earth' was the waste ground of late Roman Britain. It may be the rotted remains of late Roman wooden, or wattle and daub, buildings.) This layer marked the end of urban Lincoln. Nevertheless the city's defences were strong, and they would have presented a formidable obstacle to Germanic raiders coming up from the Wash. No Anglo-Saxon cemeteries have been found in the hinterland of Lincoln, which may mean that the post-Roman power was able to control the area. At the same time the city walls, and the aura of *Romanitas*, would have attracted the attention of status- and military-minded Anglo-Saxon leaders.[96]

The Corieltauvi *civitas* perhaps broke up after the Romans left, leaving a British princedom around Newark-on-Trent (perhaps with Anglian mercenaries posted here), a Middle Anglian princedom around the Sleaford and Loveden Hill area, while the *Colonia* at Lincoln, in the north of the former Corieltauvi territory, probably took control of what was to become the kingdom of Lindsey. (A *colonia* was originally a Roman outpost planted in conquered territory. Later it signified a Roman city of the highest status. Retired legionaries were often given lands in a *colonia*.)

Early Lindsey is evidenced in the large cremation cemeteries at Elsham Wold, Cleatham, Fonaby near Caistor-on-the-Wolds, South Elkington near Louth, and West Keal. Prehistoric and Romano-British sites were re-used, perhaps to emphasise the new ownership. The Elsham Wold cremation cemetery was excavated in 1975 and 1976, and dating evidence based on the metalwork indicates use from the early fifth century and on into the sixth century. It could have been the burial place for *laeti* settled around Kirmington, which area has produced both very late Roman and very early Saxon material. The cemetery at Cleatham (excavated in 1979, then from 1984 onwards) was in use from the fifth century until at least the late sixth century. The cemeteries at Fonaby, South Elkington, and West Keal have all produced pots decorated with *stehende Bögen*, a design which lasted little beyond 500.[97] Great square-headed brooches were found with the inhumations. Such brooches were not used in the early settlement period, and John Hines has shown that they were introduced into England with a secondary influx of people from southern Scandinavia after about 470.[98] There was a dramatic increase in the size of Anglo-Saxon cemeteries in the late fifth and early sixth centuries, and the close link with Roman sites ended. The old settlement pattern which underlay that of the Roman occupation reasserted itself. For example, there is a line of early village names in Lindsey which is not associated with the artificial line of the Roman road from Lincoln, but with the prehistoric track and spring-line sites favoured by earlier settlers.[99]

---

[96] Eagles, in Bassett, *Origins*, 1989, 208.
[97] Eagles, in Bassett, *Origins*, 1989, 210.
[98] Leahy, 2010, 63.
[99] P Stafford, 1985, 81, 83.

About the only literary record of early Lindsey is the genealogy of its kings in the so-called 'Anglian Collection' of genealogies. This begins with a certain Geot, and the line of descent from him is: Godulf – Finn – Frioðulf – Frealaf – Woden – Winta – Cretta (or Critta, Crida) – Cuelgils (or Cueldgils) – Cædbæd – Bubba – Beda – Biscop – Eanferð – Eatta – Aldfrið. The first of these with any historical basis is Winta, who can probably be dated in the middle of the fifth century. This name is found in the place-names Winteringham and Winterton which lie almost on the banks of the Humber. Winta's folk may have come up the Humber and made contact with the descendants of *laeti* on the eastern Wolds.[100]

The last name in the list is that of Aldfrith, and he is probably the 'Ealdfrid' who attested a land charter confirmed by Offa of Mercia in the late eighth century. Stenton suggests Aldfrith lived from about 750-790, that Biscop flourished about 660, and Cædbæd about 570. This last name is an anglicisation of the British name Catuboduos. Perhaps he was the ruler of a British princedom based on Lincoln, or the offspring of British-Anglian intermarriage. It seems the kings of Lindsey were not ashamed to have a *walh* ('Welshman', 'stranger') in the family tree.[101] It would appear, by the way, that the Continental Germans had a blanket term, *Walhōz*, which meant not so much 'foreigners' as people who had been Romanized. The 'Welshnut' or walnut, for example, was the nut of the Roman lands.[102]

In the second quarter of the seventh century there was an Anglian *praefectus Lindocolinae civitatis*, and this suggests that there was a city population once again, living within the old walls. Bede mentions the Prefect's name, Blaecca, and as the name alliterates suggestively with the Beda, Bubba and Biscop in the genealogy of the kings of Lindsey, he may have been of the kingly dynasty. Blaecca was converted by Paulinus, and he built a fine stone church, though by Bede's day it was roofless, and all but deserted.[103]

Lindsey has few surviving Celtic place-names. These include the river names, Trent, Ancholme, Witham, and Humber. 'Horncastle' appears to be a part-translation of the Romano-British name *Bannovalium*. The first element of that name means 'peak, horn, or spur (of land)', and the second is the word 'strong', suggesting a possible meaning 'horn-strong'.[104]

---

[100] Myres, 1989, 176-7, 180.
[101] Eagles, in Bassett, *Origins*, 1989, 206-7.
[102] C Thomas, *Celtic Britain*, 1997, 39; Davies, *A History of Wales*, 2007, 69.
[103] Bede, *HE* II. 16; Myres, 1989, 178-9.
[104] Rivet, Smith, *The Place-names of Roman Britain*, 1981, 262, 265; O Padel, in Carroll and Parsons, *Perceptions of Place*, 2013, 40.

Deira

Deira, and Bernicia to the north, both have British names and they were surrounded by Celtic kingdoms. It is possible that they were in origin British kingdoms or tribal territories that were taken over by Anglo-Saxon warbands. The border between Deira and Bernicia is thought to have been the valley of the Tees, or the North Yorkshire Moors.[105] It has been suggested that the name (the 'Deur' of *Historia Brittonum*, 61) means 'oak-forest'.[106] Deur/Deira was probably centred on the Vale of York, and included much of the hinterland of the city. It may also have included the adjoining territory of the Parisi tribe, the present East Riding.[107]

Beside the Roman road that leads north from Brough lies the great cremation cemetery of Sancton in East Yorkshire. Here, in a cemetery used for at least 250 years, there were thousands of burials, covering at least 30 acres. Among the cremation urns there are many parallels with pottery from Schleswig and Fyn, of the late fourth/early fifth centuries, and with Borgstedt in Angeln – too many for this to be mere coincidence.[108] It was no doubt these parts that Bede was thinking about when he spoke of the old Anglian homeland as largely deserted. There are also parallels with pottery in Saxon territory, further south and west around the lower Elbe.

Cemetery evidence shows that Deira was more intensively settled by Germanic incomers than Bernicia. (The Angles were settled in Deira by *c.* 450, Bernicia by *c.* 500.) That these burials are found in association with major Romano-British military centres may be thought to fit in with the broad lines of Gildas's story of the employment of Anglo-Saxon mercenaries, their rebellion and their takeover of territory. It is not hard to imagine that the rebellion of such strategically placed Anglo-Saxon forces would have had the severest effect on the British polity to which they had been attached.[109] *Historia Brittonum* 61 says that Soemil was 'the first to separate Deira from Bernicia'. This most likely means that he took it from the hands of the British, and he may have been a leading figure among the Yorkshire *laeti* of the first half of the fifth century. He was the great-great-great-grandfather of Ælle, king of Deira 568-598, so his takeover would have to be placed in the middle years of the fifth century.

Archaeological evidence seems to imply that the Deirans had reached York by the year 500, but their expansion towards the west was long delayed by the Britons of Elmet.

[105] McClure, Collins edition of Bede's *Ecclesiastical History*, 384.
[106] C Thomas, *Celtic Britain*, 1997, 50.
[107] C Lowe, *Angels, Fools and Tyrants*, 1999, 7; Dark, 1994, 128; Yorke, *Kings and Kingdoms of early Anglo-Saxon England*, 1990, 74.
[108] Myres, 1989, 69, 72.
[109] Dumville, 'The origins of Northumbria: some aspects of the British background', in Bassett, *Origins*, 1989, 215, 219; S Bassett, *Origins*, 1989, 24; S Evans, *Lords of Battle*, 2000, 19n; C Thomas, *Celtic Britain*, 1997, 127.

Essex

Sites like Mucking, dating from the early years of the fifth century, show that Essex was among the first areas of Britain to receive Anglo-Saxon settlers. The Mucking settlement was on marginal land, and it followed a Roman villa occupation. There seem to have been three key factors in its siting: a strategic location on higher ground, a likely river crossing, and a clear line of sight down the Thames estuary. It was probably on the eastern borders of the *territorium* of London, and it could have been a posting of *foederati* or *laeti* placed here by the city authorities. This perception seems to be borne out by the finds of early fifth century Saxon pottery and late Roman military metalwork.[110] The fourth-century signal tower at Wapping may have been part of the same early warning system. The Mucking cemeteries and settlement were in use from the early fifth to the early seventh century. The settlement was moved downhill in the seventh century, an example, perhaps, of so-called 'Middle Saxon shuffle'. (This phrase has been applied to a known feature of Anglo-Saxon settlement history. It refers to the shifting of settlements from upland sites to valley bottoms, roughly in the period 660-900. This may have come about through soil exhaustion, or through a number of small settlements coming together, perhaps with pressure from a great landowner such as the church.)

Evidence from Mucking, the Roman villa at Rivenhall, and the Roman town at Great Chesterford seems to show the peaceful interaction of Romano-British and Germanic people, and to throw light on the circumstances through which the territory of the Trinovantes became an Anglo-Saxon kingdom. It is possible that there was a Romano-British enclave based on the small walled town of Great Chesterford and its hinterland, which was then taken over, more or less peacefully, by the Saxons.[111] Yorke writes, 'Recent studies of the Essex landscape and the relationship between Roman and Saxon sites suggest that the structure of the Roman countryside largely survived and that any changes in rural settlement were a gradual response to changing economic and political circumstances. Early Saxon settlers would have been in the minority and their cemeteries are centred on the coast and eastern waterways'.[112]

The late Roman belt fittings and Romano-Saxon pottery found at Colchester, together with fifth and sixth century sunken-featured huts, also suggest continuity.[113] The Mersea Road and Butt Road cemeteries have produced both late Roman and post-Roman burials, and there seems to have been a sub-Roman church at Mersea Road. However, it does not seem to have lasted into the seventh century, when the East Saxons were converted to Christianity. It had no early associations with the East Saxon kings, and Colchester did not become the seat of a bishop.

---

[110] Evison and Myres, *The Antiquaries Journal*, 1968.

[111] Bassett, *Origins*, 25-6.

[112] Yorke, 1990, 46.

[113] For questions raised about so-called 'Romano-Saxon' ware see 'Limitations of archaeology' in the Appendices.

A Chilterns/London enclave?

There was a continuing Romano-British population, probably of Trinovantian folk, in the wooded North Chilterns in the fifth century.[114] The territory was centred on St Alban's or London or both. The boundaries of this British kingdom (if such it was) seem to have been the Chiltern scarp on the north side, the River Orwell in the east, the Thames on the south side.

In late Roman and sub-Roman London there is a marked contrast between that part of the city which lay west of the Walbrook, and that part to the east. The western part of the city was never so densely built up, and much of it seems to have become gardens or open ground. It was in this comparatively uncluttered area that the Augustinian mission chose to build their church of St Paul in 604 as the seat for a bishop. East of the Walbrook, however, and especially near the site of the later Tower of London there are signs of much greater activity in the last days of the Roman city. The centre of the post-Roman administration in this rather shrunken city may have been at the Cripplegate Roman fort.[115]

Archaeological evidence indicates early Saxon occupation of sites such as Mitcham, Shepperton, Hanwell, Beddington, Croydon, Orpington and Darenth, on the fertile terraces of the Thames and its tributaries. These sites are closely related to the Romano-British settlement and road system, and the Anglo-Saxons may have been placed here by the sub-Roman authorities in London as *laeti* to guard the approaches to the city.[116] Roman coinage in Anglo-Saxon graves may indicate protection money paid to them by this isolated British state. It is, however, hard to see any real signs of continuity in political and social life between Roman and Saxon London. For example the street-plan of medieval London bears no relation to the Roman grid of streets and *insulae*, other than ongoing use of some approach roads to the old Roman gates.

It is not known when the London/Chilterns area came under Anglo-Saxon control, but it may have occurred at any time after about 460.[117] It may be that the area was overrun by the Anglo-Saxons in the late fifth century, then retaken by the Britons in the Ambrosius/Arthur counter-thrust. The Chilterns seem to have finally come into Anglo-Saxon hands towards the end of the sixth century, as a result of the warring of Cutha/Cuthwulf of Wessex in 571.

---

[114] C Thomas, *Christianity in Roman Britain to AD 500*, 1983, 260; D Hooke, *The Landscape of Anglo-Saxon England*, 1998, 142; Bailey, in Bassett, *Origins*, 1989, 110.

[115] Bailey, in Bassett, *Origins*, 1989, 110; Stenton, 1967, 55-6.

[116] Bailey, in Bassett, *Origins*, 1989, 112-3; Dark, 1994, 88-9, 127; P Drewett, D Rudling, M Gardiner, *The South-east to AD 1000*, 1988, 256.

[117] Bailey, in Bassett, *Origins*, 110, 113.

'Greater' Essex

The original bounds of the East Saxon diocese of London would almost certainly have been based on the boundaries of the kingdom of Essex. On this evidence the kingdom once included not only the Essex that we know, but also Middlesex, Surrey, and south-eastern Hertfordshire, as far west as Hemel Hempstead at the foot of the Chilterns. Middlesex and Surrey may have been independent at one time, only to be taken over as Essex became a rising power. West Kent was settled by Saxons, and it may also have been Essex territory until wrested from its power by Jutish East Kent. This may have been in the time of Æthelberht of Kent, one of Bede's 'Bretwaldas'. Surrey was also lost at an early date, and then in the eighth century Middlesex, the Hertfordshire lands, and London, were taken over by Mercia.

The Middle Saxons seem to have been a loose confederation of people groups, with no central authority. Among these groups were the *Geddingas, Gillingas,* and *Gumeningas* – whence the place-names Yeading, Ealing, and Harrow. Geddi, Gilla, and Guma may have been three early Saxon leaders in west Middlesex. Harrow was 'the pagan sanctuary (*hearh*) of Guma's people', and according to Stenton this was 'the most impressive site of heathen Germanic worship in

England'.[118] Such a loose confederation would have been easy prey for powerful neighbours, first Essex and then Mercia.

In the East Saxon kingly genealogies the common ancestor from whom descent was traced was Sledd. He was married to Ricula, sister of Æthelbert of Kent, and the latter seems to have exercised considerable authority over the East Saxons. It was Æthelbert, and not Sabert, Sledd's son and successor, who built and endowed St Paul's in London. Sledd was said to be the son of Æscwine who is often identified as the first Essex king. Working backwards from Aescwine the family line reads Aescwine – Offa – Bedca – Sigefugi – Swæppa – Gesecg – Seaxnet (or Saxnot). Seaxnet was a god still worshipped by the continental Saxons as late as the eighth century.

Kent

In the *Anglo-Saxon Chronicle* for the year 449, we find the following entry: 'In this year Marcian and Valentinian obtained the kingdom and reigned seven years. In their days Vortigern invited the Angles hither, and they then came hither to Britain in three ships.' The Chronicler goes on to say that Vortigern settled the newcomers in the south-east, that they were Jutes, and their leaders were two brothers, Hengest and Horsa. It is thus that the written tale of Anglo-Saxon Kent begins. (Marcian and Valentinian were, respectively, the Eastern and Western Roman emperors in the middle of the fifth century.)

The written sources

There is, in fact, more written material for the origins of the Kentish kingdom than for any other part of Anglo-Saxon England. We have the works of Gildas and Bede, the *Anglo-Saxon Chronicle*, and the *Historia Brittonum*. We also have hints of an unfolding drama in three short pieces of Anglo-Saxon poetry, the so-called *Finnsburg Fragment*, an Episode in the *Beowulf* saga, and *Widsith*.

In his *De Excidio Britanniae*, 'On the Ruin of Britain', Gildas tells how in their despair the Britons wrote to one 'Agitius', appealing for help: 'The barbarians push us back to the sea, the sea pushes us back to the barbarians; between these two kinds of death we are either drowned or slaughtered' (*DEB* 20.1). 'Agitius' should probably be corrected to Aëtius, who was *magister militum* ('Master of the Soldiers') in the Western Roman Empire, and four times consul. The Britons got no help from him. (Bede, who dates this letter to 446, explains that the Romans could not come in answer to this call, because of the threat of Attila's Huns. These were then in the Balkans, but they might come back at any time. They did in fact invade Gaul in 451.)

Gildas goes on to tell of the folly of a *superbus tyrannus*, that is, 'proud tyrant'. (In the context of the fifth and sixth centuries the word 'tyrannus' meant 'usurper' rather than 'oppressor') This title implies lordship over lesser *tyranni*, and Gildas's words seem to suggest that the tyrant acted as the chairman of a Council, like a Roman

---

[118] Stenton, 1967, 54.

provincial governor.[119] In his melodramatic style Gildas tells how the tyrant and his council made up their minds to let in the ferocious Saxons – 'hated by man and God' – like wolves into the fold (*DEB* 23.1) These came in three 'keels', and they were encouraged by favourable auguries. They were quick to complain that their supplies were not enough. They turned on their hosts and ravaged the land from sea to sea.

The Northumbrian monk, Bede, completed his *Historia Ecclesiastica*, 'The Ecclesiastical History of the English People', in AD 731. He had good Kentish sources of information, and he helps us with the names and dates that Gildas does not supply. He sets the *adventus Saxonum* (the coming of the Saxons) in the time of the eastern emperor Marcian (AD 450-57) and the western emperor Valentinian III (425-55), in other words between the years 450-55. And he calls the tyrant 'Vurtigernus'. (In Romano-British this is 'Wortigernos' and the name has come down to us as 'Vortigern'.) The family connections of this man seem to have been mainly with east-central Wales, near the south-west border of Powys.[120]

In a well-known passage Bede says that the Germanic mercenaries were from 'three very powerful Germanic tribes', the Saxons, Angles, and Jutes (*HE* I.15). They were to receive land and *stipendia* ('pay'), and it is likely enough that failure to come up with the promised money led to the Saxon revolt. As to the leaders of the newcomers Bede notes that the first chieftains 'are said to have been Hengist and Horsa'. The *Anglo-Saxon Chronicle* tells us that they landed at *Ypwinesfleot* or *Heopwinesfleot*, (possibly Ebbsfleet). In its account of the arrival of Hengest and Horsa and their followers the *Historia Brittonum* adds something not found in the other sources, namely, that the three ships of the newcomers were 'driven into exile'. This is not at all unlikely.

Vortigern has passed into legend and the early history of Celtic Britain as (in the words of Charles Thomas) 'the archetypal national mistake-maker, if not betrayer'.[121] Elsewhere Thomas has commented that our versions of what happened all come from those who were wise after the event.[122] Vortigern's actions may in fact have been modelled on Roman policy. Since Agitius/Aëtius had refused troops to help Britain, and since any that he might have sent would, like enough, have been Germanic anyway, why not recruit direct? The threat was from the sea, so Vortigern needed men with experience of the sea – Saxons. Perhaps the coming of Jutes to Kent (and Hampshire) originated with 'related treaty settlements on the *Litus Saxonicum* in the final or sub-Roman phase of its functioning in the fifth century.'[123] The move would not have seemed unusual or unworthy at the time – it just happened to go wrong.

---

[119] R Bromwich, ed, *Trioedd Ynys Prydein*, 2006, 389; Alcock, 1975, 357.
[120] Bromwich, *Trioedd*, 2006, 389.
[121] C Thomas, *Celtic Britain*, 1997, 43.
[122] C Thomas, *Britain and Ireland in Early Christian Times*, 1971, 33.
[123] Myres, 1989, 114.

The poetry

The *Finnsburg Fragment* (also called *The Frisian Slaughter*) opens part way through a sentence and breaks off, forty-eight lines later, also in mid-sentence. The poetry concerns a deadly night onset against sixty warriors holed up in a hall. Their leader is one Hnæf, and several of his followers are named. These are Sigeferth, Eaha, Ordlaf, Guthlaf and Hengest. Two other warriors are referred to: Guthhere, one of the attackers, and a certain Garulf son of Guthlaf, who is urged (in vain) not to risk so precious a life in the first onset. The fighting goes on through five days, with none of the defenders falling. At last a wounded warrior turns away, his mail-coat riven through, his helmet pierced. Then the leader asks how can the other warriors endure their wounds? And there the *Fragment* ends.

If this was all we had, there would be little hope of understanding the tale. But there are two other sources to draw on. The poem *Widsith*, as we have seen, is a 'who's who' of Germanic kings, kingdoms, and heroes from the third to sixth centuries AD. It does not give us any more of the Finnsburg tale, though it names some of those who were part of that story, in particular, Finn Folcwalding and Hnæf of the Hocings. The other source is an Episode in the *Beowulf* epic. After the hero has grappled the monster, Grendel, and fatally wounded him, the Danish king, Hrothgar, gives a feast, and he bids his poet sing to the gathering. The man's song (lines 1066b-1159a) is, in the Anglo-Saxon manner, marked by allusion, by words with half-hidden meanings. They touch on events, and leave the audience, if alert, to grasp who and what is referred to. We who live so long after these events are sorely handicapped when it comes to fathoming the old tales. Yet we are not wholly at a loss, so let us see what we do have.

In the *Finnsburg Fragment* we hear of a treacherous night-onset against a hall defended by sixty warriors, and we have the names of Hnæf 'Battle-young', and Hengest. We also hear of a certain Garulf son of Guthlaf, 'the first man in the Frisian islands', and how one, Guthhere, sought in vain to hold him back from risking his life.

In the *Beowulf* Episode we have:

Hnæf who was 'fated to fall in the Frisian ambush',

Hildeburgh, daughter of Hoc: she had 'little cause to speak of the good faith of the Jutes', and she lost both son and brother in the fight.

Finn Folcwalda is there; most of his followers were killed in the fight.

After the fight Finn made a pact with Hengest, he being the new leader of the party of Danes and Jutes.

The body of Hnæf was burned on a funeral pyre, along with the body of Hildeburgh's son, who, we learn, was Hnæf's nephew.

Hengest was constrained by winter storms to stay with Finn. He brooded over the fact that his lord's death was unavenged. Here we have, in starkest form, the clash of two 'oughts' so beloved of the Anglo-Saxon poet. Having given his troth to Finn Hengest ought to keep his word, but then he really ought to avenge his lord.

With winter passed, 'the son of Hunlaf' laid the best of blades, a 'battle-gleaming sword', across Hengest's knees.

After a sea-crossing, presumably to the Dane-land and back, Guthlaf and Oslaf came again. In the renewed fighting Finn was slain, and the 'Scylding crewmen' took Hildeburgh and restored her to her people.

This is poetry and not historical narrative, but it does not follow that the events and the players were never part of true life. There is nothing here that could not have happened, and the tale that is told in the poems fits well with what we know of pagan Anglo-Saxon culture and outlook. So, while acknowledging that we are engaging in supposals, let us try to guess what may have happened on the southern rim of the North Sea in the middle of the fifth century.

Untroth and revenge

We will begin by supposing that there were two rising powers in the region. In the west the Frisians under Finn 'Folcwalding' were building a kingdom that would stretch from the Rhine mouths eastwards as far as the Weser. At the same time the Danes under Hnæf were moving out of their original homeland in southern Sweden and starting to take over the islands at the entrance to the Baltic. The scene was the more fraught because there were other folk, the Jutes, caught in the middle. The Jutes were a folk asundered, two parties harbouring a great hatred towards each other. For them the fight at Finnsburg was the latest chapter in their bitter feud. What was at stake, and who was the Garulf whose life should not have been put at risk needlessly? In its list of Dark Age rulers the poem *Widsith* names a certain Gefwulf of the 'Ytum' (Jutes?), followed by Finn Folcwalding of the Frisian kin (lines 26-7). Alan Bliss thinks it may well be that Garulf and Gefwulf are the same man, and that Gefwulf is more likely to be the true name. *Widsith* is, after all, an older and better authority than the *Fragment* as it has come down to us in the 1705 transcription made by the Reverend George Hickes. (Hickes was a Church of England clergyman, excluded from ministry as a 'non-juror', that is, one who would not swear an oath to William III because he had previously sworn loyalty to James II. He afterwards spent much of his time gathering material about the languages of northern Europe. He said that he came across the *Fragment* on a single leaf in a book in Lambeth Palace Library. This leaf has not been seen since, so Hickes' work cannot be checked.) Bliss goes on to suggest that Hickes also got the name of Gefwulf's father wrong – he calls him Guthlaf. There is another Guthlaf in the poem, named among the defenders of the hall. If there really were two men of that name involved in the fight one might have expected some comment or explanation. It seems more likely that Hickes made another copying error here, and Bliss says that on palaeographical grounds a correction to 'Guthulf' would be likely enough.[124]

---

[124] Bliss, ed, *Finn and Hengest*, 1998, 33.

We will suppose, then, that Hoc, the father of Hnæf, had overthrown the Jutish kingdom (until then a 'buffer' between Frisian and Dane) and that he was helped in this by infighting among the Jutes. Perhaps Guthulf had slain, unrightly, a Jutish chief, and when the Danes made war against him that chief's followers left him to his fate, then afterwards acknowledged Hoc's lordship. But others, very much Guthulf's men, were not to be reconciled to the usurping Dane. They took the young Gefwulf, Guthulf's son, and sought refuge with Finn and the Frisians. And they hoarded in their hearts a deep bitterness against those Jutes who, as they saw it, had betrayed their lord. By the time of which the poems tell Hoc had passed on, and there were two rivals, Finn and Hnæf, who had good reasons to be wary of each other. Where would the Danes make their next thrust? What trouble might the Frisians stir up for the Danes, using the Jutish exiles?

Our next supposal is that the two leaders, Finn and Hnæf, saw that from threat could come thriving, through making a marriage alliance. For Finn it would mean a check on Danish thrustfulness, while Hnæf could look to Finn to keep his Jutes under firm hand. So a marriage was arranged between Finn and Hnæf's sister, Hildeburh. A son was born to them, and he was named Frithuwulf. When he was weaned he was sent as foster-son to Hildeburh's brother, Hnæf. There he stayed until, at fifteen, he came to war-years. Then, with summer over and the onset of winter not far away, Hnæf took Frithuwulf, and, with sixty warriors (Danes, Jutes, and others), sailed into Frisia. They were warmly welcomed by Finn, but not by Finn's Jutes. For them the duty of revenge outweighed the duty of hospitality, and in the outcome they would not let Hengest and other 'traitor' Jutes go in peace. There followed the night-onset, the deaths of Hnæf and Frithuwulf, a patched-up peace, a winter of brooding, then, in the spring, Hengest's revenge on Finn. This was about AD 451-2.

Hengest the 'wrecca'

What now for Hengest? The word used of him in the *Beowulf* Episode, line 1137, is 'wrecca', the root of today's English 'wretch'. To the Anglo-Saxons it meant an exile, even an outlaw. In Old English songcraft it is used of men driven from their homeland by usurpers or invaders, or by feuds, or their own wild deeds. Hengest, then, was now a footloose adventurer with a warband, looking for work. It was at this time that Vortigern was looking for troops to hire, and somehow the two parties were brought together.

Hengest sailed with his men across to Kent, and the island of Thanet was given to them. It was a key base from which to intercept shipping in the Dover Straits. Perhaps Vortigern thought to guard against any move by the Aurelians – Ambrosius and the pro-Roman party – to link up with Roman forces in Gaul, and bring back Roman protection and control. It is possible that the Jutish settlements in Hampshire were also the result of a treaty settlement, whereby the Portchester end of the Saxon Shore network could be held.

Vortigern seems to have been weak and shifty, and he could not hold the loyalty of a man like Hengest, 'an experienced man, shrewd and skilful' (*Historia Brittonum*, 37).

The latter sized up the weakness of Vortigern's position and, with the latter's ready agreement, brought over another sixteen longships of warriors. Hengest's fair daughter, 'a beautiful and very handsome girl', also came over. Geoffrey of Monmouth names the girl 'Renwein' or 'Rowena'. This may be the Anglo-Saxon name, 'Hrothwyn', a name not known from elsewhere, but one that preserves an 'h' alliteration with the name 'Hengest'.[125] In the Welsh *Trioedd* ('Triads') she is R(h)onwen 'the pagan woman'. Rachel Bromwich thinks this is the true form of the name, and that its meaning is 'White' or 'Fair lance', a fitting name for a slender girl. Her name was nevertheless understood in Wales to be *rhawn* plus *gwen*. The former usually means 'horse hair' but it was also used of a girl's hair, and the latter means 'white' or 'fair'. The Welsh poets looked on Rhonwen as the mother of the English nation, and by extension a kind of 'summing-up' of that folk.[126]

The story given in the *Historia* goes on to tell how Vortigern became drunk at a feast given by Hengest, and Satan entered into his heart, so that he looked on the maiden and wanted her. Speaking through Hengest's interpreter, Ceretic, he asked for her hand, offering as bride-wealth up to half his kingdom. After taking counsel of his elders Hengest asked for the whole kingdom of Kent. Vortigern agreed, without any reference to the king, Gwyrangon. The *Historia* adds that Vortigern then gave Gwyrangon secretly into the hands of the Saxons.

The war in Kent

The betrayal of the Kentish king seems to have provoked a reaction. Vortigern found himself side-lined, and the British fought back under the leadership of his son, Vortimer. Both the *Chronicle* and the *Historia* describe a campaign marked by four battles, but the final outcomes are not the same. In the *Chronicle* record the first battle was at *Ægelesþrep* in 455, where Horsa was slain. Then there was a battle at *Crecganford* (456), after which the Britons 'forsook Kent, and fled to London in great terror'. The third battle was at a place near *Wippedesfleot* (465), where twelve Welsh nobles were slain, together with a thegn named Wipped. Lastly, in 473, at an unnamed battle-site 'Hengest and Æsc fought against the Welsh and captured innumerable spoils, and the Welsh fled from the English like fire'.

According to the *Historia Brittonum*, 43-44, Vortimer fought 'four keen battles' (in the event only three are named). The first was on the river Derguentid (Derventio or Darent), the second at a place called Episford in English, or 'Rhyd yr afael' in Brittonic. Here Horsa, and Vortigern's son Cateyrn (Catigirnos or Catigernos) were slain, so this must be the *Ægelesþrep* of the *Chronicle*. The third battle was fought 'in the open country by the Inscribed Stone on the shore of the Gallic Sea', and the barbarians were beaten. 'They (the barbarians) fled to their keels and were drowned as they clambered aboard them like women.' The fighting ended in stalemate, with the Jutes penned up in Thanet, threatened and terrified by the forces of Vortimer, while the Britons lacked the warships to get across to the island.

---

[125] Chadwick, 1907, 46n.
[126] Bromwich, ed, *Trioedd*, 2006, 488-9.

After a while the Jutish host sailed away, though this proved to be only a ruse. Vortimer died soon after, poisoned by Rhonwen, in Geoffrey of Monmouth's account.[127] According to *Historia Brittonum*, 44, 'Before he died he told his followers to set his tomb by the coast, in the port from which (the English) had departed, saying "I entrust it to you. Wherever else they may hold a British port or may have settled, they will never again live in this land." ' But they ignored his command and buried him instead at Lincoln. In the more primitive tradition found in the Welsh Triad 37R Vortimer's bones were actually buried in the chief ports. In this Triad Vortigern is 'Gwrtheyrn the Thin' (that is, 'lacking in substance'), and he is guilty of one of the Three Unfortunate Disclosures. If the bones of Gwerthefyr the Blessed, that is, Vortimer, had stayed hidden no Saxon Oppression would have come to this island. But for love of a woman – 'Rhonwen the pagan woman' – Vortigern revealed where they were.

After the death of Vortimer, his father, Vortigern, came back, and so did Hengest. The latter now turned to treachery. He spoke of peace and a long-term treaty, and it was agreed that the leading men of the two sides would meet, with everyone leaving his weapons behind him. Vortigern was perhaps over-confident, seeing that Aëtius, who he had perhaps long feared, had been murdered in 454, and Rome itself had been sacked by the Vandals in 455. There seemed to be little likelihood that Rome would ever again step in to help its friends in Britain. So the British leaders came to the meeting unarmed. Hengest and his men, however, came with knives hidden in their shoes. When Hengest gave the word, 'Saxons, draw your knives', his men took out their daggers and slew the Britons. Vortigern alone was spared, and to save his life he yielded up more land (*Historia Brittonum* 45-6).

Mapping the tide of war

Many writers judge the *Chronicle* and the *Historia* to be in conflict. But this can be said only if the places named can be identified. From the *Chronicle* we have the name of the landing place – *Ypwinesfleot* or *Heopwinesfleot* – and those of three battle sites, *Ægelesþrep*, *Crecganford*, and *Wippedesfleot*.

As regards 'Ypwinesfleot' Nicholas Brooks has said that this seems to be significantly close to, but not the same as, 'Yppelesfleot', that is, Ebbsfleet on Thanet.[128] (Yppelesfleot is 'the creek or inlet of a stream where hips grow'.) 'Ægelesþrep' (Ægel's 'thorp' or farm) is often taken to be another name for Aylesford, but this involves the assumption that the familiar word 'ford' was substituted for 'threp'. 'Crecganford' is said to be 'close to, but not an acceptable form of, *Cræganford*, Crayford'.[129] The identification 'depends on the bare possibility that all extant manuscripts of the *Chronicle* go back to an original in which the name was misrepresented.'[130]

---

[127] See the *Historia Regum Britanniae*, VI, 14.
[128] N Brooks, *Anglo-Saxon Myths: State and Church 400-1066*, 2000, 41.
[129] Brooks, 41.
[130] Stenton, 1967, 17.

As for 'Wippedesfleot', a 'fleot' is a creek, of which there are many around the Kent coast, and we have no way of knowing which one might be referred to. On the face of it the name looks as if it has been made up on the basis of 'Wipped', the thegn who died there. The text reads: 'In this year Hengest and Æsc fought against the Welsh near *Wippedesfleot* and there slew twelve Welsh nobles; and one of their thegns, whose name was Wipped, was slain there.' Who 'their' refers to – the Jutes or the Welsh – cannot be determined on linguistic grounds. The Latin of the bilingual Manuscript F, written about 1100, irons out the ambiguity by saying of Wipped that he was 'a very rich man on Hengest's side'. Richard Coates wonders if there might be a Welsh explanation of the name. He suggests it may contain the ancestor of Welsh *gwybed* 'gnats', giving the meaning 'gnats' creek or inlet', compare Welsh river-names such as *Gwybedog* 'fly-infested'.[131]

We have seen that the *Historia's* first battle seems to have been fought on the river Derventio or Darent. The next was fought at Episford (Horseford)/'Ægesþrep'. The third battle was 'by the Inscribed Stone on the shore of the Gallic Sea'. Such is the geographical 'evidence'. What are to make of it?

The Darent is not far from the Cray, so we might suppose that this is the same battle as the *Chronicle*'s 'Crecganford', or at least part of some back-and-forth fighting. It might be that the Britons had advanced down Roman Watling Street, were checked on the Darent, then defeated on the Cray. The battle at Ægesþrep/Episford might have been fought as one side pressed forward along the Pilgrims' Way and sought to force the passage of the Medway. The battle by 'the Inscribed Stone on the shore of the Gallic Sea' is the only one where the *Historia* clearly claims victory. The *Chronicle*'s battle of Wippedesfleot (Wipped's Creek, or Gnats' Creek) must also have been fought by the sea, and it may be the same battle. If so, and if Wipped was an Anglo-Saxon, it might be a case of the 'vanquished valour' relished by the Anglo-Saxon poet, with Wipped going down fighting, and taking twelve Welsh warriors with him.

For Frank Stenton the antiquity of the accounts of the Kentish war 'is shown by the extreme difficulty of identifying the place-names which occur in them ... These names must have been taken over by the original West Saxon annalist as an integral part of an ancient tradition, and it is greatly to his credit that he did not translate them into forms intelligible to himself or his readers'.[132] Brooks, however, follows Wallenberg in seeing mangled forms, drawn from oral tradition, of known place-names. Brooks goes on, 'The West Saxon dynasty of Egbert (802-39) may have had ancestors in the Kentish royal family, and a West Saxon *scop* (court poet), ignorant of Kentish geography, could have garbled the place-name forms in a way that would not have been acceptable to a Kentish audience.'[133] Esmonde Cleary sees the

[131] R Coates, '*Wippedesfleot* in the Anglo-Saxon Chronicle', *Journal of the English Place-Name Society* 49, 2017, 41-47.
[132] Stenton, 1967, 17.
[133] N Brooks, 2000, 41-2, and J K Wallenberg, *Kentish Place-Names*, 1931, 83-4, 286-8, 320-3.

recorded names as 'conscious and inaccurate archaisms by the compilers of the *Chronicle*'.[134] This, however, is no more than guesswork.

An aside: Towards a chronology of Hengest's career

Bede's dating of the first coming of Germanic groups to Britain gives us one fairly fixed point, within the years 450-455. Tolkien suggests a date of about 450/51 for the *Freswæl* ('The Frisian Slaughter'), and about 453 for Hengest's coming into Britain.[135] We may have one clue about Hengest's years in that he is called a *hyse* 'youth, son' (but also 'man, warrior') in the *Finnsburg Fragment*. Another clue is the coming to the kingship (of Kent) of Æsc/Oisc in 488, presumably on the death of Hengest (though the *Chronicle* does not say that in so many words). Tolkien suggested a date around 420/25 for the birth of Hengest, making him 25-30 years old at the time of the *Freswæl*, and 63-68 years old when he died. Hnæf was perhaps about 30 years old at the time of Finnsburg, and his sister-son about 15 years old.

Tolkien suggests a birth date for Oisc of about 450. But if 455 is a reasonable date for the death of Horsa, it would mean that Oisc was only five years old when he took Horsa's place at Hengest's side. We would then have to say that the chronicler, or his source, had made the shared leadership happen too early. But the *Chronicle* seems fairly sure about its facts here, naming Æsc/Oisc alongside Hengest in 456, 465, and 473. Perhaps, then, Oisc was born about 440, so that he came to warrior years in 455. He would then have been about 72 years old at the time of his death (the *Chronicle* says that he was king for twenty-four years from 488). We could also put back Hengest's birth year a little, say to 415. This would make it easier to fit Rhonwen /Hrothwyn into the time scheme. If Hengest had fathered her, say, about 438, he being then some 23 years old, Rhonwen would have been 16 or 17 years old at the time Vortigern saw her.

The settlement

The Germanic settlers who came into Kent were, in the traditional account, Jutes. Whence did these folk come? Bede seems to have regarded them as northern neighbours of the Angles, but some archaeological evidence suggests strong links between Jutland, the Rhineland, and a few parts of Britain (north and east Kent, coastal Sussex, and the Isle of Wight). This might mean that the Jutes who settled in Kent (and further west) had earlier migrated to the Rhineland. Or perhaps there were independent, parallel cultural developments in Britain, Scandinavia, and Frankish Gaul. Or, again, the likenesses might have come about simply through trade and diplomatic gifts.

---

[134] Esmonde Cleary, 1989, 71.

[135] Bliss, *Finn and Hengest*, 1998, 72-6.

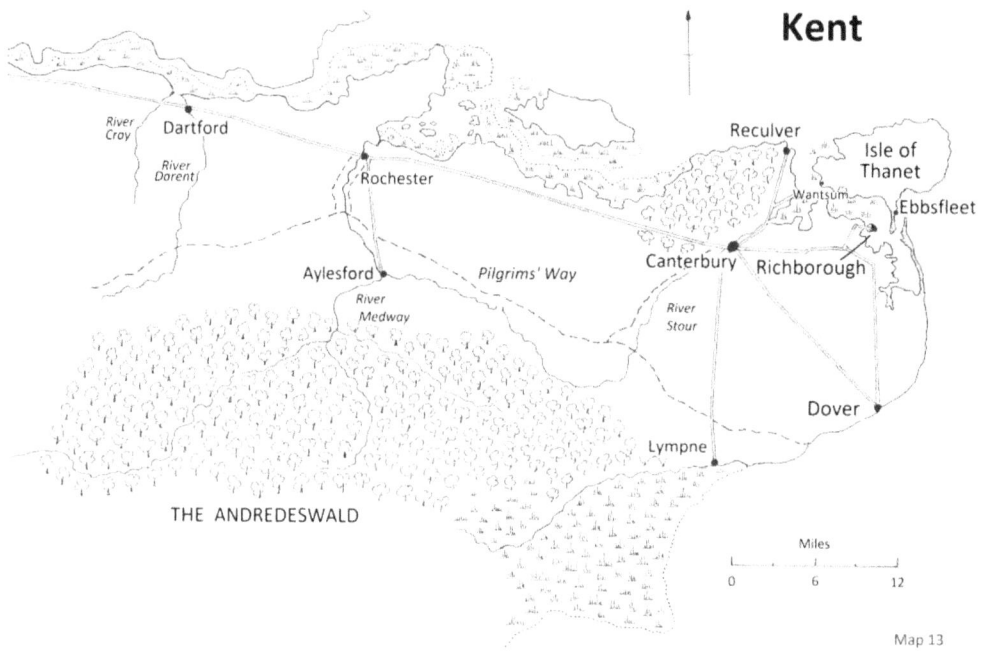

Kent

River Cray
Dartford
River Darent
Rochester
Reculver
Isle of Thanet
Wantsum
Ebbsfleet
Aylesford
Pilgrims' Way
Canterbury
Richborough
River Medway
River Stour
Dover
Lympne
THE ANDREDESWALD
Miles
0   6   12

Map 13

The Kent to which the new settlers came seems to have been larger than the shire we know today (15,000 hides in the seventh-century Tribal Hidage, more than twice the Sussex hidage). Iron Age Kent, the land of the Cantiaci tribe, had included parts of what we know as Sussex and Surrey. It may be that the Weald to the north and east of Pevensey, now in Sussex, was at that time part of Kent, together with eastern Surrey.

Fifth century Kent was heavily wooded. What we know as Sheppey was then several islands, the Isle of Thanet was truly an island, and the Romney and Walland marshes were mostly under water.[136] The earliest Germanic settlements were on the light, fertile soils of the Canterbury/north-east Kent region, along the coast, and up the river valleys. For it was the rivers that gave a way in (and a way out, if things went wrong). Boats could get further upstream in the fifth century, than they can today. There were early settlements in the Stour valley as far as Wye or Ashford, and up the Medway to Teston or Yalding.

The areas of early Germanic settlement were also the areas of Romano-British activity, and Alan Everitt argues strongly for continuity of settlement in Kent, and for a largely peaceful Jutish-Saxon takeover. Roman remains are to be found in the neighbourhood of almost every major Jutish settlement. At Richborough and Reculver

---

[136] Hart, 'The Tribal Hidage', in *Transactions of the Royal Historical Society*, 1971, 154, 154-55n.

there were Roman forts, at Sturry there was a Roman settlement and a quay by the river, and at Eastry there was a Roman ritual site. At Worth there was a temple and a burial ground. The church at Lyminge stands on the site of a Roman temple. In the neighbourhood of Milton Regis, which was a seat of the Kentish kings, there are at least twenty-five major archaeological sites, mostly dating from the Roman period. At Faversham there are a good number of late Roman buildings and a rich and extensive Germanic cemetery, clearly implying continuity of occupation. Faversham was a centre of metal-working in Roman times, and this may have been continued in the Anglo-Saxon period. The meaning of the name seems to be 'The smith's *ham*', with the first element probably coming from Latin *faber*. Finds at the Roman burial ground at Martyrs' Field, outside Canterbury, show that the Anglo-Saxons made use of that burial ground in the fifth/sixth centuries. At Deal, too, graves of Romano-Britons and Anglo-Saxons have been found close together. The goal seems to have been to stand in rightful heirship. (For the same reason, like enough, the early English also buried their dead in prehistoric barrows, or at sacred sites.)

There is a similar story in Saxon west Kent. Boats could get as far as Otford by way of the River Darent, and Roman Watling Street in the north, and the ancient trackway known as the Pilgrims' Way in the south also provided ready access to the valley. Excavated sites and casual finds point to the existence of a series of Anglo-Saxon settlements, dating from the mid-fifth to mid-seventh century, along this valley, in the Cray valley, and along the lower Thames. A total of eighteen cemeteries and five settlements are known. Three substantial cemeteries date from the second half of the fifth century: Riseley, South Darenth, and Orpington. The largest cemetery in the area is that at Northfleet, clearly an important site of late-fifth to mid-sixth century date. And one of the most striking features of the cemetery distribution is that it seems to be related to the Roman countryside, suggesting that the incoming Saxons of the fifth century chose to settle on Romano-British villa estates.[137] At almost every major Roman site in the shire there are early Saxon or Jutish burials.

At places like Eastry, Woodnesborough, Sturry, Rainham, Maidstone, Rochester, and Dartford, it is noteworthy that the main street of the Roman settlement is still the main street today. There is further evidence from place-names. First there is the name of the shire itself. To the ancient geographer-historians Kent was 'Kantion' or 'Cantium', 'the corner land', one corner of what was believed to be a three-cornered island (the other 'corners' being Land's End and Orkney). The name was passed on to the Anglo-Saxons (it is 'Cantia' in Bede), and the Germanic folk who settled in Kent called themselves the 'Cantware' or 'Kentings'. It has been suggested that the ongoing life of British names in coastal Kent is probably the result of the conservative needs of Saxon seafarers in the fourth century. The name of Thanet is Celtic, as are the names of rivers such as the Medway, the Darent, and the Cray. The British word *ceto* ('wood', 'forest') is found in five place-names: Chatham,

---

[137] Susan Tyler, 'Anglo-Saxon settlement in the Darent valley and environs' in *Archæologia Cantiana*, Volume CX, 1993, 71-81.

Chattenden, Chetney, and the lost Chathurst and Chetham, all lying within the former Blean Forest that stretched for some forty miles between the Thames estuary and the Stour Levels.

Altogether, there are about thirty-five place-names that certainly have Celtic roots (including Dover, Reculver, Lympne, Lyminge and others), a further dozen or so that may be Celtic, and between twelve and twenty for which a Celtic root has been suggested by reputable scholars (though challenged by others). All are in areas of early Jutish settlement. There are more Celtic place-names in Kent than in the 'highland zone' county of Devon, though they are still only a small percentage of the whole. There are also some names with 'walh' (the Old English for 'Welshman', 'stranger', 'Briton'), suggesting the presence of Celtic-speaking settlements. Stenton also notes a number of heathen names (which one would think should go back to the period before the Christian mission of 597). Augustine and his fellow-missionaries came to a land where there was a living heathenism, and even today, after 1,400 years, five places of former heathen worship can be identified within twelve miles of Augustine's church of Canterbury. Stenton adds that it is not surprising the conversion advanced by generations rather than by decades.[138]

In sum, while acknowledging that there was probably a break in the story of human settlement in some parts of Kent (Canterbury is cited), the overall picture is of continuity, and of a largely peaceful takeover. The Germanic incomers may have taken over the *civitas* from post-Roman 'tyrants' or kings, or have had control handed to them. (The story in the *Historia Brittonum* is of the transfer of power by means that were legal – if underhand – before a resort to war.) This picture of peaceful takeover would not be at odds with the tale of war found in the *Chronicle* and the *Historia Brittonum*. Fifth-century war-bands were small, and for the common folk the tide of war would, like enough, have meant little more than new landlords and new men gathering taxes.

Canterbury

At Roman Canterbury, the *civitas* capital of the Cantiaci, the civic life withered in the 4th century AD. The baths had fallen out of use by the 350s. The public sewer system broke down, so that blockages led to the backing-up of foul water. The latest small coins are dated 380-90 (but were current for much longer). Sometime in the first part of the fifth century a family was buried within the temple precincts. This was against Roman law, which banned burials within cities, so clearly official control had broken down. These were a man, a woman, girls of about 11 years and 8 years, and the old family dog. The woman was laid with one girl in her arms, and the other at her feet, and the man was laid with the old dog on his lap. The females had Roman keys, chains and bangles, and imported glass beads. It has been suggested that these deaths are evidence of disease amid decay.[139] As the fifth century wore on

---

[138] F M Stenton, 'The Historical Bearing of Place-Name Studies: Anglo-Saxon Heathenism', 1941, in D M Stenton, ed, *Preparatory to Anglo-Saxon England*, 1970, 297.
[139] M Lyle, *Canterbury: 2000 years of history*, 2002, 36; Esmonde Cleary, 1989, 151.

the west part of the town was flooded by the Stour. 'Dark earth' layers of varying depths seal nearly all excavated Roman buildings. Anglo-Frisian pottery (handmade and not fired in a kiln) and some forty Anglo-Saxon-type sunken-floored huts, dated about 450, have been found in one *insula*, on top of levelled Roman buildings.

The economic life of the city also died, and the layout of the Roman streets was utterly lost. But it is likely that Canterbury was never totally deserted during the so-called 'Dark Ages'. Brooks writes that almost two centuries later when Augustine landed in Kent, there were still stone buildings in Canterbury, and these were known to have been Christian places of worship under the Romans, for Bede tells us that Æthelberht gave Augustine permission to repair them. Two such churches are the one which Augustine received as a cathedral, and St Martin's, where Bertha and Luidhard had worshipped, and where excavation has confirmed the existence of a small rectangular structure built with Roman materials. Another church, St Peter's, may preserve the site of a Roman church for it heeds the lines of the Roman, rather than the medieval, street pattern. The parish churches of St Dunstan, St Sepulchre, and perhaps St Paul coincide with Roman cemeteries, indicating continuity of Christian site, and perhaps even of Christian practice, since the fourth century.[140]

West Kent and East Kent

It seems that the early Jutish kingdom of Kent was made up of the eastern half of the shire only. There had long been an east/west divide. Caesar noted differences between the West Kent folk and East Kent's Belgae. In the early Anglo-Saxon period the fact of there being two Kentish bishoprics (Canterbury and Rochester) suggests that the east/west division 'was a significant administrative division within the kingdom before the arrival of Christianity'.[141] West Kent belonged, economically, with East Surrey. Both regions looked to the Weald and practised 'transhumance' stock rearing, the seasonal movement of sheep and pigs to pastures deep in the woodland of the Weald, to be fattened on the pannage of oak, chestnut, hornbeam and beech. The system goes right back to the early days of the Anglo-Saxon settlement, and perhaps to Romano-British times and beyond. As for Anglo-Saxon grave goods from West Kent, these are more akin to those of the Saxons of Essex, Surrey, and the Thames valley than to those of East Kent. It seems not unlikely that West Kent was once part of the Essex kingdom, and that there may have been a tug-of-war between Essex and East Kent over the West Kent lands. Near Rochester, where Watling Street from London crossed the Medway, the burial ground of a well-armed community has been found. There is another at Aylesford, on the Pilgrims' Way track along the North Downs. It would seem these were marcher settlements of the East Kent kingdom.[142] West Kent was most likely taken over by the East Kent leadership sometime in the late sixth/early seventh century. It has been noted that a pair of gold and copper-alloy clasps from the early seventh-century Taplow barrow show a Kentish connection. 'It is likely that a political

[140] Brooks N, *The Early History of the Church of Canterbury*, 1984, 16-22.
[141] B Yorke, 'Joint kingship in Kent c. 560 to 785', *Archaeologia Cantiana*, volume 99, 1983, 5.
[142] Drewett and others, 1988, 257, 275.

reality underpins this link, connected perhaps with Kentish territorial expansion in the Middle Thames region during the earlier seventh century.[143]

A related question is that of joint kingship. In Kent there seems to have been a senior king based in Jutish Kent, with a junior partner (generally a close relative) in the Saxon west.[144] The need to keep a firm eye on the important marcher land of West Kent, may provide an explanation of the origins of dual kingship, which system lasted until the third quarter of the eighth century.

Early development of the Kentish kingdom

Two means have been suggested for the growth of the early Anglo-Saxon kingdoms: 'competitive exclusion', and 'core-periphery interaction' using prestige-goods. Both could apply to Kent. The first model involves competition between local political groupings with the winners becoming progressively more powerful, a process likened to the FA Cup competition. This is, in truth, a back-projection from the era chronicled by Bede, when dynasties were striving for power. Such developments might be furthered through population growth, alliance, marriage, or warfare, until one group gained enough land and resources to give it a competitive edge over neighbours. Then it might either absorb them or place them in a relation of dependency. This may be what happened as Jutish East Kent took over Saxon West Kent.

As to core-periphery interaction and the prestige-goods model, the Kentish kings had the advantage of nearness to a rich continental neighbour, namely, Frankland (France) under the Merovingians. From here came new ideas, new politics, and many of the luxury goods (garnet jewellery, glassware, bronze bowls) found in sixth-century Kentish burials. Such goods may have come in as trade goods, marriage gifts, or gifts between rulers. Having control of such high-worth goods would have been a key tool in building strength, standing, and lordship within Kent and beyond.

The Oiscingas

Bede gives us two short family trees for the Kentish kingly house. In *HE* 1.15 he traces the line of Hengest and Horsa back through Wihtgisl, Witta, and Wecta to Woden. In *HE* II.5 he says that 'Æthelberht was the son of Eormenric (or Irminric), the son of Octa, the son of Oeric whose surname was Oisc, whence the kings of Kent were known as *Oiscingas*. Oisc's father was Hengest'. A variant on these traditions is found in the *Historia Brittonum* 58, and in the genealogy of Æthelberht II of Kent in the so-called 'Anglian collection' of genealogies (eighth/early ninth centuries). In *HB* 58 Hengest's son is Octha or Ocga (presumably Octa), who is the father of Ossa or Oese, and he of Eormenric the father of Æthelberht. At some point the more readily understood name 'Æsc' was substituted for the archaic Oisc.

---

[143] L Webster and J Backhouse, *The Making of England: Anglo-Saxon Art and Culture AD 600-900*, 1992, 56.

[144] B Yorke 'Joint Kingship in Kent', 1983, 15, 19; N Brooks, 'The creation and early structure of the kingdom of Kent', in Bassett, ed, *Origins of Anglo-Saxon Kingdoms*, 1989, 67-74.

The key figure is Oisc. He (and not Hengest) gave his name to the dynasty, so presumably a claimant to the kingship of Kent had to show descent from him. Was he truly the son (or grandson) of Hengest, or have two kinship lines been artificially merged? (It has been suggested that Oisc was perhaps a lesser pagan god, for the name 'Oisc' seems to be an early spelling of 'Oesc', and 'Oisc' goes back to an earlier *Oski, or *Anski. It is related to the Norse word for a god, *áss*.)

How far back can we trust this kinlore? Barbara Yorke is reasonably confident that Eormenric or Irminric was the name of the father of Æthelberht. (Note that the element 'Eormen' or 'Irmin' is rare in Anglo-Saxon names, but relatively common among the Frankish royal house and aristocracy.[145]) Barbara Yorke also thinks that Oeric/Oise was probably a historical figure. But by this stage (in her view) we are in 'the problematic world of divine ancestors'. Hengest she sees as belonging to the world of Germanic heroic poetry,[146] perhaps one of those heroes of war and adventure that kingly houses liked to add to their lineage.

So are we faced with two traditions of the founding of the kingdom of Kent, the brothers Hengest and Horsa featuring in one, Hengest and his 'son' Oisc in the other? In defence of the record as it stands it might be said that it was only in the time of Oisc that the kingdom was set on a sure footing. Also, there are other cases from the early English period where a kingly house took its name not from the known founder, but from his son or from another. The *Historia Brittonum* says that Wehha was the first king of the East Angles (*HB* 59), but, as we have seen, the later kingly house called themselves the Wuffingas, after Wehha's son Wuffa. The kings of Mercia were known as the Iclingas, taking their name from Icel, who probably lived about the 460s. Yet there were war-leaders in Mercian tale much better-known than Icel, both before his time (Offa of Angeln) and after (Penda).

King Æthelberht

According to Bede (*HE* II.5), and the *Chronicle* annal for 616, Æthelberht died in that year, after a reign of fifty-six years. This would be a truly long reign for the time, and it has been suggested that a fifty-six year life-span has been confused with the reign length. Now because Æthelberht married a Frankish princess named Bertha we can turn for help to the sixth-century *Historia Francorum* of Gregory of Tours. Bertha was the daughter of Charibert I, who lived from about 517 until 567. In 561 he became king in Neustria, Aquitaine and Novempopulana, with his capital at Paris. In Book IV, 26 (written between 575 and 581), Gregory notes, 'Moreover king Charibert married Ingoberga, by whom he had a daughter who afterwards married a husband in Kent and was taken there.' It is usually assumed that the daughter was Bertha. And some writers read these words as meaning that she was only born after Charibert had become king. They also take it that Æthelberht was not yet king at the time of his marriage, and that the marriage took place during the time

---

[145] B Yorke, 1990, 27.

[146] B Yorke, 'Fact or Fiction?' *Anglo-Saxon Studies in Archaeology and History* 6, 1993, 47; 'Joint kingship in Kent', *Archaeologia Cantiana*, 1983, 3-4.

that Book IV was being written, say about 578.[147] Bertha's mother, Ingoberga, is thought to have lived from 520-89. In *HF* IX.26, Gregory reports Ingoberga's deathbed will (of 588-9), which states that she had a daughter who married the son of a king in Kent. Again, some take this to mean that even then Æthelberht had not begun his kingship. (But Ingoberga might simply be referring to Æthelberht's status at the time of the marriage.)

This matter of possible confusion in the chronology of Æthelberht's life and kingship is serious. If there was muddle in Canterbury, the oldest centre of Anglo-Saxon Christianity, it would weaken confidence in all early Kentish dates, and indeed early dates from the other Anglo-Saxon kingdoms too. Might Bede have misunderstood the records, taking a statement that Æthelberht had lived for 56 years to be a reference to his reign length? Yet surely so careful a historian would have cross-checked the truth of a fifty-six-year reign. It is not impossible that his Kentish informants could have talked with folk about what they had heard from their grandparents, and maybe about what those grandparents heard from their elders in turn. So the oral tradition could take one back to about 600, though not much further than that.

One possibility might be that Æthelberht served for many years as under-king to his father, in West Kent. The fifty-six years would then be the whole of his years in government, first as under-king and then as sole king. To sum up, we might guess that Æthelberht was born about 545, that he became under-king in West Kent about 560, and married about 578, Bertha being then sixteen or seventeen years old. We might further suppose that his father, Irminric, lived from about 520-590, his grandfather Octa from 480-550, with Oeric/Oisc living from about 440-512. If this series of seventy-year life-spans is deemed not believable, we would then have to acknowledge that we seem to have lost a generation.

The fact that Æthelbert is named as the third Bretwalda ('Britain-wielder or ruler') indicates something of his authority and reach. We have seen that his sister Ricula was married to Sledd of the East Saxons and it is possible that Kent played a key role in bringing the family of Sledd to power. Links with the East Angles may also have been particularly significant. The East Angles are the only other Anglo-Saxon people whom Æthelbert is recorded as having tried to convert.

Bernicia

To the north of Deira, between the Tweed and Tyne, lay the short-lived British state known variously as Bernaccia, Berneich, Brynaich, or Brennych in Old Welsh.[148] The name may mean 'the land of the mountain passes'.[149]

---

[147] See, for example, N Brooks, 'The creation and structure of the early kingdom of Kent', in Bassett, ed, *Origins*, 1989, 66-7; D Kirby, *The Earliest English Kings*, 1991, 26.

[148] *Historia Brittonum*, 56; Alcock, 1975, 35; J Davies, *A History of Wales*, 1994, 59; Ashley, *The Mammoth Book of British Kings & Queens*, 1998, 273.

[149] C Thomas, *Celtic Britain*, 1997, 50.

Gildas and archaeology could imply that Anglo-Saxon mercenaries were settled at military sites from York to Catterick in the 480s, to defend the British state against the Picts.[150] Bamburgh and Lindisfarne were in the territory of the Votadini, and if the region was unstable this might provide a context for the suggestion that the Votadini invited the first Angles to settle in their territory, or at least acquiesced in such settlement, probably in the fifth century.[151] The settlement was, like enough, at Dinguoaroy (or Din Guoaroy), a British promontory fort on the site of the later Bamburgh. However, there have been sporadic Anglo-Saxon finds at Aldborough, Catterick, Darlington and Norton, and it may be that there was a northward movement up the Roman roads from Deira.[152]

A number of scholars have written of a small Anglian warrior aristocracy ruling over a largely British population in the 5th-7th centuries.[153] Ida is said to have been the founder of the Bernician kingly dynasty. His grandfather, Oessa (or Esa/ Eosa), is named as the first Bernician leader to come to Britain, so if Ida's reign was (as the *Chronicle* states) from 547-559, Oessa would have lived *c.* 500. The *Historia Brittonum* 61 credits Ida with the conquest of the Bamburgh area. The original nucleus of Bernicia was probably in the Tyne area, and the Tees valley seems to have formed the boundary with Deira in the seventh century. The penetration of inland Bernicia most likely followed two main routes, from the Tyne estuary, and from the Lindisfarne/Bamburgh area (between the Coquet and the Tweed). The name 'Lindisfarne' echoes that of the Lindiswara of Lindsey, suggesting that some of those folk migrated northwards and joined Ida's followers.[154] Likewise the name of Bede's monastery, *In Gyrvum* (now Jarrow) recalls the name of the Gyrwe folk of the Peterborough district. Either some of these folk also migrated northwards, or the Durham Gyrwe were named from a local fen area ('gyr' is an Old English word for 'fen' or 'mud'.[155])

---

[150] Dumville, in Bassett, *Origins*, 1989, 214-5.
[151] Kirby, 2000, 58, and 204, note 42, citing L Alcock.
[152] Myres, 1989, 197.
[153] Alcock, 1975, 310; Dark, 1994, 250; S S Evans, *Lords of battle*, 2000, 21.
[154] Myres, 1989, 199.
[155] Myres, 1989, 175; Ekwall, *English Place-names*, 1960, 268.

Chapter 5   The South

Sussex

Sussex is divided into self-contained blocks by south-flowing rivers. It lacks good natural harbours between Pagham, near Chichester, and Pevensey, and it has formidable chalk cliffs between Brighton and Beachy Head. To the north the great Wealden forest would have been a hindrance to movement. The British people of Sussex were the Regni, part of the original Atrebates tribe.

The *Anglo-Saxon Chronicle* has three entries relating to the coming of the Saxons to Sussex, and they concern a certain Ælle, whose story is perhaps taken from a lost saga. (Nothing is known of his earlier life.) Under the year 477 the *Chronicle* tells us that Ælle came to Britain with his three sons Cymen, Wlencing, and Cissa with three ships. They landed at *Cymenesora*, slew many Welsh and drove the rest into *Andredesleag* (the Sussex Weald). In 485 Ælle fought against the Welsh near the bank of *Mearcrædesburna*. Then in 491 Ælle and Cissa besieged *Andredescester* (the Saxon Shore fort of Anderida, that is, Pevensey) and slew every Briton there.

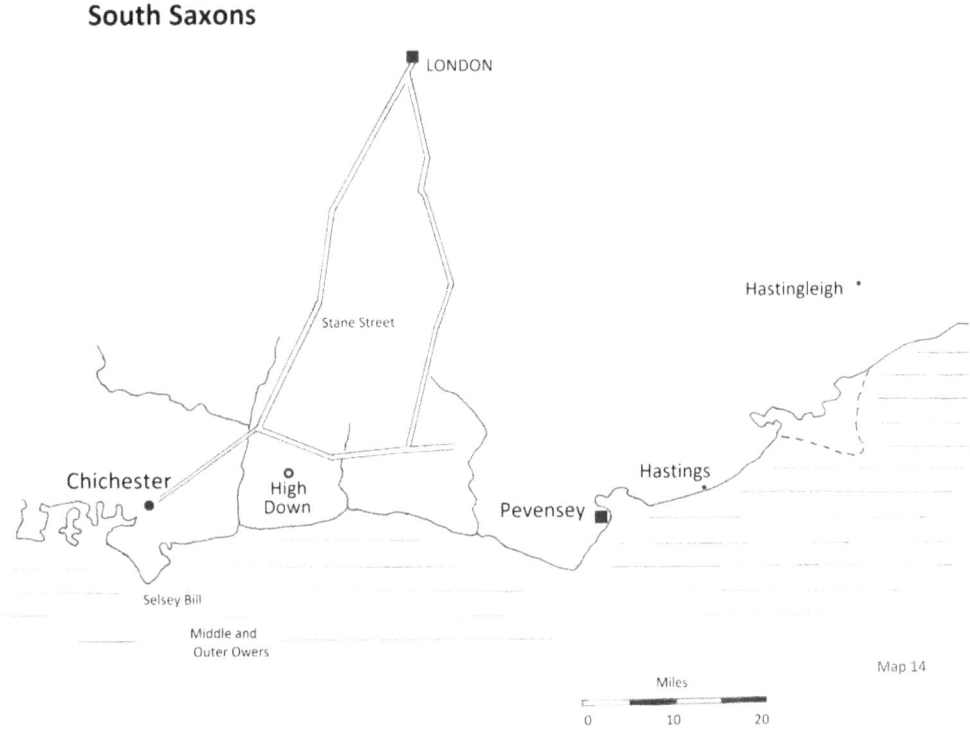

South Saxons

Map 14

The situation across the Channel may be relevant here. Saxons seeking to settle within the western empire would have found Gaul more attractive than Britain. It was the richer province, and its coastal defences seem to have been less formidable than those of the Saxon Shore in Britain. By the middle of the fifth century Saxon folk had pushed into much of northern Gaul, and in 463 under their king Eadwacer they took Angers. They were then dislodged from that city by Childeric, king of the Franks, acting as an ally of the empire, and the Franks went on to extend their power further. In 486 Clovis son of Childeric overthrew the semi-Roman state of Soissons, the last remnant of the western empire. The Franks were now the masters of northern Gaul, and there was no further scope for the settlement of other Germanic peoples. The outcome may well have been that the Saxons turned to Britain, to Sussex and to Wessex.[156] The timing fits well enough with the *Chronicle* account.

Where might the Saxons have begun their penetration of Sussex? Martin Welch thinks the original South Saxon kingdom was in the eastern half of the Sussex downland,[157] but Stenton believes it began in the west, where the *Anglo-Saxon Chronicle* places it. The *Cymenesora* landing-place, now under the sea, would have been south of Selsey Bill. P Hunter Blair suggested the location was the group of ledges and rocks known as the Middle Owers and Outer Owers, about seven miles south-south-east of Selsey Bill. The Mixon rocks, closer to Selsey, have also been suggested. The archaeological evidence demonstrates that the Roman shoreline would have been here (and was not breached by the sea until the 10th or 11th century[158]). Chichester's capture is not mentioned, but it would be a likely result of Ælle's landing and victory. Chichester seems to have been almost deserted between the fifth and ninth centuries, and Pevensey became the base for the defence of Sussex against the newcomers.

High Down was another important part of the defences. It probably began as an isolated community of mercenaries in or near a prehistoric hill-fort on the Downs above Worthing. This was a defensible position with excellent visual command of the shoreline and coastal shipping for many miles both to the east and west. The site remained in use for some time after the end of Roman rule, as witnessed by Anglo-Saxon inhumations accompanied by late-fifth- and sixth-century brooches and weapons.

The *Mearcrædesburna* where Ælle fought with the British in 485 has been plausibly interpreted as 'the stream of the agreed frontier'. The stream in question may have been the Cuckmere. There seems to have been a South Saxon concentration between the Cuckmere and the Ouse, west of Beachy Head, an area where there do not seem to have been any Roman villas. Five fifth-century cemeteries, one of them associated with a contemporary settlement, are located in the downland of this

---

[156] Stenton, 1967, 12; Alcock, 1975, 112.

[157] M Welch, 'The kingdom of the South Saxons: the origins', in ed, Bassett, *Origins*, 83.

[158] Stenton, 1967, 17-18; P H Blair, *Roman Britain and Early England*, 1963, 176; Hume Wallace, *The Underwater Book: The Search for Roman Selsey*, 1968.

region. It has been suggested that the Ouse-Cuckmere settlement was a block of territory ceded to the Saxons by the British authorities.[159] (Or Saxon settlement may simply have spread, in the fifth century, across the Downs from High Down to Cuckmere.) If the Cuckmere was Ælle's eastern boundary then he may have felt he had good reason to eliminate any British garrison at *Anderitum* (Pevensey). Stenton comments that the rarity of British place-names in Sussex 'points to English colonization on a scale which can have left little room for British survival.'[160]

In the Tribal Hidage Sussex is assessed at 7,000 hides to Kent's 15,000, and, as already noted, it may be that the Weald to the north and east of Pevensey was once attached to Kent. The Roman road pattern in this region links it to Rochester, Canterbury, Lympne and Dover rather than to the South Downs and the *civitas* capital of Chichester, and it seems probable that the Hastings region was administered in the Roman period from Canterbury rather than from Chichester.[161] The *Hæstingas*, who gave their name to this region, seem to have been a small semi-independent tribal group, comparable to the small people groups of the East Midlands listed in the Tribal Hidage. The three surviving place-names which include the personal name 'Hæst' seem to occur on the margins of their territory at Hastingford in the west, Hastings on the south coast and Hastingleigh near Ashford in Kent in the east. It may be that the *Hæstingas* originated in south-east Kent and colonised the eastern Weald, perhaps in the seventh to eighth centuries. The Hastings area seems to have maintained its identity within Sussex throughout the historical Anglo-Saxon period. A Northumbrian chronicler noted that in 771 Offa of Mercia conquered the *gentem Hestingorum*, and the *Hæstingas* and the South Saxons were still seen as separate folk groups up to within fifty years of the Norman conquest.

An aside: The Tribal Hidage

The Tribal Hidage is a list of thirty-five people groups, and the 'hidage' of their lands, using the Anglo-Saxon 'hide' as the measure. The most likely purpose of the Hidage list is the assessment of tribute payments, to be made by smaller dependent states to their overlord. The actual hidage attributed to each people-group very likely depended on such factors as fertility of the soil, population density, and the exact relationship with the overlord. We cannot be sure where and when it was drawn up, and on whose command. Some historians see it as a Northumbrian initiative, limiting the power of their great rivals, the Mercians. Others see it as a Mercian document, to be dated perhaps in the 670s, or maybe as late as the 790s in the last years of the powerful King Offa.

---

[159] M G Welch, *Early Anglo-Saxon Sussex*, BAR no.112, 255-7, and see his chapter in Bassett, *Origins*, 81.

[160] Stenton, 1967, 18.

[161] Welch, 'The kingdom of the South Saxons: Origins', in Bassett, *Origins*, 1989, 78, 83.

Ælle and the Bretwaldaship

Bede (*HE* II. 5) tells us that Ælle was the first king to rule over all the southern English kingdoms. At first glance this may seem unlikely, and there has been a tendency to dismiss the record. But, on the other hand, we may ask why Bede, or the authority which he followed, should choose such a seemingly obscure figure as the first chief among English kings, unless he was following some old tradition. Ælle might have widened his authority to the north, pushing up Stane Street, and another Roman road through the Wealden forest. These roads do not seem to have gone out of use, and by these routes Ælle may have thrust inland, perhaps as far as the upper Thames.[162] And there is another circumstance which may have some bearing on the story. Gildas states that he was born in the year of the siege of 'Mons Badonicus'. This episode is represented by all the Welsh authorities as a great disaster for the Saxons, and it was followed by a period when there was no war between the Britons and the Saxons. Now if the dates assigned by the *Chronicle* to Ælle's conquests are at all near the truth, his overlordship must be placed before the battle of Mons Badonicus. Is it not possible that this defeat broke up the Anglo-Saxon coalition and that the peace of forty-four (or more) years which followed was due to their broken alliance? The lengthy gap between Ælle and Ceawlin, the next Bretwalda, strengthens the impression of the English advance being halted at this time. (The story of the West Saxon invasion, during the post-Badon peace, is of course a difficulty, and to this we shall have to return.) Welch notes that, 'We can accept that Ælle was an extraordinary military leader of great renown'.[163]

After Ælle nothing more is known of Sussex history until the baptism of a king named Æthelwalh shortly before 675. (Sussex was the last part of England to receive the Christian faith.) Wulfhere of Mercia gave to this Æthelwalh the lands of the Meonware, and also the Isle of Wight, probably in the first half of the 670s. This was presumably a reward for military help against the Gewisse.[164]

The Isle of Wight and the Hampshire coast

The Isle of Wight and the Hampshire coastlands opposite were taken over by Jutish folk. When the chronicler Florence of Worcester wrote of the death of William II 'Rufus' he noted that this happened in the New Forest, 'which in English is called *Ytene*', that is, '(the forest) of the Jutes'. This tribal name is also preserved in *Ytingstoc*, modern Bishopstoke, on the east bank of the River Itchen. The name is also found in *Ytedene* meaning 'the valley of the Jutes', a lost hamlet near East Meon. These may be the western, northern, and eastern limits of Jutish authority. Bede's account seems to say that the western end of the Isle of Wight lay opposite the Jutish/Gewisse (West Saxon) border, and the eastern end opposite the Sussex border. This would mean that the lands lying roughly between Lymington and Hayling Island were Jutish. The folk known as the Meonware were probably a Jutish group centred on the River Meon. (The hillfort of

---

[162] Myres, 1989, 138-9.
[163] Welch, in ed Bassett, *Origins*, 1989, 83.
[164] Welch, in ed Bassett, *Origins*, 1989, 75, 78.

Winchester Hill was in Meonware territory.) The Jutish coastal plain would have been separated from the chalklands to the north by the woodland which was known as the Forest of Bere. The Netley Marsh area had poor soil and it was boggy; it may have been a no man's land between the Jutes and the Gewisse.

The coming of the Jutes into the west

It may be that the Jutish settlements in both Kent and Hampshire were the outcome of treaties made on the *Litus Saxonicum* in the final or sub-Roman phase of its functioning in the fifth century. It has been suggested, for example, that the Hampshire/Isle of Wight territory may once have been a separate *pagus* (local government area) of the Belgae, perhaps centred round Portchester, which was then ceded or conquered.[165]

The *Anglo-Saxon Chronicle* tells how Port and his two sons, Bieda and Mægla (the latter probably a Celtic name), came to the Portsmouth area in 501 This is commonly dismissed as an invention based on the place-name, and the suggestion has a certain plausibility. But Stenton notes that it does not account for the other evidence for Port as an Old English personal name, and it does not explain why the entry should have been made up.[166] Next, under 514, the *Chronicle* records the coming of Stuf and Wihtgar to a place called *Cerdicesora*. It names them West Saxons, but there is good evidence that they were Jutes, perhaps the sons of Cerdic's sister and a Jutish noble. Asser, the biographer of King Alfred, makes it clear that in ninth-century Wessex they were believed to be Jutish and the founders of the royal house of Wight. Writing of Osburh, the mother of Alfred, Asser says she was the daughter of Oslac, King Æthelwulf's butler, and that Oslac was descended from the line of Stuf and Wihtgar, two brothers. They had received authority over the Isle of Wight from their uncle King Cerdic and from Cynric his son (their cousin), and they had killed the few British inhabitants of the island whom they found there.[167] It may be that Cerdic left the lands of his original conquests (see under 'Wessex') in the hands of Jutish allies, then moved on in search of adventure, and of other lands for settlement.

The *Chronicle* has a further 'Jutish' entry. Under the year 530 it says that Cerdic and Cynric 'took possession' of the Isle of Wight'. How are we to understand this? About 150 years later, in 686, the West Saxon Cædwalla seized Wight in a bloody takeover. The question has been raised whether the *Chronicle* narrative, with its traditions about Port and Stuf and Wihtgar, could have been written to give historical justification for the late seventh century Saxon takeover.

---

[165] M Ashton and C Lewis, *The Medieval Landscape of Wessex*, 1995, 25.
[166] Stenton, 1967, 20n.
[167] Asser, *Life of King Alfred*, translated by S Keynes and M Lapidge, 1983, 68.

Early Wessex

River Thames

Oxford

Icknield Way

Fairford

Frilford

Abingdon

Dorchester

Kemble

Lechlade

Badbury Hill

Liddington Castle

The Ridgeway

River Thames

Barbury Castle

The Wansdyke

Cerdices beorg

River Bourne

River Test

Old Sarum

Winterbourne Gunner
Petersfinger

River Itchen

Winchester

River Avon

Bishopstoke

Ytedene

Old Winchester Hill

Charford

River Meon

Ytene Forest

Portchester

Badbury Rings

Stone

Portsmouth

Chessell Down

Map 15

Miles

0   10   20

100

It seems clear that Bede saw both the Isle of Wight and the Hampshire coastlands as distinct polities, and not originally part of Wessex. In his view a people could flourish as Christians when they had their own king and their own bishopric. In the *Historia Ecclesiastica* thirteen political entities meet Bede's definition of a *gens* (people), having their own kingly house and their own bishopric (or the potential for that). These were Kent, the East Saxons, the East Angles, the West Saxons, Mercia, Hwicce, the South Saxons, Deira, Bernicia, the Isle of Wight, Lindsey, the Middle Angles, the Magonsæte. From its inclusion in this list it is clear that the Isle of Wight was a self-governing area, with its own royal family. (In *HE* IV. 16 Bede names one of its kings, Arwald.) It was assessed as an independent province in the Tribal Hidage. And Bede clearly regarded the mainland Jutish province as having a similar status to the kingdom of Wight. Both are described as a *gens* and their territories are *provinciae*.[168] Perhaps the mainland Jutish royal house was afterward blotted out from the record. (Neither the Island nor the mainland provinces were to have their own bishopric. After their conquest by Cædwalla they were added to Winchester diocese.)

As an aside, note that the name of king Cædwalla (an anglicised form of Welsh Cadwallon) points to there being a British strain in his ancestry. Yet there are no British names in any other branch of the family, and it is unlikely that the strain goes back to Cerdic (another British name).[169] Kingship in Wessex was a personal, and not a hereditary, dignity, and it could be claimed by any representative of any line which could trace descent from Cerdic. Seventh-century Wessex was notable for having many kings and only a superficial unity.[170]

After the reign of Cædwalla Bede stopped using the term 'Gewisse' or 'Geuissae', saying that it was the name formerly used (*antiquitus*) by the West Saxons. 'Cædwalla abandoned the old tribal name of his people for one which could be seen as expressing a wider hegemony over other Germanic peoples'.[171]

Genealogy and archaeology

The matter of Kentish/Wight links finds further support in the genealogy of the Kentish kings. In *HE* 1.15 Bede says that Hengest and Horsa were the sons of Wihtgisl, son of Witta, son of Wecta, son of Woden. Wecta is actually the Latin name for the Isle of Wight.

Common features in grave goods (especially female dress accessories) from Kent, the Isle of Wight, southern Hampshire, and West Sussex, suggest some relationship among the élite families in these areas in the later fifth and sixth centuries. Their shared tastes were in part derived from Francia and in part from Scandinavia. The rich female burial at Chessell Down on the Isle of Wight is comparable with the

---

[168] Yorke, in Bassett, *Origins*, 91.
[169] Stenton, 1967, 69n.
[170] Stenton, 1967, 65-6.
[171] Yorke, in Bassett, *Origins*, 93-4.

richest Kentish burials. The woman was buried with three great Kentish square-headed brooches on her breast, as well as the more usual brooches on either shoulder (one of which was a rare Frankish import). The rest of her jewellery consisted of a silver and a gold ring, an elaborate necklace of beads, and a headband of gold braid in Frankish fashion. Between her legs were a crystal ball and a perforated spoon, and at her sides were an iron weaving batten and another large iron artefact (possibly a key). At her feet there was a bronze pail from Byzantium, and two silver-rimmed wooden cups. These objects are characteristic of the rich female graves at Sarre in Kent. In fact the material is so thoroughly Kentish in character as to suggest the thought that she was a Kentish princess married into the royal house of Wight, in the second half of the sixth century.[172]

---

[172] Yorke, *Kings and Kingdoms*, 1990, 27; Yorke, *Wessex in the Early Middle Ages*, 1995, 37; Yorke, in Bassett, *Origins*, 1989, 88-9.

Chapter 6 Moving inland

Surrey/Berkshire

The settlement of Surrey began before there were any organised kingdoms in the Thames valley. The Saxon burial-grounds at Croydon, Beddington, and Mitcham are among the oldest in the whole Thames basin, and place-name evidence shows that the Wey valley was a region of primary Saxon settlement.[173]

Surrey is the *suthrige* 'the southern district'. It lies to the south of Middlesex, and if that county was indeed once part of the Essex kingdom, then Surrey is naturally explained as Essex's southern region. We have seen that the central and eastern parts of Surrey had economic ties with western Kent. The western division of Surrey, on the other hand, was of a piece with the Sonning and Reading *regiones* extending up the Thames valley, and having economic ties with the sandy heaths on the borders of Hampshire and Berkshire.

The Tribal Hidage does not include any unit which certainly represents Surrey. Hart notes that the combined hidage of the mysterious provinces of the *Noxgaga* (5,000 hides) and *Ohtgaga* (2,000 hides) is 7,000 hides, and this is the hidage of independent kingdoms such as Sussex, Essex, and Lindsey. He believes that we may fairly regard them as divisions of the same people. Furthermore, he thinks that *Noxgaga* is almost certainly corrupt, and might be corrected to Woxgaga, who may be the Woccingas folk, the inhabitants of the region of Wokingham, Wokefield, and Woking. As for *Ohtgaga*, the element *Oht-* could be expected to develop into an Ox- place-name. Hart goes on, 'For purely topographical reasons it is likely that the Ohtgaga were situated in East Surrey, and I am inclined to the view that the Noxgaga and Ohtgaga between them occupied the territory of the modern counties of Surrey and Berkshire.'[174]

It seems likely that in the late sixth and seventh centuries, as the Essex rulers of Surrey wrestled with the kings of East Kent for lordship over West Kent and its Wealden wealth, so they fought against Wessex, with Surrey as one obvious bone of contention.[175] Did Surrey ever have a kingly line of its own? We know of a certain Frithuwold who gave lands for Chertsey Abbey in the seventh century. Possibly he was the last in a line of native Surrey kings, but it is thought more likely that he was sub-king, under Wulfhere of Mercia, of a wider Thames valley/Chilterns area.[176]

---

[173] Stenton, 1967, 55.

[174] Cyril Hart, 'The Tribal Hidage', in *Transactions of the Royal Historical Society*, Fifth Series, 21, 1971, 148; P Drewett and others, 1988, 275).

[175] Dumville, 'Essex, Middle Anglia and the expansion of Mercia in the South-East Midlands', in Bassett, *Origins*, 1989, 135.

[176] J Blair, 'Frithuwold's kingdom and the origins of Surrey', in Bassett, *Origins*, 105-7.

Place-names around
Oxford where names
from 'heroic' story
are embedded

Church
Hanborough

Begbroke

Witney

River Cherwell

Beckley

Elsfield

Roman road
Dorchester to
Bicester

OXFORD

North
Hinksey

South Hinksey

River Thames

River Thames

N

Frilford

Abingdon

River Thame

Miles

0   5

Long Wittenham

Little
Wittenham

Dorchester

River Thames

Map 16

Middle/Upper Thames

As we saw earlier there is good evidence of an early Germanic presence in the Middle/Upper Thames region. First, at Dorchester-on-Thames burials and grave goods have been found which suggest the presence of Germanic troops and their womenfolk either in the last days of official Roman rule or very soon after they left. The town seems to have been the *vicus*[177] for its area. For example, a late Roman altar found there was dedicated by a man holding an official position as *beneficiarius consularis*.[178] There were burials north and south of the town of men equipped with belt fittings and brooches of the kind normally used by barbarian *laeti* or native paramilitary personnel. Indications of (Germanic) sunken-featured buildings and post-

---

[177] A Roman *vicus* was, a) a local administrative unit, or b) a provincial civilian settlement.
[178] A soldier attached to a provincial governor's staff.

Roman structures within the walls show that town life in some form went on well into the fifth century. The Silchester road went out of use, but the road running north to Alchester is still traceable. Furthermore, the fact that the first West Saxon bishopric was at Dorchester supports the view that the Upper Thames was the original heartland of the 'Gewisse'.

Second, Saxon folk settled at a small Roman villa at Barton Court Farm, Radley, near Abingdon, at some time in the fifth or sixth centuries. They did not settle at the villa site itself, but at the place now known as Barrow Hills.

Third, there are sixth-century cemeteries at Lechlade, Fairford, and Kemble. Myres thinks the Thames valley sites, with their pottery, buckles and belt-fittings, show links to the continental Saxon homelands between the Elbe and Weser, of the 350-450 period.

Did these Saxons make their own way to the Middle/Upper Thames, coming up from the Wash (using rivers such as the Ouse and Cam), rather than by way of the Thames? Or were they 'planted' here by the British authorities, a buffer of *laeti* along their frontiers? It was noted earlier (see under 'Areas of friction') that the Upper Thames area was on the border between the Catuvellauni and the Dobunni.

Another suggestive point is the occurrence, noted by F M Stenton, of a number of 'heroic' names in place-names in the country round Oxford, and these cannot be wholly fortuitous. First, there is Hinksey, which contains the personal name 'Hengest'. Then Witney and Wittenham contain the name 'Witta' (a king of the Suevi, named in the poem *Widsith*). Beckley and Begbroke come from the name 'Becca' (ruler of the Baningas, in *Widsith*), and Handborough is from 'Hagena' (ruler of the Holmryge, in *Widsith*). The name 'Elsa', which is prominent in the saga of Theodric of Verona, occurs in Elsfield. Seacourt (*Seofocan wyrð*), the name of a lost village west of Oxford, contains the name 'Seofeca', a sinister counsellor of king Eormenric in one of the most famous of ancient stories. 'Frithela' or 'Fridla' is the name of one of Seofeca's victims in the story, and it occurs in the compound *Friþela byrig* in the tenth century boundaries of Seacourt, and in the name of Frilford, a few miles away, to the south of Oxford.[179] Clearly the people who chose thus to name these places knew that these were folk famous in the old tales that were handed down.

An aside: Eormenric and Seofeca

It was said of Eormenric that he was 'more cunning than all in guile, more generous in gifts'.[180] Seofeca is named in *Widsith*, line 116. In other sources he is 'Sibich' or 'Sifka'. Like Shakespeare's Iago he does evil for the love of it. However, in the *Thidreks saga* (an Old Norse work which is now the source for many medieval German legends) his actions are given a more believable motive – revenge. It is said

---

[179] Chambers, R W, *Widsith: a study in Old English Heroic Legend*, 1912, 33-4.
[180] Chambers, 29, 34, citing the Würzburg Chronicle.

that during his absence from the country Eormenric seduced his wife, and Sifka then set to work to destroy the tyrant by evil counsels. By the advice of Sifka, and of Sifka's wife, Eormenric brought about the death of his own sons – of two unintentionally, and of the third deliberately. That king then brought about the deaths of his two nephews from Harlung land, the Emerca and Fridla of *Widsith*, line 113. Finally Eormenric was persuaded to attack his nephew, Thitrek (Theodoric the Great, ruler of Italy, 493-526).

Wessex

The archaeological and place-name evidence thus suggests that Wessex had its beginnings in the Middle/Upper Thames region. How are we to understand this in the light of the picture in the *Anglo-Saxon Chronicle* where the story begins on the Hampshire coast? The *Chronicle* reads as follows:

> '495. In this year two *ealdormen*, Cerdic and Cynric his son, came to Britain with five ships [arriving] at the place which is called *Cerdicesora*, and the same day they fought against the Welsh.'

Where was 'Cerdicesora'? It is usually identified with Stone on the Solent coast, close to the mouth of the Beaulieu river, but Cunliffe thinks Christchurch, at the mouth of the Avon, is more likely.[181] The name 'Cerdic' is British, and it is hard to believe that the *Chronicle* would have given this name to one of the West Saxon leaders if the tradition was not in fact true. (The name is usually identified with Old Welsh *Ceretic* (W *Ceredig*), and this is commonly held to represent Old British *Coroticus*. But Ekwall thinks it more likely that the source is a British *Caratīc-*, identical with Welsh *caredig* 'beloved', the source of Old Welsh *Caratauc* (W *Caradog*). He holds, further, that the original West Saxon form was probably *Ceardic*, which later became *Cerdic*, see Ekwall, *English River Names*, 1968, lxviii-lxix.)

There is no independent authority for Cerdic's kindred line – it has been 'borrowed' from that of the Bernician kings, with 'Giwis' (clearly linked with the name 'Gewisse') instead of 'Bernic' (whose name is clearly linked with 'Bernicia'). Perhaps he could not claim descent from any important Germanic family. Reed thinks he was the offspring of a Jutish chief, a companion of Hengest, and a British noblewoman from Kent.[182] We have seen that there was one, 'Ceretic', who acted as interpreter between Vortigern and Hengest (*Historia Brittonum* 37).

If we accept, for the moment, the landing at *Cerdicesora*, and follow the next few entries in the *Chronicle*, a reasonably coherent story of step-by-step conquest unfolds. Cerdic and Cynric fought the Britons at Netley (508), *Cerdicesford* (519), and *Cerdicesleag* (527). (The chronicler, Æthelweard, believed *Cerdicesford* to be Charford, on the Hampshire Avon.)

Regarding the archaeology it seems that there were Anglo-Saxon cemeteries in the Itchen valley north of Winchester before the end of the 5th century. A number of

---

[181] Cunliffe, 1993, 278.
[182] Reed, *The Rise of Wessex*, 1947, 40-41.

Anglo-Saxon cemeteries, from the period 500-550, have been found south and east of Salisbury. Ten graves at the Winterbourne Gunner cemetery (four miles north-east of Salisbury) were excavated in 1960. A throwing axe ('francisca') of Frankish type was found in Grave VI. According to Böhner's classification the date should be AD 450-525. Also in Grave VI there was a late Roman strap end, with an engraved beast of 4th/5th century workmanship. A figure-of-eight buckle, inlaid with bronze wires, from Grave VI, is thought to date from the last half of the 5th century. The design of brooches found in Graves VII and IX is adapted from Kentish disc brooches, and they seem to have been well-worn before they were put into the graves. A provisional view would be that the associated settlement began not later than about 520, and that the settlers came up from Southampton Water.[183]

There are two groups of graves at the Petersfinger cemetery, south-east of Salisbury, a group orientated west-east, and another orientated north-south. The first group appears to be earlier, as in two instances north-south graves cut into the west-east graves. It is possible that the west-east graves are of the same period and settlement group as those at Winterbourne Gunner, where the graves are also west-east. Among the west-east burials there was a warrior with a fine Frankish sword. The cemeteries at Charlton and Harnham also show Frankish links, possibly spread from Kent.[184] Perhaps the communities using the Winterbourne Gunner and Petersfinger cemeteries were Germanic *laeti*, employed by a post-Roman authority in the Salisbury area.[185] Both places are at strategic points where roads to Old Sarum ford the river Bourne.

This, then, is the *Chronicle's* picture of Wessex origins, with the supporting archaeology. The picture presents us with a number of puzzles. First, there is the fact of the archaeological and place-name evidence for early West Saxon settlement in the Middle/Upper Thames region. Is the *Chronicle's* picture (in the annals for 495-534), of Cerdic landing on the Hampshire coast and working his way northwards, simply wrong? Did Cerdic in fact establish himself in the upper Thames valley, in the 530s, then work south? Or, was it that the settlements in the south were small and marginal in the early days of the migrations, but from them sprang the leaders, Cerdic and his kin, who then made themselves lords of the Upper/Middle Thames settlers? Or were these Thames Saxons a quite different group of settlers, who moved south and clashed with the Saxon/Jutish group advancing northwards?

Another puzzle is that, as already noted, southern Hampshire and the Isle of Wight were Jutish, and remained so until conquered by Cædwalla of Wessex in 686-8.

And, third, the *Chronicle* says that it was in 519 that Cerdic and Cynric 'obtained the kingdom of the West Saxons'. Yet according to the same source they had been around

[183] J Musty and J E D Stratton, 'A Saxon cemetery at Winterbourne Gunner, near Salisbury', *Wiltshire Archaeological and Natural History Magazine*, 59, 1964, 86-104.
[184] Bruce Eagles, 'Anglo-Saxon presence and culture in Wiltshire c. AD 450 – c. 675', in Peter Ellis, editor, *Roman Wiltshire and after*, 2001, 218-9.
[185] D J James, 'Sorviodunum – A Review of the Archaeological Evidence', *WANHM*, 95, 2002, 16.

since 495. What are we to make of this? Myres theorises as follows: When Cerdic and Cynric are first mentioned in the *Chronicle* they are described as *ealdormen*, which perhaps indicates that they had some administrative role under the Roman authority. Perhaps Cerdic was the head of a partly British noble family with extensive territorial interests at the western end of the *Litus Saxonicum*, entrusted, in the last days of Roman or sub-Roman authority, with its defence. The remit might also have included responsibility for a possible Romano-British enclave around Silchester. It has been pointed out that a high proportion of the coins from the Silchester excavations can be dated to AD 388-395, and that many are very worn, suggesting the site was occupied well into the fifth century. To the north-west and west of Silchester there are a number of linear dykes, facing away from the town, perhaps forming a frontier between the Saxons of the Middle Thames and the Silchester enclave.[186] Very late Roman material has been found at Lowbury Hill, which is on the Berkshire Ridgeway, overlooking the upper Thames basin. If Cerdic was originally a military commander within the post-Roman defence system he may have sought to fill a gap in Silchester's defences at 'the central watershed of southern England'.[187] In later Anglo-Saxon terminology a man holding such military responsibility could be described as an 'ealdorman'. And such a man might be tempted, once effective Roman authority had faded, to go further. Perhaps he took matters into his own hands, eliminated any competing British chieftains (such as the mysterious Natanleod of annal 508), renounced any superior authority and 'began to reign' independently.[188]

Duplications?

The suggestion has been made that the answer to the chronological puzzle is to be found in a theory of duplications. F M Stenton has noted that traditions were handed down in heroic verse, and much of the content would have been determined by the interaction between the poet and his hearers. The leading place in a narrative might be given to different characters at different times, according to the mood of the moment or, this being poetry, the needs of alliteration (so vital to Anglo-Saxon poetry). A later writer might then be in danger of taking two versions of one story as the records of separate incidents. Stenton thinks the annal for 514 represents a tradition in which the West Saxons, Stuf and Wihtgar, not Cerdic and Cynric, played the leading role. He says this raises the question whether the battle at *Cerdicesleag*, thirteen years after the landing of Stuf and Wihtgar, might be a duplicate of the battle at *Natanleag* (Netley Marsh) thirteen years after the coming of Cerdic and Cynric. Then there is that annal for 519 which tells us that Cerdic and Cynric obtained the kingdom a full twenty-four years after their coming to Britain. A related issue is the matter, already discussed, of the Isle of Wight and the mainland areas opposite being settled by Jutes rather than by Saxons.

---

[186] J Wacher, *The Towns of Roman Britain*, 1974, 276.
[187] Myres, 1989, 156-7, 161-2.
[188] Myres, 1989, 146-8.

The question of duplications has been discussed more recently by David N Dumville in a paper on the West Saxon Genealogical Regnal List.[189] Dumville lists the supposed duplicate entries thus:

494/5	Arrival of West Saxons	514
500/1	Taking of land and kingdom	519
508	Battle with Britons	527
516	End of Cerdic's reign; Cynric king	534

When the dates of this parallel series of events are compared, the difference varies between eighteen and twenty years. This chimes in with a key fact of early time reckoning. The Greek astronomer Meton (about 430 BC) grasped the fact that there are cycles of nineteen years. He noted that 235 lunar months were almost exactly equal to 19 solar years. Put another way, new moons recur on the same solar days or nights as 19 years before, with only a small margin of error. The Metonic cycle was adopted in the Easter calculations of the Church. Might the same series of events have been entered twice, in two successive nineteen-year cycles?

From a careful comparison of the reign-lengths of later Wessex kings Dumville believes that the boundary of an undisputed AD chronology can probably be put at 641/2, the date of the end of the reign of Cynegils, the first Christian king of Wessex. (This, by the way, suggests that from the first setting up of Christian institutions a good system for handing on chronological information was set up, and this without, seemingly, any tampering with reign-lengths.)

Dumville then added up those reign-lengths which he thought were the most likely original readings, and suggested that the beginning of Cerdic's reign should be placed 104 years before 641/2, that is, in 537 or 538 (instead of the 494/5 of the *Chronicle*). This led Dumville to conclude that the record had been moved back by *two* 19-year periods. He suggests that Cerdic's arrival date should become 532, and the years of his reign run from 538-554. Kirby notes that, 'The year 532 … depends on the assumption that West Saxon history really was dominated by a single line of kings after Cerdic, ruling in succession, that all their names were known, and that all the regnal figures were correctly preserved.'[190] In fact we do know of one missing name, that of the obscure Creoda. There is enough evidence to show that Creoda was Cerdic's son and Cynric's father. He appears between Cerdic and Cynric in the pedigree of king Ine, and in versions B, C, D of the 855 entry in the *Chronicle*. His name may survive in a minor Wiltshire place-name, *Creodenhyll*. Yet for some reason the compiler of the *Chronicle*-archetype left his name out of the record (though not completely). Might this be an example of the practice known as *damnatio memoriæ* ('condemnation of the memory'), the creation of an 'unperson'?

---

[189] D N Dumville, 'The West Saxon Genealogical Regnal List and the chronology of Wessex', *Peritia*, Volume 4, 1985, 21-66.
[190] Kirby, 2000, 40.

This could mean the removal of a name from the historical records, condemning a person to oblivion, even denying them access to the afterlife. Pliny the Younger records the case of the emperor Domitian, assassinated, then subjected to an official *damnatio memoriæ* by the Senate. Nearer home, we have the cases of Osric of Deira and Eanfrith of Bernicia, who committed apostasy after the death of Edwin, and were soon 'justly punished' (in Bede's words), Osric falling in battle, and Eanfrith in a foolhardy peace embassy. Bede goes on to tell how it was settled that the memory of them should be wiped away, and their year added to the time of the king who came after them, the godly Oswald (*HE*, III.1).

If Creoda suffered such a fate, what could have led to this? Was the man deemed guilty of some outstanding act of treachery? Did he perhaps accept a humiliating vassalage after the crushing British victory at Badon Hill? That might be something the later chroniclers wished to forget.

Why should the beginnings of West Saxon dynastic history in the *Chronicle* have been set 38 years earlier (if this has indeed been done) than the Genealogical List had it? Was the aim to narrow the gap between Wessex on the one hand, and Kent (the earliest recorded Anglo-Saxon kingdom), on the other? Or was it felt that the sequence of Bretwaldas (overlords) of the southern English needed to be more evenly spaced out? The first Bretwalda was Ælle of Sussex, who, in the *Chronicle's* dating, was active in the 470s to 490s. After him there was Ceawlin of Wessex, whose dates were 560-92. Such a reign length seems necessary for the campaigning carried out by that formidable warrior-king, though Dumville's suggested dates for him are 581-88. He says that seven years – short, glorious, and violent – would fit the *Chronicle's* Ceawlin very well.[191]

The West Saxon royal genealogy

Kenneth Sisam has gone into the matter of 'old names of kings and shadows' in West Saxon royal genealogy.[192] He notes that R W Chambers brings out the perfect alliterative structure of the Cynric to Woden genealogy in the *Chronicle* (under the years 552, 597 and 855). Thus we have:

(Cynric Cerdicing),	Cerdic Elesing,
Elesa Esling,	Esla Giwising,
Giwis Wiging,	Wig Freawining,
Freawine Friðogaring,	Friðogar Bronding,
Brond Bældæging	Bældæg Wodening.

Chambers thought that these lines were likely to be truly old, going back to a time when the names of forebears, both real and imaginary, were recorded by memory,

---

[191] Dumville, *Peritia*, 1985, 51, 58, 59.

[192] Kenneth Sisam, 'Anglo-Saxon royal genealogies', in *Proceedings of the British Academy*, 39, 1953, 287-346, recently reprinted in the collection *British Academy Papers on Anglo-Saxon England*, Oxford University Press, 1990.

and 'were doubtless chanted by retainers of the West-Saxon kings in heathen days'.[193] Perhaps the perfect alliteration is too good to be true. Sisam believes that from Ecgberht, grandfather of Alfred the Great, back to Ingild, the brother of Ine, the Wessex genealogy may reasonably be trusted, and that from Ingild to Cerdic the genealogy is 'defensible', though there is conflicting evidence of Cerdic's immediate successors. But when we consider his forebears 'all is fiction or error'. We have already seen that, like enough, Cerdic's true roots are unknown, though this does not mean that Cerdic himself is a fiction.

As time went on gods, heroes, and biblical figures were brought into genealogies. One of the most striking additions is that of the god Woden. He is named in all the kingly lines other than that of Essex, where we have the god Seaxnet instead. Clearly the Church did not see Woden as a god, but it seems that a hero of old bearing the same name could be accepted. Perhaps it was a means of defining royalty, a way of claiming that all these kingly lines (and the folkdoms they 'summed up') were boughs of the one tree.[194]

---

[193] R W Chambers, quoted in Sisam, 1953, 158.
[194] Webster and Backhouse, editors, *The Making of England*, 1991, 45-7.

Chapter 7 The Britons fight back

From a number of sources we have indications that at some time before the middle of the sixth century there was a check to the Anglo-Saxon advance, even a reverse migration, with English settlers moving out. Stenton comments, 'No Germanic race ever took to the sea without some urgent reason.'[195]

First, in *DEB* 25-26 Gildas tells how, after the first storm of the barbarian onset, the Britons recovered under the leadership of a certain Ambrosius Aurelianus. The tide of war flowed back and forth, with victory going first to the Britons, then to their enemies. Gildas goes on: 'This lasted right up to the year of the siege of Badon Hill, pretty well the last defeat of the villains, and certainly not the least. This was the year of my birth; as I know, one month of the forty-fourth year since then has already passed' (*DEB* 26:1).

Next we have the evidence of Procopius of Caesarea (*c.* 500 - *c.* 554) who can only have gained his information about Britain from Frankish visitors to Constantinople. In his *History of the Wars* he wrote that Britain was inhabited by three races named *Angiloi, Frissones* (Frisians), and Britons. Their fertility led to large numbers migrating, every year, to the land of the Franks, where they were settled in emptier parts of the country. As a result the king of the Franks claimed lordship over Britain.

Third, a monk of Fulda, writing a little before 865, spoke of the ancestors of the Saxons migrating from Britain to the Continent, coming to Cuxhaven in 531, a time when Theuderich, king of the Franks, was warring against the Thuringians. The incomers helped him in the war, and were afterwards given land to the north of the River Unstrut.

Fourth, the *Anglo-Saxon Chronicle* records a steady advance by Cerdic and Cynric until the battle at *Cerdicesleag* in 527. Then in 530 these two 'obtained possession of the Isle of Wight', perhaps a piece of consolidation. After this there seems to have been no further advance until a second phase of the conquest began with the taking of *Searoburh* (Old Sarum) in 552. In Kent and Sussex, too, there are no references to further progress at this time.

Stenton concludes: 'it may at least be claimed that when four independent authorities agree in suggesting a single coherent story, it is unlikely to be very far from the truth'.[196] As to what happened to interrupt the Anglo-Saxon advance the answer seems, clearly, to be the siege of Badon Hill referred to by Gildas. The battle is not named in Anglo-Saxon sources. This may be because the memory of the defeat was too painful, though on the other hand the Anglo-Saxon poets could write movingly of great defeats (as in the poem, *The Battle of Maldon*) as well as great victories. They admired 'the worth of defeated valour'.[197]

---

[195] Stenton, 1967, 6.
[196] Stenton, 1967, 31.
[197] J R R Tolkien, quoted in H Mayr-Harting, *The Coming of Christianity*, 236.

Twelve battles

According to the *Historia Brittonum*, 56, Badon was in fact the climax of a series of twelve battles, and the British war leader was Arthur (not Ambrosius). The writer says:

'Then (after the death of Hengest) Arthur fought against them (the English) in those days, together with the kings of the British; but he was their leader in battle. The first battle was at the mouth of the river called Glein. The second, the third, the fourth and the fifth were on another river called the Douglas, which is in the country of Linnuis. The sixth battle was on the river called Bassas. The seventh battle was in Celyddon Forest, that is, the battle of Celyddon Coed. The eighth battle was in Guinnion fort, and in it Arthur carried the image of the holy Mary, the everlasting Virgin on his (shield) and the heathen were put to flight on that day, and there was a great slaughter upon them, through the power of Our Lord Jesus Christ and the power of the holy Virgin Mary his mother. The ninth battle was fought in the city of the Legion. The tenth battle was fought on the bank of the river Tryfrwyd. The eleventh battle was on the hill called Agned. The twelfth battle was on Badon Hill and in it nine hundred and sixty men fell in one day, from a single charge of Arthur's, and no one laid them low save he alone, and he was victorious in all his campaigns.'

It is noteworthy that seven of the twelve battles were fought on rivers, and two on hills. That said, it must be acknowledged that none of the battle sites can now be identified with anything like certainty. What can be said of the overall strategic position about the year 500? We will digress for a moment, and look at the western side of Britain, a hundred or so years later. There were two key developments here, first, the Anglo-Saxon taking of the Gloucester region, then their capture of Chester. The first move drove a wedge between the Britons of south Wales, and those of south-west Britain. The second cut off the Britons of north Wales from those of Cumbria. Were there any such key points on the east side of the country, where the Britons might have driven wedges and separated the various groups of Anglo-Saxon incomers? The Lincoln area might be one such. To hold, or re-take, Lincoln would have driven a wedge between the Angles of Deira and those of East Anglia. Again, holding the London area would keep separate the Saxons of Essex and Middlesex, and those of west Kent and Surrey.

What about tactics? The British warrior aristocracy of this time would have fought as light cavalry, able to move four to five times faster than infantry. They would have been able to deter the Anglo-Saxons from raiding in small parties, and hinder the gathering of larger armies. But they could not allow themselves to be encumbered with spades, pick-axes and such, with which to build an overnight camp, so they must have sought ready-made defences. In much of lowland Britain there were small walled towns 8-12 miles apart. Elsewhere Iron Age hill forts could have been brought back into use.

On the whole, Dark Age warfare was mobile, with little use made of strongholds and prepared positions[198] though there were occasional sieges. The open Wiltshire downland, westwards from Silchester, was good cavalry country.[199] And the vital horse-raising areas were the Cotswolds, Salisbury Plain and Hampshire.

How did Dark Age armies find one another? From the striking correlation of Dark Age battle sites with Roman roads and major ancient tracks such as the Ridgeway, it is evident that Dark Age armies made good use of roads. A commander would surely have enlisted local people as guides, though recorded instances are hard to find from this period. And he would no doubt have made use of scouts on horseback, to find the enemy quickly, so that he could then concentrate a larger force against a weaker enemy. It has been suggested that 'Arthur' must have had a good intelligence system, enabling him to know where the invaders were gathering dangerously, where to cut their communications, and where to corner them.[200]

Keeping all these considerations in mind let us look at the names of the battle-sites. Something can be said about 'the country of Linnuis', about 'Cat Coit Celidon', and 'The City of the Legion'.

Kenneth Jackson derived 'Linnius' from 'Lindenses', meaning 'the people of Lindum or Lincoln'.[201] If this is right then four battles in that region (key for Anglo-Saxon penetration) makes good enough sense. Alcock, however, discusses a small emendation, and this at a point where, he says, the manuscripts do in fact diverge. He arrives at the reading *lininuis*, which would derive from Lindinienses, the name of one section of the Durotriges tribe (of Dorset, and parts of Somerset, Wiltshire and Hampshire). The Lindinienses were the people who lived around Lindinis, which is usually taken to be Ilchester. This is an area where there might well have been British-Saxon fighting in the time of the supposed Arthur. Some hill-forts that went out of use in the Roman period were elaborately refortified at this time, no doubt as a counter to the threatened advance of Saxons from Wessex.[202] The most striking example at present known is the great fortress at South Cadbury. Around AD 500 the innermost line of the multiple Early Iron Age ramparts was strengthened with a great timber-framed superstructure of rubble stones, and there is some evidence for at least one large timber hall within the ramparts.

'Cat Coit Celidon', that is, 'The battle of the Caledonian Forest', presumably took place somewhere in southern Scotland. And the 'City of the Legion' would be either Chester or Caerleon. Suggestions have been made about the other sites, but in truth these are only guesswork. And so to Badon.

---

[198] Alcock, 1975, 344-5.
[199] Nick Griffiths, 'The Roman army in Wiltshire', in ed Peter Ellis, *Roman Wiltshire and after*, 43.
[200] Lindsay, *Arthur and his times*.1958, 217.
[201] Jackson, 'Once again Arthur's battles', *Modern Philology* 43:1, August 1945, 44-57, cited in Ashley, *A brief history of King Arthur*, 2010, 147.
[202] Alcock, 1975, 66; Myres, 1989, 215-6.

Context for Badon?

We do not know where Badon was, or when the siege took place. It is not even clear who was the besieged – Britons or Saxons – or who led the opposing forces. However, we have seen that there were Anglo-Saxons settled early in the Middle/Upper Thames area, close to the ancient trackway known as the Icknield Way and the Thames crossing in the Dorchester/Wallingford area. Once across the Thames an invader could reach an important road-meet, namely, the point where the Roman road from Winchester was joined by that from Silchester before going on north-westwards to Cirencester. The invader would also be able to follow the Ridgeway to reach the north-facing linear defence work (probably post-Roman) known as the Wansdyke. The dyke gives maximum visual command of the Ridgeway, and it was perhaps built to block an Anglo-Saxon advance southwards from the Thames valley.[203] A number of writers see this as a key area to attack and defend. David Nicolle and Angus McBride think that fighting between Saxons and Britons centred on Wiltshire, the Icknield Way, and Cambridgeshire.[204] Lindsay, too, thinks the area most hotly contested between Briton and Saxon was around the point where the Icknield Way crosses the Thames.[205] Peter Fowler suggests that East Wansdyke was being hastily built in the 490s to meet an imminent Saxon attack from the Thames valley. As it happened the attack did not materialise, because of the victory at Badon, and building work was at once abandoned.

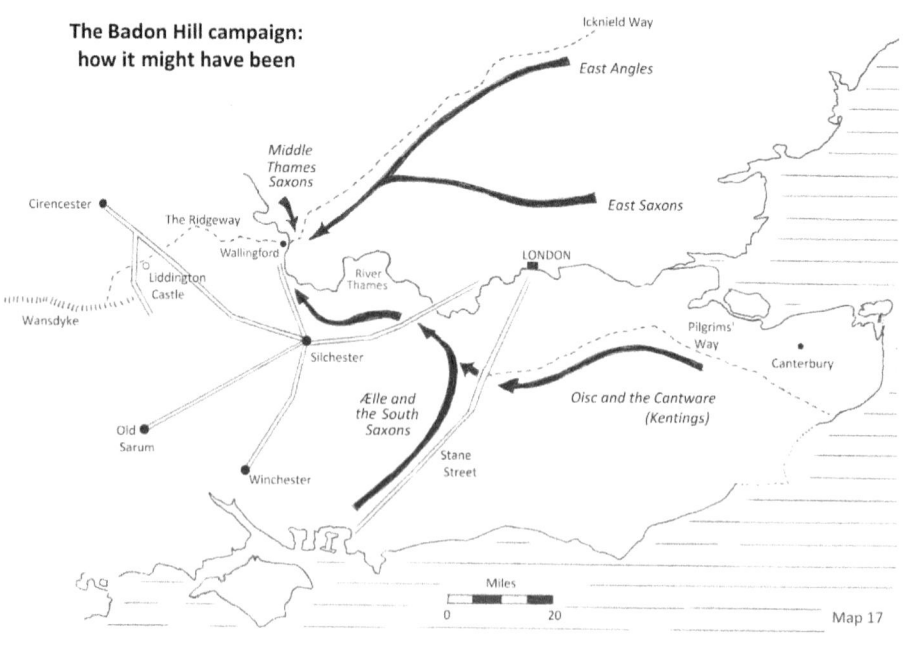

[203] Myres, 1989, 155-6.
[204] D Nicolle and A McBride, *Arthur and the Anglo-Saxon Wars*, 1994, 10.
[205] J Lindsay, 1958, 201.

116

Where was Badon?

There seems no reason to doubt that Gildas's 'Mons Badonicus' must be his Latinization of a name later anglicized as Badbury. Many (perhaps most) scholars take it that this was a hill-fort, though some think it may have been a walled settlement. According to Alcock, the 'd' in the Latin 'Badonicus' or 'Badonis' is a 'th' sound (as in 'that') and this would become Baðon in Old English. If Badonis was the native British name for Bath, Old English may have assimilated to 'Bath'. Alcock concludes that Mount Badon was probably a hill outside Bath. Higham thinks it may have been the city itself, with its Roman walls, that was besieged.[206]

There are certainly other places in Wessex which could have given rise to the Badbury name. Of the suggested sites perhaps the least unlikely are Liddington Castle and nearby Baydon, and Badbury Rings in Dorset. Of the last-named it must be said that it seems too far from any point of serious friction between Briton and Saxon. Could there have been a Jutish thrust across the lower Avon – an attempt to bypass the barrier of Bokerly Dyke? It seems unlikely, for at this time (c. 500) the Jutes had hardly had time to even begin to settle the Hampshire coastlands. And a British victory here, over a single enemy, could scarcely have been decisive.

Myres argues that Gildas probably intended the name 'Mons Badonicus' to identify a wider area than that marked by a hill-fort and a road-meet. He suggests it could mean 'the hill-country of Badon', and this brings us to the two most probable suggestions: 1) a hill-fort known for centuries as Liddington Castle, and 2) a site some three miles to the south-east, close to the village of Baydon. The latter is set high between deep valleys to the north and south. However, there are no indications of defensive earthworks here.[207] The situation of Liddington/Baydon had obvious strategic importance in the post-Roman age, being on the Ridgeway, and close to a road-meet. Grinsell, on the other hand, while acknowledging that Liddington could be the place, suggests a possible alternative, Badbury Hill camp, between Faringdon and Highworth, a little to the west and south of Oxford.[208]

When did the siege happen?

Gildas seems to date it in the year of his birth, 44 years before his time of writing. And the time of writing is usually taken to be before 547, because in, or about, that year Maglocunus of Gwynedd (one of five rulers named by Gildas), is credibly reported to have died in the 'great death' or plague noted in the *Annales Cambriae*. This gives a date of 'about 503', and it is thus awkward that the *Annales* date Badon in 516. Bede, with a manuscript of Gildas at least 300 years earlier than any we possess today, understood the text to mean that Badon took place forty-four years after the *Adventus Saxonum*, 'the coming of the Saxons'. For Bede the *Adventus* is dated somewhere between 446 and 455, and Badon, therefore, between 490 and 499. The whole date range is thus 490-516.

---

[206] See Alcock, 1975, 70, 359; N J Higham, *The English Conquest*, 1994, 166.
[207] Myres, 1989, 159-60.
[208] L V Grinsell, *The archaeology of Wessex*, 1958, 277.

As to who besieged whom, who commanded the opposing forces, and the ebb and flow of the battle, we can only ponder what might have happened. *The following paragraph, it must be stressed, is but guesswork!*

First, the leaders: was it Ambrosius who led the Britons, or, as in the *Historia Brittonum*, Arthur? Was Cerdic, later of Wessex, an ally, or did he cannily stand aside? And what of the Saxons? Ælle of Sussex was the first of the Bretwaldas named by Bede, and in the *Chronicle* record he was the victor in battles fought at 'Cymenesora' (near Selsey Bill), 'Mearcrædesburna' (the river Cuckmere, perhaps), and 'Andredescester' (the Saxon Shore fort at Pevensey). And he may have won war-fame before coming to Britain. Would his renown have given him enough weight among the Angles, Saxons, and Jutes of south-east Britain to enable him to summon them to his standard? Oisc of Kent, whose supposed death date of 512 is within the 490-516 date range, might have marched along the Pilgrims' Way to join Ælle somewhere on the Roman road called Stane Street. They might then have headed across country to the London-Silchester road, next turning north from that town to reach the Thames crossing at Wallingford. Here they might have met up with war-bands of East Angles and East Saxons marching down the Icknield Way, and others from the Dorchester-Abingdon area. Ælle's war aims may have included the elimination of the Silchester enclave and the strangulation of any remaining Romano-British petty-state centred on London. He may have hoped to press on south-westwards along the Ridgeway, to take the Wansdyke defensive line from behind, and to deny the Britons the cavalry country of the Wiltshire downs. But the outcome was a Saxon disaster. Perhaps a British host, taken off guard by this raid in force, took refuge in the Liddington hill-fort, then broke out in a cavalry charge and turned the tables on the attackers. Or maybe the Saxon host was cornered, besieged for three days, then destroyed in a determined attack. Maybe Ælle fought to the last, surrounded by his war-band or 'comitatus' – the forebears of Angenmær, Geofa, Pafen and Pæcca, Wighelm and Willa, Beada, Hægel and others.[209] Perhaps a heroic poem, now lost, sang of their deeds, their 'defeated valour'.

'Arthur'

Scholars are still divided on the question, 'Was Arthur a historical figure?' Myres, on one side of the argument, notes that Gildas makes no mention of Arthur, and, 'His silence is decisive in determining the historical insignificance of this enigmatic figure'.[210] Another, wary, answer is that 'At this stage of the enquiry, one can only say that there may well have been a historical Arthur; that the historian can as yet say nothing of value about him.'[211] Others go further, holding that there must have been an Arthur-like figure, someone who turned the tide of war for a short while, perhaps even reversed the Anglo-Saxon advance.

---

[209] These names lie behind the South Saxon settlements of Angmering, Jevington, Pevensey, Patching, Wilmington, Willingdon, Beddingham, and Hailsham.

[210] Myres, 1989, 15.

[211] Thomas Charles-Edwards, 'The Arthur of history', in Bromwich, Jarman and Roberts, eds, *The Arthur of the Welsh*, 1991, 29.

The earliest reference to Arthur comes in *Y Gododdin*, the Welsh poem describing a disastrous raid against the Angles, about the year 600. From the spelling it would seem the couplet referring to Arthur could be a ninth century addition, but a date of about 600 is not impossible. Charles Thomas notes that the naming of Arthur in *Y Gododdin* confirms his historicity, because there are no references to legendary or unhistorical figures elsewhere in the poem, and many of those named are independently attested. Thomas thinks Arthur was a roving general with a band of horsemen, and that he could have been the victor of Badon.[212]

The most likely derivation of Arthur's name is from the Latin *Artorius*, and there is evidence that this name was known in Britain in the second century. An inscription records that a certain Lucius Artorius Castus, *praefectus castrorum* of the Sixth Legion stationed at York, was sent at the head of two legions to suppress a rebellion in Armorica, in the 190s. He could have left descendants, or perhaps namesakes, in Britain.[213]

If Arthur was a historical figure he might have lived from *c*. 460 to *c*. 530. We might suppose that he succeeded to the leadership of the Britons after the death of Ambrosius, perhaps *c*. 480. Alcock suggests Arthur may have been *magister militum per Britannias*, leader of the combined forces of the small British kingdoms of sub-Roman Britain. These forces may have been raised by the city administrations to which Honorius had remitted authority, or they may have been personal war-bands. Such war-bands may have numbered about 1,000 men.[214] Titles for Arthur in Welsh poetry are *tywyssawc cat* 'leader of battle', and *tywyssawc llu* 'leader of the army'.[215]

Camlann and after

After the stunning victory of Badon Hill the Britons had the upper hand. The poet of *Armes Prydein* called for the invading Saxons to be asked to compensate for the damage they had done before they should be allowed to leave the land of Britain. Compensation was required not merely for physical damage but for insult. This is the concept known as *sarhad* or sometimes *wynebwerth* ('worth of face'), underlying the laws. The honour of a man, or of a group, was as precious a thing as his body and property. Damage done to a person who was protected by a third party might oblige the offender to compensate the third party as well as the person injured.[216]

British ascendancy was not to last. Nearly a generation after Badon there took place the fight at Camlann. Depending on when we date Badon this could have happened at any time between 511 and 537 (the date given in the *Annales Cambriae*).

---

[212] Thomas, *Britain and Ireland*, 1971, 40-41; he cites T Jones, 'The early evolution of the legend of Arthur' *Nottingham Medieval Studies*, VIII, 1964, 3-21.

[213] P Salway, *Roman Britain*, 1981, 213n; S Frere, *Britannia*, 1967, 166; R Bromwich and others (eds), *The Arthur of the Welsh*, 1991, 6.

[214] Alcock, 1975, 358-9.

[215] M Holmes, *King Arthur, A military history*, 1998, 15.

[216] W Davies, *Wales in the Early Middle Ages*, 1996, 136-7.

Rachel Bromwich discusses Camlann in her edition of the Welsh Triads, for five of the Triads mention the fight.[217] She gives the root of the name as either *Cambolanda* 'crooked enclosure' or *Camboglanna* 'crooked bank'. The site of the battle was perhaps the Roman fort of *Camboglanna* or Birdoswald on Hadrian's Wall.

Concerning Camlann note, first, that according to the Triads the battle came about through a quarrel among Arthur's women. Triad 84 includes it among the 'Three Futile Battles of the Island of Britain', brought about 'because of Gwenhwyfar's contention with Gwenhwy(f)ach' (her sister). Triad 53 refers to the 'Three Ill-omened Hard Slaps', one of which was struck by Gwenhwyfach upon Gwenhwyfar. (The other futile battles were the Battle of Goddeu, which arose because of the bitch, the roebuck and the plover, and the Contest of Ar(f)derydd, whose roots are traced to the lark's nest. The Battles were futile because they were brought about by such barren causes.[218]) The medieval Welsh poet, Tudor Aled (*c.* 1465-*c.* 1525/7), in lines to Gruffudd ap Rhys, spoke of the fight as less than just.[219] He also said that the battle 'happened over two nuts'[220]

Note, second, in the 'weaving' or 'plotting' before the battle, Arthur was over-generous to Medrawd and Iddawc. The latter had a name as 'The Agitator of Britain', and he is said to have won his nickname by distorting Arthur's messages to Medrawd.

Third, the Camlann battle was noteworthy for its 'fury and intensity'.[221]

Fourth, there are different traditions about the number who escaped after the battle – was it three or seven? A note in one of Evan Evans's manuscripts gives the names of seven survivors: Sandde 'Angel's Form' escaped because of his beauty, Morfran son of Tegid (Tacitus) because of his ugliness, St Cynfelyn from the speed of his horse (Arthur's horse, 'Hengroen'), St Cedwyn from the world's blessing, St Pedrog from the strength of his spear, Derfel the Strong from his strength, Geneid the Tall from his speed. Petroc/Petrog 'Shattered Spear' was renowned for his wielding of the spear, but after Camlann he vowed never to take up worldly weapons again.[222] The Welsh tale of *Culhwch and Olwen* (lines 225-232) knows of only three survivors: Morfran, Sandde, and Cynwyl.

It has been suggested that the British were fatally weakened by the plague in the 530s,[223] whereas the Anglo-Saxons, lacking Mediterranean links, may not have been affected. The Britons were surely weakened as much, perhaps more, by their own infighting.

---

[217] Bromwich, ed, *Trioedd*, 2006, 167-170. The five are numbers 30, 51, 53, 59, 84. Camlann is not mentioned in *Historia Brittonum*.
[218] Bromwich, ed, *Trioedd*, 2006, 217.
[219] Bromwich, ed, *Trioedd*, 2006, 169.
[220] Blake and Lloyd, *Pendragon*, 2002, 188, citing T Gwynn Jones *Gwaith Tudor Aled*, 1926; see also *Pendragon*, 288n.
[221] Bromwich, ed, *Trioedd*, 2006, 169.
[222] Bromwich, ed, *Trioedd*, 2006, 482-3.
[223] E Foord, *The Last Age of Roman Britain*, 1912, 256.

Five 'tyrants'

Gildas attacked five 'tyrants' of his day, Aurelius Caninus, Constantine, Cuneglasus, Maglocunus, and Vortiporius.

Gildas condemned Constantine of Dumnonia as an oath-breaker. After swearing good behaviour he stabbed two royal youths and their guardians, in a church, while disguised as an abbot. Moreover, after his own successive adulteries, he put away his lawful wife. This Constantine may have been the Custennin Gorneu (Constantine of Cornwall) of later Welsh tradition.[224] The *Annales Cambriae* note, under the year 589, the late conversion to Christianity of a certain Constantine.[225]

Aurelius Caninus (or Caninius) has been thought to be king of Glywysing, or the Silures of south-east Wales, or the Gloucester area, or all of Somerset, Gloucester and Glamorgan.[226] Gildas accused him of committing 'parricides, fornications, adulteries' and of having 'an unjust thirst for civil war and constant plunder'.[227]

Vortipor was the 'bad son of a good king', guilty of 'the rape of a shameless daughter after the removal and honourable death of your own wife.' There is a rough pillar of stone which once stood at Castell Dwyran on the borders of Carmarthenshire and Pembrokeshire, some three miles from the traditional court of Dyfed at Narberth. It is inscribed, in Latin and ogam, with the name Vorteporix, and it is generally accepted as the man's epitaph. Vortipor is named 'Protector', a title given to officer-cadets of the imperial bodyguard. There is no question that Vortipor was ever a Protector, but perhaps the kindred still had hazy memories of a forebear who had been such, and went on using the title as a hereditary honour. Davies adds that Magnus Maximus occurs in the pedigree of Vortipor, and that it was he who allowed the migration of the Deisi from Ireland to Dyfed. Perhaps one of Vortipor's forebears had been in his service.[228] Other suggested names for this patron are Constantine III, or Ambrosius.[229]

Cuneglasus was 'driver of the chariot of the Bear's Stronghold'. Gildas chooses to read Cuneglasus' name as 'red butcher', but it is rather 'blue (or grey) hound', or 'Tawny Hound'. His father was Eugen, the uncle who Maglocunus/Maelgwyn slew. Cuneglasus put away his wife in order to marry her villainous sister, a widow who had vowed perpetual widowhood.[230] He was perhaps king of Ceredigion or Powys.[231]

---

[224] C Thomas, *Celtic Britain*, 1997, 51.

[225] See *DEB* XXVIII-XXIX; C Thomas, *Christianity in Roman Britain to AD 500*, 1983, 253; Snyder, *An Age of Tyrants*, 1998, 246.

[226] C Thomas, *Celtic Britain*, 1997, 116; Higham, *The English Conquest*, 1994, 178; Ellis, *Celt and Saxon*, 1993, 70; Lloyd Laing, *Celtic Britain*, 1979, 124; Alcock, 1975, 122; J Morris, *Arthurian Period Sources* 3, 1995, 163.

[227] Gildas, *DEB* XXX, 1; Snyder, *An Age of Tyrants*, 1998, 246.

[228] Davies, *A History of Wales*, 2007, 51.

[229] Snyder, *An Age of Tyrants*, 1998, 118.

[230] *DEB* XXXII, 1-2, and notes on page 152-3); Snyder, *An Age of Tyrants*, 1998, 246.

[231] C Thomas, *Celtic Britain* 1997, 51, 116; Dark, 1994, 79.

The five 'tyrants' named by Gildas

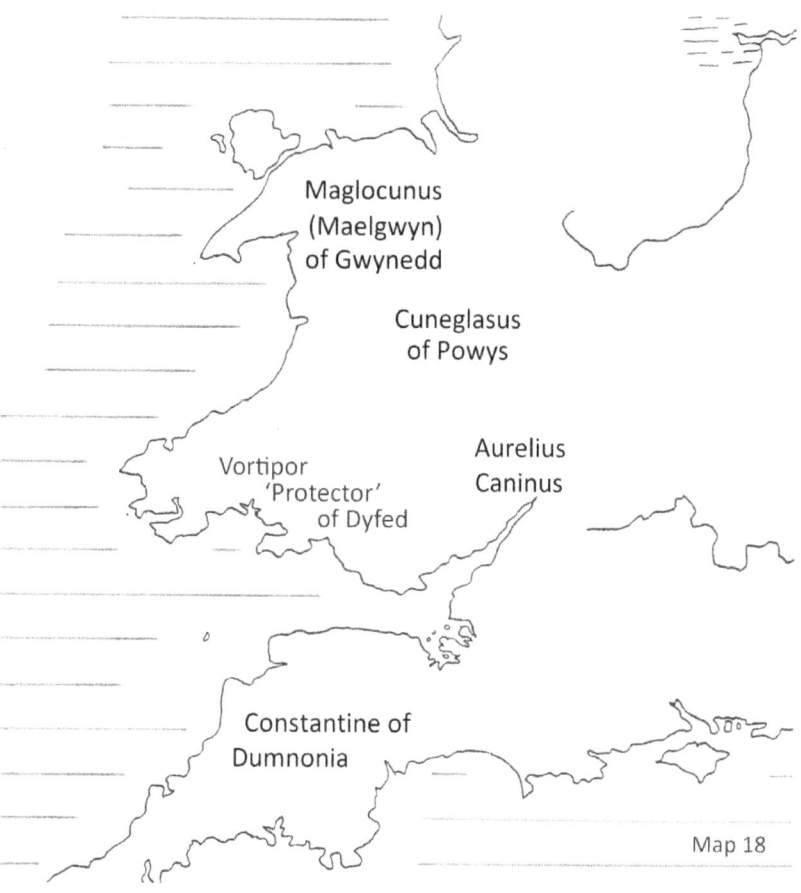

Maglocunus
(Maelgwyn)
of Gwynedd

Cuneglasus
of Powys

Aurelius
Caninus

Vortipor
'Protector'
of Dyfed

Constantine of
Dumnonia

Map 18

The fifth of the tyrants was Maglocunus ('Princely Hound'), that is, Maelgwyn Hir (the Tall). Gildas calls him 'dragon of the island' – a royal title. He also calls him 'first in stature and also power', and *Historia Brittonum* calls him 'the great king' – indicating a claim to headship by Gwynedd.[232] Perhaps at first he was a sub-king based on Anglesey, who then seized the over-kingship from his uncle, the king of the Ordovices based in Merioneth, killing him and those loyal to him. Later he put away his wife, becoming a monk and a pupil of 'the refined master of almost all Britain'.[233] (This may have been Illtyd, who lived in the late fifth/early

[232] W Davies, *Wales in the Early Middle Ages*, 1996, 104.
[233] *DEB* XXXIII, 1, 4; XXXIV, 1; XXXV, 2; XXXVI, 1, and note on page 153; Dark, 1994, 78.

sixth century, and founded the monastery and school of Llanilltyd Fawr. Gildas may have been a pupil there, as well as Maelgwyn.) The king forsook his early devotion to the church[234], and became a ruthless chieftain. He murdered his own wife and nephew in order to take the nephew's wife. Morris names his wives as Sanant of Powys, and Walldewen.[235] According to Gildas the first marriage was unlawful, though Gildas does not say why. Maelgwyn went on to murder his second wife. His seat was at Degannwy.

In sum, Maelgwyn was tall, probably fair-haired and handsome, attractive to women, a patron of the arts. He had bouts of remorse accompanied by generosity to the church. He died in a plague, perhaps the 'yellow plague' which began in Persia about 541/2, and reached Britain about 547-9. According to legend he took refuge from the plague in a church, but his curiosity overcame him and he looked out through the keyhole, being thereby caught by the infection. This fulfilled a curse pronounced upon him by the bard Taliesin, whose property he had taken.[236] His sons were Rhun and Ennianus/Einyawn.

---

[234] G Ashe, *Caesar to Arthur*, 1960, 241; Snyder, *An Age of Tyrants*, 1998, 246.
[235] J Morris, *Arthurian Period Sources* 3, 1995, 166.
[236] Lady Charlotte Guest, trans, *The Mabinogion*, 2002, 295, 299.

Chapter 8   Westward expansion

Middle Angles

The settlement of the Middle Anglian area, between the Mercians and the East Angles, probably began before the end of the fifth century, with penetration by way of the Wash river system. The area eventually stretched as far south as the Thames. (The later diocese of Leicester may indicate the extent of Middle Anglian territory.)

The topography of this area south of the Wash has been greatly altered since the Anglo-Saxon period, first by the silting up of river estuaries, causing radical changes to their courses inland, and secondly by drainage of the fens in the late eighteenth and early nineteenth centuries. In the period of the settlements communications were poor, and isolated fenland tribal units kept their identity. The Tribal Hidage lists a number of small people groups who settled here. Their common name of 'Middle Angles' suggests related peoples who had migrated separately from the Continent, among whom no single war-leader or family was able to gain the headship. It is likely that in the sixth century Wessex, Mercia, Northumbria, and East Anglia would also have been patchworks of small people groups such as we see in the Middle Anglia of the Hidage. Among such groups were the Rodingas of Essex, the Hæstingas of Kent and Sussex, and the Readingas, 'the people of Reada', or 'people of the red one', in the Reading area. There were the Horningas – probably 'the people of the horn of the land', that is, the Thames loop above Dorchester – the Sunningas, 'Sunna's folk', of Sonning, Sunningdale, Sunninghill, Sunningwell, and possibly Sunbury, also the Basingas, 'Basa's folk', of Basing and Basingstoke, and many others.

Among the Middle Anglian groups were the North and South Gyrwe. That the Gyrwe constituted a kingdom of their own is shown by Bede who wrote that Thomas, the first English bishop of East Anglia, came *de prouincia Gyruiorum*, 'from the kingdom of the Gyrwe'. Bede (HE IV, 19) also refers to Tondberht as an ealdorman of the South Gyrwe. Peterborough Abbey was located by Bede *in regione Gyruiorum*, and a 'late but reliable authority' places Crowland *on middan Gyrwan fenne*. From Bede, too, we learn that the Gyrwe were divided into north and south sections as early as *c*. 660. We may be reasonably sure that the dividing boundary between north and south was the River Must, which ran along a course closely related to that of the modern River Nene. Ermine Street may well have formed the western boundary, and the old course of the Western Ouse was probably the southern boundary.[237]

---

[237] Hart, 1971, 143.

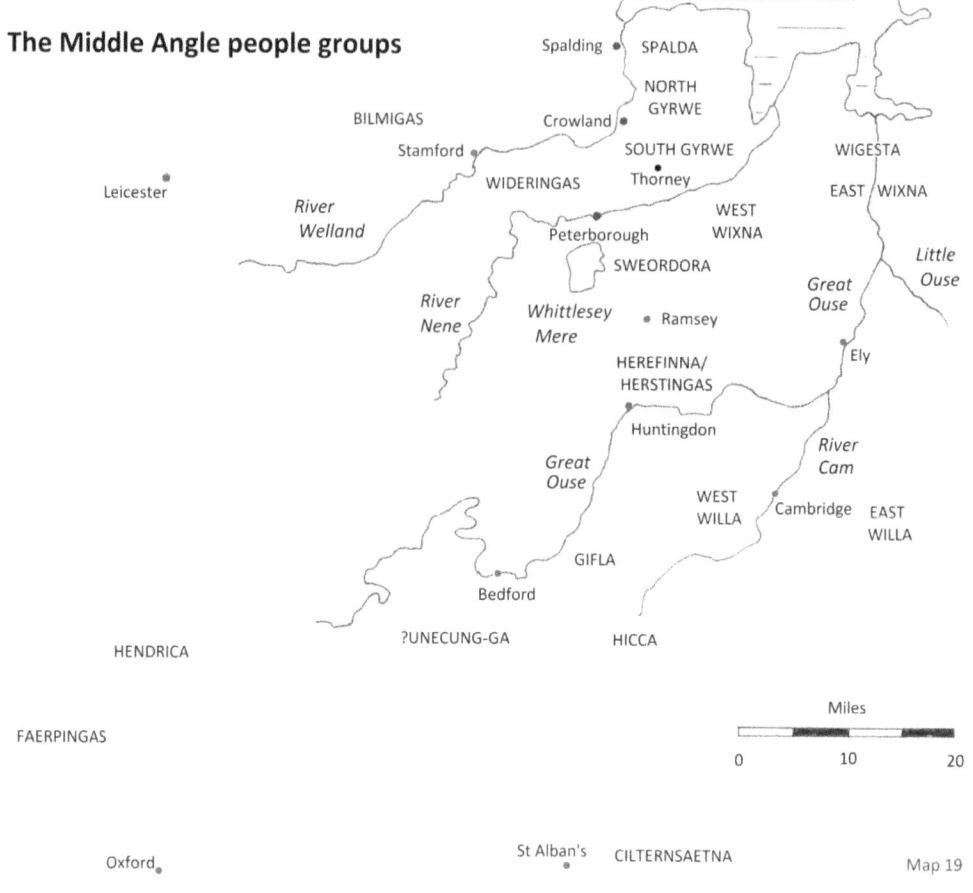

The Middle Angle people groups

Spalding • SPALDA

NORTH GYRWE

BILMIGAS   Crowland •

Stamford •   SOUTH GYRWE   WIGESTA

Leicester •   WIDERINGAS   Thorney •   EAST / WIXNA

River Welland   WEST WIXNA

Peterborough •   Little Ouse

SWEORDORA   Great Ouse

River Nene   Whittlesey Mere   • Ramsey

HEREFINNA/ HERSTINGAS   Ely

Huntingdon   River Cam

Great Ouse   WEST WILLA   Cambridge   EAST WILLA

GIFLA

Bedford •

?UNECUNG-GA   HICCA

HENDRICA

Miles

FAERPINGAS

0   10   20

Oxford •

St Alban's •   CILTERNSAETNA   Map 19

Other groups were: the *Spalda* (of the Spalding area), the *Wigesta* (probably of the Norfolk marshland), the *Bilmigas*, the *Widerigga* of the Soke of Peterborough, and the *Herefinna* (perhaps the *Herstingas* of the Huntingdonshire woodlands). The *Sweordora* were from the Sword Point region on the edge of Whittlesey Mere, and the *East and West Wixna* probably settled the Isle of Ely/Wisbech area. The *Gifla* settled the Ivel valley in Bedfordshire, the *Hicca* were probably centred on Hitchin, and the *East and West Willa* possibly settled on the Cam and the land south of the fenlands. The *Unecung-ga* (perhaps a corruption of 'Uuecling-ga') might be the *Wæclingas* of St Alban's and Watling Street. The *Hendrica* were perhaps settled on the flat land north-west of the Chiltern escarpment, and the *Færpingas* in the Charlbury, Oxfordshire area. The *Ciltern sætna* probably occupied all the land between the Chiltern ridge and the Thames. They were at the southernmost limits of the territory penetrated from the Wash.[238]

---

[238] Hart, 1971, 151.

During the middle Saxon period when stronger states were striving for lordship over smaller neighbours, it is likely that the Mercians and the East Angles were rivals for Middle Anglian territory. The South Gyrwe seem to have been absorbed into East Anglia by the end of the seventh century, but the Mercian kings became overlords of the lion's share of Middle Anglia. It seems that in the mid-seventh century the Mercians welded a patchwork of formerly independent peoples into one convenient territorial unit separating Mercia from East Anglia, Essex and Wessex.[239]

Mercia

Mercia was to become the leading political power in the late seventh- and eighth centuries, but very few Mercian primary sources for its early history have survived. No Mercian chronicle exists, and Bede was not in touch with any of the major Mercian religious houses. The fact that Cwichelm of Wessex, seemingly alarmed by the growing power of Edwin of Deira, sought to have him assassinated, makes it hard to believe that early Mercia, between the other two powers, was then of much political consequence.

Old English *Mierce* means 'borderers, dwellers on the march'. It has often been assumed the border in question was that with the Northumbrians, but in the seventh century the two kingdoms were separated by groups such as the *Pecsætan* of the Peak district and the British *Elmetsæte* of the Leeds area. It seems more likely that the border where the Mercians dwelt was the border with the Welsh.

The distribution of heathen burial-grounds makes it clear that the first Mercian settlements were in the Trent valley, and perhaps a little way up its tributaries. Gelling discusses a gloss in the Tribal Hidage which, reconstructed, reads *Ærest Myrcnaland*. This is in fact a district name, and it means 'original Mercia', 'the first land of the Mercians'.[240] It is likely that the settlers were folk who moved westwards from earlier settlements in eastern England, coming by way of the Leicestershire Soar, and ultimately by rivers such as the Welland that drain into the Wash. Other settlers may have come from the north, down the Trent.

The early Mercian settlements seem to have been relatively small, relatively late, and relatively poor.[241] Professor Wendy Davies would place the beginnings of the settlement in the early sixth century, though Stenton says that objects found by archaeology need not be dated earlier than the mid-sixth century.[242]

The traditional forebear of the Mercian house was Icel. He was the son of Eomer in the genealogies, and Chadwick believed this was the Eomer named in *Beowulf* (lines 1961ff). He suggested that Eomer was perhaps born about 420, and that it was in his

---

[239] Dumville, in Bassett, *Origins*, 1989, 134.
[240] Gelling, in Bassett, *Origins*, 1989, 191-2.
[241] So Brooks, 'The settlement of the Mercian kingdom', in Bassett, ed, *The Origins of the Anglo-Saxon kingdoms*, 1989, 162.
[242] Stenton, 1967, 42.

lifetime the migrations to Britain took place.[243] Icel comes five generations before Penda in the Mercian royal genealogy in the 'Anglian Collection': Icel – Cnebba – Cynewald – Crida/Creda/Creoda – Pypba – Penda. Depending on how we date the reign of Penda, and on whether we allow twenty-five years or thirty for a generation, Icel may be dated somewhere between *c.* 450 and *c.* 525.[244] The Mercian royal genealogy asserts that these kings were descended from 'the men who had ruled the whole Anglian race before its migration to Britain'.[245]

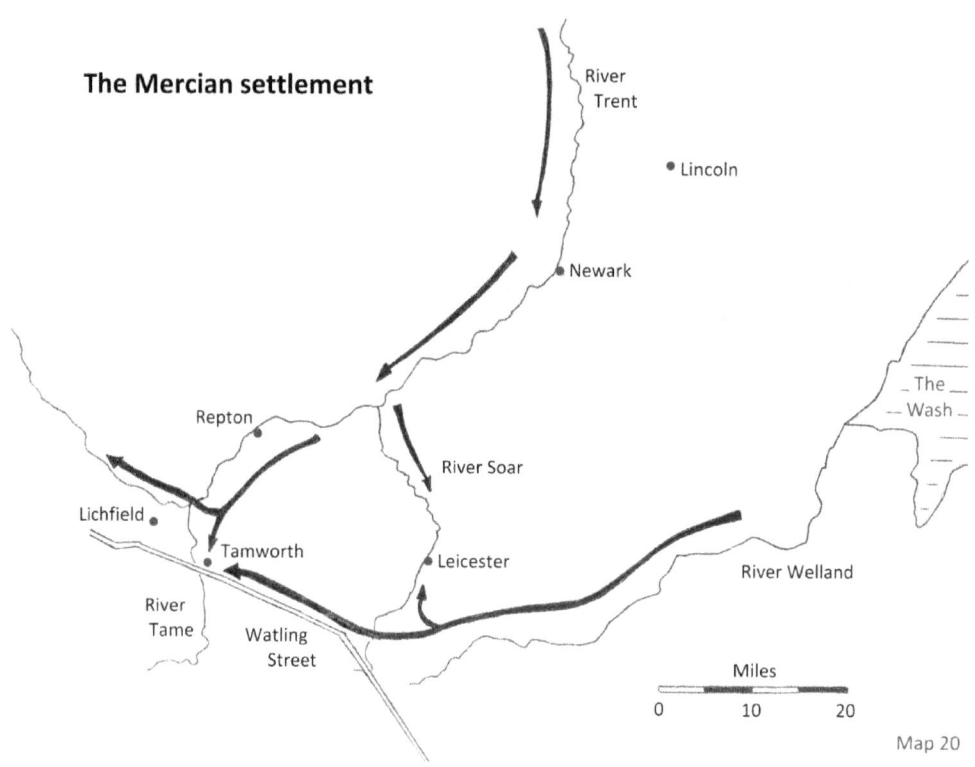

Map 20

A group of post-Conquest annals claims that Creoda, the grandfather of Penda, founded the kingdom of Mercia in 585. These annals are found in the writings of the twelfth century chronicler, Henry of Huntingdon (who seems to have had access to lost material, probably of a seventh-century date[246]), and the thirteenth century chroniclers Roger of Wendover, and Matthew Paris. These annals also provide

---

[243] Chadwick, *The Origin of the English Nation*, 1907, 15, 144.
[244] Gelling, *The West Midlands*, 1992, 79, citing Brooks in Bassett, *Origins*, 1989, 163.
[245] Stenton, 1967, 39.
[246] Stafford, 1985, 81.

succession dates for Pybba, Cearl, and Penda. This Cearl gave his daughter, Coenburg, to the exiled Edwin of Deira, and she bore him two sons. This would seem to place the reign of Cearl towards the end of the sixth century.[247] Professor Wendy Davies has argued tentatively for the historicity of these annals.[248] Cearl does not appear in the Anglian Collection of genealogies. Perhaps he was a usurper, and Penda reclaimed a throne that was rightfully his.[249]

The Mercia of the Hidage may have comprised much of Staffordshire and Leicestershire, with south Derbyshire and north Warwickshire. The heart of the kingdom was on the Middle Trent, the territory of the Tomsæte ('the dwellers by the river Tame'). It is possible that the Mercian royal line began as the leaders of this people.[250] Here, on the south bank of the Trent, were the later seat of the Mercian bishops at Lichfield, the Mercian royal monastery at Repton, and the royal vill of Tamworth used by eighth- and ninth-century kings. The later monastery of Breadon-on-the-Hill in Leicestershire was also in Tomsæte territory. It has been noted that the Tribal Hidage does not list the Tomsæte, and if the Hidage was a Mercian work this omission might imply that the Tomsæte enjoyed royal exemption from assessment.[251] The name 'Lichfield' comes from British *Llwytgoed* 'the grey wood') referring to the woodland from which the Romano-British town of *Letocetum* (Wall, Staffordshire) took its name. 'Girt by forest and marsh', Lichfield was perhaps the nearest that Chad, missionary to the Mercians, could find to an island, another 'Lindisfarne', in the sea-less Mercian kingdom.[252]

In 1927 Stenton drew attention to the concentration of place-names in the West Midlands which seem to preserve the rare names of Creoda, Pypba, and Penda. Among the 'Creoda' names are Credenhill in Herefordshire, and Curdworth in Warwickshire. The 'Pypba' names are Pedmore, Pepper Wood, Pepwell, and perhaps Peplow in Shropshire. Among the 'Penda' names are Pinbury in Gloucestershire, and Pendiford, Worcestershire. The fact that two Icel names in the East Midlands (Ickleton, Cambridgeshire and Ickleford, Hertfordshire) are on the Icknield Way, warns us that alternative etymologies are possible. Brooks writes, 'None the less it is clear that place-names formed from Creoda, Pypba and Penda are concentrated in the West Midlands … They are not found elsewhere. Such a distribution may suggest that the late accounts of the creation of a Mercian kingdom by Creoda and of its subsequent rule by Pypba and Penda do indeed represent some form of dynastic tradition … For the place-names certainly indicate that these three personal names achieved a unique popularity in this area'.[253]

---

[247] C Peers, *Offa and the Mercian Wars*, 2017, 54.
[248] See Brooks, in Bassett, *Origins*, 1989, 163.
[249] Peers, 2017, 55.
[250] Yorke, *Kings and Kingdoms*, 1990, 102.
[251] Gelling, *The West Midlands in the Early Middle Ages*, 1992, 85.
[252] Brooks, in Bassett, *Origins*, 1989, 169.
[253] Brooks, in Bassett, *Origins*, 1989, 164.

The growth of Mercia

If the Tribal Hidage was a Northumbrian document it might reflect a Northumbrian policy of divide and rule. It would mean that Oswald of Northumbria limited Mercia to its core heartlands, and in laying down the Hidage for the smaller kingdoms he would make it clear that they were no longer part of the Mercian kingdom. They were now in his 'sphere of influence'. The massive 30,000 hide assessment for Mercia would suggest a penal element imposed by the Northumbrians.[254]

Whether the Hidage was the work of Oswald or not it was after he had passed from the scene that the Mercians were able to expand, moving out from their original settlements around the Trent in three ways: 1) north-eastwards into the Peak District, Lindsey and Elmet, 2) south-eastwards along Watling Street, assimilating small people groups of Middle Anglian stock (Hart calls this 'Outer Mercia'[255]), 3) south-westwards into east-central and south-east Wales, and north-west Wessex.

East-central Wales was an area where, in the late fourth century, each major river valley running east-west to the Severn contained a Roman town, and each town presumably acted as a focus for fiscal, judicial and economic practices. Thus we have: Viroconium/Wroxeter, Bravonium/Leintwardine, Magnis/Kenchester, Ariconium/Weston-under-Penyard. These settlements were linked by a major Roman road, running north-south and using the Church Stretton Gap. The status of hereditary ruling British families, masked during the Roman period, re-emerged after the Romans left. Perhaps the towns of Wroxeter, Leintwardine, Kenchester, and Weston-under-Penyard became the centres of small kingdoms.

As the Anglo-Saxons began to settle these borderlands a number of -sætan names appeared – those of the Pencersæte of Staffordshire (in the valley of the River Penk), and the Wreocensætan, Magonsætan, and Arosætan. Areas with -sætan names do not have fifth- and sixth-century Anglo-Saxon cemeteries in such numbers as the other territories mentioned in the Tribal Hidage. The folk-names incorporate British elements (such as 'Wrekin' and 'Magana'), and they are perhaps territories built around the earlier Romano-British communities. Their populations are likely to have been as much British as Anglo-Saxon.

The rise of Ceawlin of Wessex

The deeds of Ceawlin and his kin are recorded in the *Anglo-Saxon Chronicle* entries for 556 to 593. In Myres' view there are echoes of poetic wording in the account, especially in the annals for 584 and 592. He sees these as evidence of a lost saga recalling the drama.[256] Ceawlin should probably be viewed as a man who welded different Saxon groups together within a framework of military success, as Penda would do in Mercia in the mid-seventh century.[257]

---

[254] Brooks, in Bassett, *Origins*, 1989, 167-8.
[255] Hart, 1971, 138-9.
[256] Myres, 1989, 163.
[257] Yorke, in Bassett, *Origins*, 96.

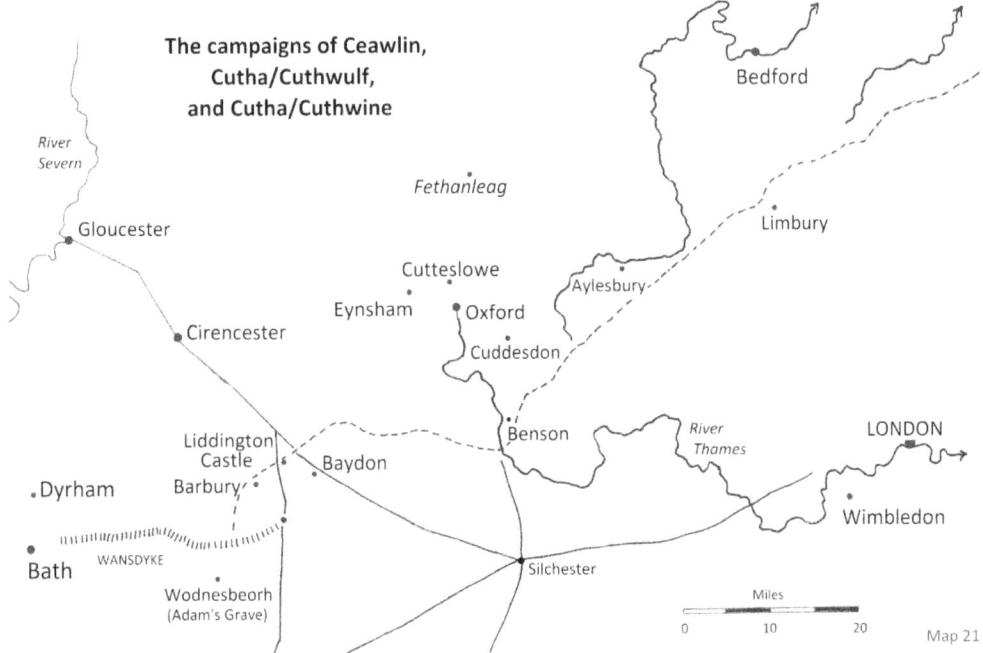

The campaigns of Ceawlin,
Cutha/Cuthwulf,
and Cutha/Cuthwine

River
Severn

Gloucester

Fethanleag

Bedford

Limbury

Cutteslowe

Aylesbury

Eynsham   Oxford

Cirencester

Cuddesdon

Liddington
Castle   Baydon

Benson

River
Thames

LONDON

Dyrham   Barbury

Wimbledon

Bath   WANSDYKE

Wodnesbeorh
(Adam's Grave)

Silchester

Miles

0   10   20

Map 21

Ceawlin and kin seem to have been based in the upper Thames, and to have been independent of the Cerdicings moving up from the south. From the *Chronicle* we learn that the two groups came together to fight the Britons at Barbury in 556. But thereafter it is Ceawlin and Cutha (or Cuthwulf) who take the lead. Ceawlin 'succeeded to the kingdom' in 560, and in 568 he and Cutha fought Æthelberht of Kent at *Wibbandun* and drove him back into Kent. Then in 571 Cuthwulf gained the victory in the battle of *Bedcanford* or *Biedcanford*. Stenton comments that there is no more important annal than this. The names of the captured towns (Limbury, Aylesbury, Benson, and Eynsham) give us some idea about where 'Bedcanford' was fought, but despite a superficial likeness to 'Bedford' it is hard to establish any connection with early spellings of that name. And the place of Cuthwulf in the Wessex kingly family is quite uncertain. (Yorke believes that Cutha/Cuthwulf was the brother of Ceawlin, and Cutha/Cuthwine his son.[258])

Stenton thinks that the battle in 571 resulted in the recovery of lands probably won earlier, but lost by the Anglo-Saxons after Badon Hill.[259]

---

[258] Yorke, *Kings and Kingdoms*, 143.
[259] Stenton, 1967, 27-8.

131

In 577 Ceawlin, this time with Cuthwine, fought with the British at Dyrham and slew three leaders. Two of them, Coinmail and Farinmail, had Celtic names. The third name, Condidan, is Roman, from some such name as Candidianus. The forms of the names are archaic, and they certainly came from a written source much older than the Alfredian chronicle, perhaps sixth century.[260] It looks as if Ceawlin was striking against a perceived British threat to the security of the upper Thames settlements. By this victory the Saxons won Gloucester, Cirencester, and Bath, and drove a wedge between the Britons of the West Midlands and those of Dumnonia in the south-west. After the battle West Wansdyke, south of Bath, was perhaps built as a new line of British defence.

In 584 Ceawlin and Cutha fought the Britons at *Fethan leag*, which seems to be Stoke Lyne, in north-east Oxfordshire (*Fethelee* in 1198).[261] The *Chronicle* says that Cutha (probably here a shortened form of Cuthwine) was killed in this battle, and that Ceawlin took villages and countless booty, but 'departed in anger to his own [territories].' This was clearly a northward thrust from the upper Thames valley which may well have ended in disaster and cost Ceawlin his overlordship.[262] Myres notes that Cutteslowe, on the Banbury road three miles north of Oxford preserves the memory of the *hoga de Cudeslowe*, which could have been Cutha's burial mound. Unfortunately the mound was demolished by royal order in 1261, because it had become a haunt of highway robbers. After burying Cutha Ceawlin perhaps headed for Cuddesdon, a few miles south-east of Oxford (which name also includes Cutha/Cuthwine). Recent excavation has revealed another princely interment at this site, and it is likely that this was a *villa regalis* of the Thames valley Saxons.[263]

Next Ceawlin may have been tempted to strike southwards, perhaps seeking to take the West Wansdyke from behind, but at *Wodnesbeorh* (almost certainly Adam's Grave, near Alton Priors in Wiltshire) disaster overtook him. Ceawlin was expelled, and his reign seems to have ended in confusion. The *Chronicle* records that Ceol(ric) began to reign in 591 which suggests that it was he who overthrew Ceawlin. Next after Ceolric came Ceolwulf, who is credited with continually warring against both Britons and Angles.

---

[260] Stenton, 1967, 29; Myres, 1989, 168.
[261] Stenton, 1967, 29; M Gelling, *Signposts to the Past*, 1988, 14.
[262] Stenton, 1967, 29-30.
[263] Myres, 1989, 169-170.

Chapter 9   The Western marches

Hwicce

The name of Wychwood Forest is the only surviving memorial of the people known as the Hwicce. They occupied all Worcestershire except the north-west, all Gloucestershire except the Forest of Dean, and west Warwickshire.[264] This was, more or less, the original area of the diocese of Worcester, created for the Hwicce in 679 or 680. Furthermore, Hooke thinks this kingdom closely represented the earlier Dobunnic kingdom, and that British Christianity survived here.[265] The ancient ridgeway of Ditchedge Lane marked one boundary of the Hwiccan kingdom. It ran past the prehistoric stone circle of the Rollright Stones.

The cemeteries indicate colonisation by Angles moving down from the north-east in the late 5th century. The distribution of penannular brooches points to links between the River Avon settlers in south Warwickshire and both the Cambridge / Peterborough area, and the borders of Lincolnshire and Kesteven. Saucer brooches (more common than cruciform brooches in the Avon valley cemeteries) may be imports from the Thames valley Saxons. The Hwicce were thus a people of mingled Anglian and Saxon stock.[266] Among small people groups that became part of the kingdom of the Hwicce (they are named in charters of that territory) are the Pencersætan of the country south-west of Birmingham, the Stoppingas – the extended family/tribe of Stoppa, and at one time an embryonic kingdom – and the Husmerae or Usmere, who were settled in the area where modern Kidderminster now stands.[267]) In the 6th century the Anglo-Saxons of the Hwicce lands were a minority group beside their British neighbours.[268]

Magonsæte

This name may be based on 'Magana', the area around the Roman town of Magnis (Kenchester). The name seems to be associated with the Welsh word for 'the rocks', and the feature referred to may be the rocky outcrop of Credenhill.

The boundaries of the later diocese of Hereford are thought to have followed those of the province of the Magonsætan[269] The eastern frontier of the province was marked by the woodlands of Malvern and Wyre and, further to the north, those of Morfe. There was also thick woodland along the northern frontier, where it adjoined the territory of the Wreocensæte in the vicinity of Wenlock Edge.[270]

---

[264] D Hooke, *The landscape of Anglo-Saxon England*, 1998, 139; Stenton, 1967, 43.

[265] D Hooke, *The Anglo-Saxon landscape of North Gloucestershire*, 1990, 1.

[266] Stenton, 1967, 44.

[267] Stenton, 1967, 44.

[268] M Gelling, *The West Midlands in the Early Middle Ages*, 1992, 30-31, 34, 40, 48.

[269] Hart, 1971, 140.

[270] D Hooke, *The landscape of Anglo-Saxon England*, 1998, 142.

Chester

WREOCENSÆTE

Wroxeter

The Western marches

MAGONSÆTE

HWICCE

• Magnis

• Gloucester

Cirencester

Miles

0   20

Map 22

It has been noted that this was a large region with little to bar the way for would-be settlers. It was not defensible to the east, north-west, or south. There are many places where the Severn could be readily crossed. There is no 'corridor' that might be blocked with dykes, and the woodlands of its boundaries were not dense enough, and could not bar passage. Moreover, there was no natural refuge anywhere, no upland area, for example, where British folk might form an enclave, no fenland with an 'Athelney' hidden away, where a defeated ruler might, Alfred-like, bide his time.[271] Watling Street was also available to incomers.

There is no archaeological trace of pagan Anglo-Saxons in Cheshire, Shropshire and Herefordshire. On the other hand, in Herefordshire 'Celtic names which may be considered at least as old as the Roman period are relatively numerous, however, and it is important to note that some Welsh names for places of administrative importance, though post-Roman in form, may be taken to represent a continuous linguistic history'.[272] The most likely way for Anglo-Saxon settlers to establish themselves in Herefordshire was for them to have come from the Worcester area, where there are pagan burials at Wyre Piddle and Upton Snodsbury. The pagan cemeteries of south Warwickshire and the nearer parts of Worcestershire are not large, but they provide evidence of a community of Anglo-Saxon farmers c. 500.

The transference of power to the Anglo-Saxons in the lower Severn valley (following the British defeat at Dyrham in 577) seems to have had little effect further north and west. Thus it may have been only after Penda's victory at Maserfelth in 642 that he was able to strengthen his hold on territory west of the Severn. He now bestowed wide lands in this region on a certain Merewalh. The Lugg valley was probably the heartland of Merewalh's family holdings. Rennell and Sheppard see this area as the original Magana from which the Magonsæte took their name.

We know something of Merewalh (whose name means 'illustrious Welshman') because he was the father of three daughters – Mildthryth, Mildburg, and Mildgyth – who entered the religious life. Such was their fame the French monks of Wenlock Priory commissioned Goscelin, a professional writer of saints' lives, to put together a life of St Mildburg, the foundress.[273] (Goscelin was a monk from Flanders or Brabant. He lived in the eleventh century.) From this we know that Merewalh (c.625 - c.685) was converted to Christianity after 660 and then took a Christian bride, Eormenbeorg, of the Kentish royal family. (She was his second wife.)

The prevalence of 'M' names in the family is very noticeable. It seems that Merewalh had a brother named Mearchelm ('helmet of the Mercians') and a son named Merefin. We also know of a Mildfrith who ruled in the mid-eighth century.[274] These names alliterate not only with each other, but with the name of the

[271] See Gelling, in Bassett, *Origins*, 1989, 185-6.
[272] Gelling, in Bassett, *Origins*, 1989, 196.
[273] Gelling, in Bassett, *Origins*, 1989, 192; Stenton, 1967, 47.
[274] Stenton, 1967, 47, citing William of Malmesbury, *Gesta Pontificum*, ed Hamilton, 299.

Magonsætan themselves. This seems to go against Goscelin's statement that Merewalh was the third son of Penda, for there are no 'M' names in the genealogy of the Mercian royal house. In Stenton's view this was a local dynasty, originally independent of the Mercian kings, though it seems they could not claim descent from the ancient gods (in which the essence of early Germanic kingship lay).[275] Yet, Mildburg calls Æthelred (undoubtedly one of Penda's sons) her uncle. Also Merewalh was buried at Repton, as were at least three members of the Mercian royal house. Was Merewalh an Anglo-Saxon who took the name as a compliment to his Welsh subjects, or a Briton, rewarded by Penda for his help at Maserfelth?[276]

Writing of the 'Westerna' in the Tribal Hidage Hart says: 'There can be no doubt that we have here an early name of the Magonsætan, the people centred on the district of Magana, now Maund, seven miles south-east of Leominster.' He suggests that the appendix to Florence of Worcester may be right when it calls king Merewalh *Westan Hecanorum rex*, and lists the bishops of the Magonsætan under the title 'Hecana'. Elsewhere in the appendix to Florence Merewalh is styled *Rex West-Anglorum* (King of the West Angles), and Hart suggests that this is ethnically and topographically correct, distinguishing these folk from the East and Middle Angles. Hart argues that if the Magonsætan were the Western 'Hecana' then a glance at the map indicates that the eastern 'Hecana' must be the Hwicce. He says we cannot avoid thinking that 'Hecana' is a corruption of Hwiccena, the Old English genitive plural of the tribal name Hwicce. Hart suggests further that the East and West Hwicce, perhaps with the Wreocensætan, formed the West Angles.[277]

Pecsætna

All agree that this folk-group dwelt in the Peak District. The beginning of the Pecsætan settlement in Derbyshire should probably be placed in the latter part of the sixth century.[278]

Wreocensætan

The Wreocensætan of the north Shropshire plain took their name from the Wrekin, as did the Roman city of Viroconium/Wroxeter. The 7,000 hides of their territory must represent the old hinterland of the city.[279] Urban life went on there for some while after the Romans left. On the site of the basilica of the baths at Wroxeter a large wooden-framed building was put up in the sixth century. It was of two storeys, and it had projecting wings or towers flanking the entrance. It was clearly the work of a powerful, vigorous character, influential enough to privatise public land, and able to command a considerable labour force. Among these workers were skilled craftsmen familiar with the Roman measuring system for building. This building was not a citadel, and clearly the builders were not expecting trouble

---

[275] Stenton, 1967, 47, 47n.
[276] See Gelling, in Bassett, *Origins*, 1989, 191; Kate Pretty, in Bassett, *Origins*, 176.
[277] Hart, 1971, 139-141.
[278] Stenton, 1967, 41.
[279] Pretty, 'Defining the Magonsæte', in Bassett, *Origins*, 1989, 174.

– Wroxeter was far from the reach of the pirates of the Irish Sea and the Bristol Channel. It has been suggested that it may have been the home of the bishop (bishops were drawn mainly from the aristocracy), though it has been said that there is a lack of evidence for Christianity in 5th century Wroxeter.[280] It is possible that the *frigidarium* of the baths nearby was converted into a chapel.

A re-used Roman tombstone has been dug from the eastern rampart bank at Wroxeter. The inscription reads, *Cunorix macus maqui coline*, 'Hound-King, son of the son of the Holly'. It is written in Latin letters but with an Irish spelling, and it has been dated by Professor Kenneth Jackson to 460-75. If the man was a cleric, or even a Christian, this would probably have been stated. It seems most likely that he was a pagan, and that he had some military role. However, there is no way of knowing whether he was employed by the city council, by some 'tyrant', by a bishop, or whether he was acting on his own account.[281] Viroconium was abandoned about 550,[282] the people perhaps relocating to the hill-fort of Wrekin.

The Wreocensætan are likely to have been as much British as Anglo-Saxon. (The Anglo-Saxon element in the Wrekin area appears to be no earlier than the second half of the seventh century.[283]) The 'Wocen sætna' of the Tribal Hidage must be the same folk, the letter 'r' having dropped out. The boundary with the Magonsætan appears to have run along Wenlock Edge. It could be that the Wreocensætan occupied all the land up to and including the Wirral.

---

[280] Gelling, *The West Midlands*, 1992, 27.
[281] R White and P Barker, *Wroxeter, Life and Death of a Roman City*, 1998, 106.
[282] Davies, *A History of Wales*, 2007, 62.
[283] Stenton, 1967, 41; Dark, 1994, 153-4.

Chapter 10   Wars in the North, Lords of war

Welsh tradition (in such sources as *Historia Brittonum, Annales Cambriae, Trioedd Ynys Prydein*) tells of colourful characters, with colourful names, in northern history. The historicity of the stories may be uncertain, but the general picture – of rivalries, warring, treachery – may well be a true one. We hear of a certain Eleuther of the Great Army, who established a strong kingdom in the York/Catraeth area in the mid-sixth century. His sons Gwrgi and Peredur sought to defend the kingdom against the Angles. They also had to confront the renegade warlord Gwenddolau, whose father Ceidiaw had taken North Rheged and then sought to expand into Brigantian territory. *Annales Cambriae*, 573, tells how Gwrgi and Peredur defeated him at the battle of Arfderydd/Arthuret. The latter's court adviser, Myrddin (Merlin), is said to have gone mad as an outcome of the battle, and to have lived in the Caledonian forest like a wild animal. In 580 Peredur and Gwrgi were defeated and killed by the Angles, led by Theodoric 'Flamebearer' son of Ida, and York fell to the incomers.

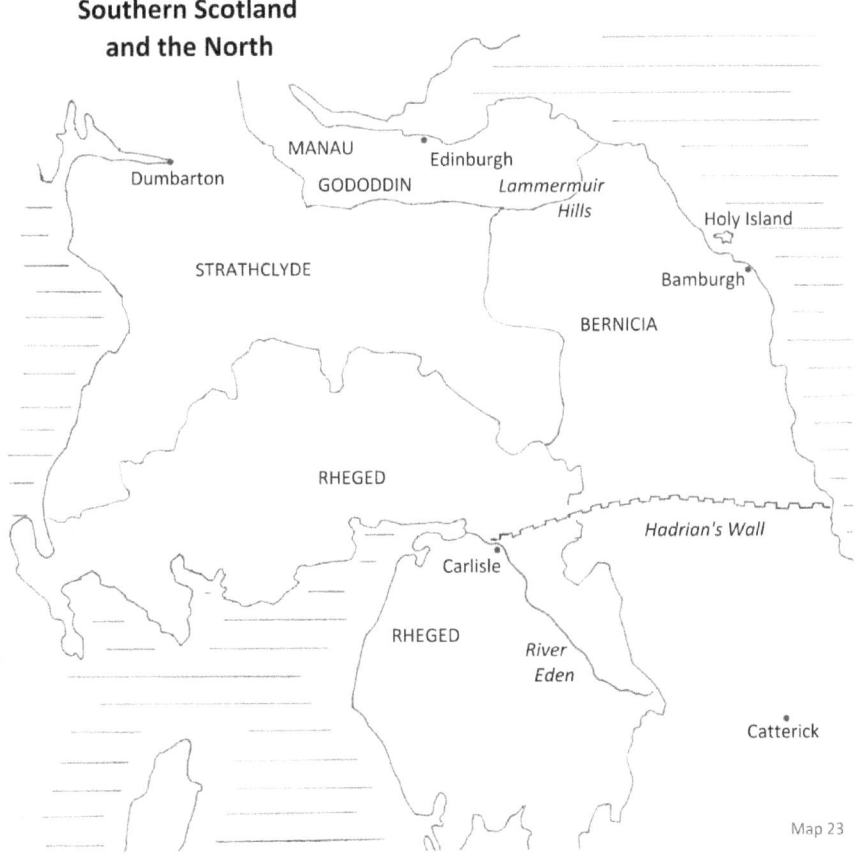

Southern Scotland and the North

Map 23

Rhun son of Maelgwyn was challenged for the kingdom of Gwynedd by Elidyr Mwynfawr, who was married to Maelgwyn's daughter, Eurgain. Rhun defeated and slew him, then dealt Elidyr's allies, the Men of the North, a great overthrow. This was about 561/2.

About 590 Urien Rheged 'Pillar of Britain', Rhydderch Hen of Strathclyde, Gwallawg of Elmet, and Morcant allied against the Angles. They succeeded in trapping, on Lindisfarne, either Theodoric or Hussa (the order of succession of the kings, and their dates, are not wholly clear, but Theodoric may be dated 572-9, followed by Hussa 582-92).[284] The siege lasted three days and three nights, and was going well, then a follower of Morcant murdered Urien. *Historia Brittonum* 63 says he acted from jealousy, 'because his (Urien's) military skill and general-ship surpassed that of all the other kings'. It has also been suggested that Lindisfarne was Morcant's home area, and he wanted to win the victory and the spoils himself.

About 595 Owain son of Urien is said to have forged a new alliance. He was named *dwyrein ffossawt*, 'scourge of the eastlands', because of his raids against Bernicia or Deira or both.[285] But then he died in the disastrous attack on Catraeth, *c.* 600.

Æthelfrith

Another notable heathen lord of war (after Ceawlin) was Æthelfrith. He was king in Bernicia from 592-604, and went on to conquer Deira from Æthelric, the elder brother of Edwin, so becoming king of all Northumbria, 604 to 616. It was he who turned Bernicia from a small state clinging to a stretch of the Northumbrian coast into the leading power in the north. He made his power felt by the Scots of the borderlands, the Britons of Cumbria and North Wales, and the Angles of Deira. To the Britons he was Æthelfrith *Flesaur* ('The Twister' or 'The Artful'.[286])

Bede (*HE* I. 34) introduces him thus: 'He ravaged the Britons more extensively than any other English ruler. He might indeed be compared with Saul who was once king of Israel, but with this exception, that Æthelfrith was ignorant of the divine religion. For no ruler or king had subjected more land to the English race, or settled it, having first either exterminated or conquered the natives.' Bede saw likenesses in the military successes of Saul and Æthelfrith, and also in the fact that the latter was replaced by Edwin, the first Northumbrian king to become a Christian, as Saul was replaced by David.[287]

---

[284] Dumville, 'The Origins of Northumbria', in *Origins*, 218; P B Ellis, *Celt and Saxon*, 1993, 74.
[285] Evans, *Lords of Battle*, 20.
[286] Alcock, 1975, 36; *Historia Brittonum* 57.
[287] See note in Bede, *Ecclesiatical History*, Judith McClure and Roger Collins eds, 374.

Holy Island

Bamburgh

**The wars of Æthelfrith,
Edwin, Oswald and Oswiu**

River
North
Tyne

Denisesburn/
Heavenfield

✗?

Hadrian's
Wall

Corbridge

✗?

see map 25

South Tyne

Catterick

River
Wharfe

Marston
Moor

York

River Aire

Towton

Leeds

River
Went

Hatfield
✗ Chase

Doncaster

River
Don

River
Idle

Chester

River Trent

Oswestry ✗

River Tern

Pengwern?

Shrewsbury

River Severn

Miles

0   20   40

Map 24

'Y Gododdin' and the Catraeth raid

Romanised *civitates* were not formed in northern Britain,[288] but by the later years of the sixth century three substantial Brittonic-speaking kingdoms had emerged in southern Scotland: Strathclyde, Rheged, and Gododdin. Strathclyde was, like enough, the lineal successor of an Iron Age kingdom of the Damnonii, and it was centred on Dumbarton. The most notable king of Strathclyde was Rhydderch Hael (the 'Generous'). Rheged included the territory of the Novantae of Galloway, the Selgovae of Dumfriesshire, and the Carvetii of the Carlisle area, down into northern Lancashire. The heart of the kingdom seems to have been the Eden valley, and the land around the Solway estuary. Carlisle may have been the centre, but Urien (the most famous king of Rheged) is said to have had his court at Llwyfenyd (probably Lyvennet in modern Cumbria).[289] Gododdin occupied the lands around the head of the Firth of Forth. It was successor kingdom to the Votadini (see below) who are believed to have enjoyed friendly relations with the Romans. The latter may have treated them as *foederati*, a bulwark against the Picts.[290] The kingdom of Gododdin, or Manau Gododdin (Manau was a subsidiary district, just beyond the Antonine Wall) had probably emerged by the mid-fifth century. At one time it stretched as far south as the River Wear, but as Bernician strength grew Gododdin was pushed back to the Lammermuir Hills. These three British kingdoms, together with the kingdom of Elmet in the Leeds area, made up what was later known to the Welsh as *Yr Hen Ogledd*, 'The Old North'. And the leading families and ruling classes of these kingdoms were known as the 'Men of the North'.

About the year 600 the Britons of Manau Goddodin launched a raid against Æthelfrith. The raid ended in disaster for the Britons, but it became the subject of a famous Welsh poem, *Y Gododdin*. (Sims-Williams says that early Welsh poetry is dominated by 'ideas of past defeat, present oppression, and prophesied revenge.') *Y Gododdin* is not a narrative poem but a series of elegies for heroes who died in battle at a place called Catraeth.

The story of the battle would have been familiar to the original listeners, but we have to try to work out the context of the poem for ourselves. There have been various interpretations of the events recorded in the poem. The 19th-century Welsh scholar Thomas Stephens identified the Gododdin with the Votadini of the Romano-British period, and Catraeth as Catterick in North Yorkshire. Ifor Williams in his *Canu Aneirin* (first published in 1938) accepted Stephens' conclusions, and he identified the *Mynydawc Mwynvawr* of the text with *Mynyddog Mwynfaw*, king of the Gododdin, who had his chief seat at *Din Eidyn* (modern Edinburgh). The events described took place 'around 600'. Mynyddog gathered about him 300 chosen warriors, some from as far afield as Gwynedd in North Wales. There were many minor political entities at this time, each with its lord, and it is probable that many of these joined Mynyddog and fought at Catraeth. One, Gwallawg, may have been the ruler of Elmet who fought

---

[288] Dumville, in Bassett, *Origins*, 1989, 217.
[289] Dark, 1994, 72.
[290] A O H Jarman, *Aneirin: Y Gododdin*, 1990, xviii.

alongside Urien of Rheged at the siege of Lindisfarne. He is the subject of at least two panegyric poems by Taliesin. Jackson suggests that a force of 300 men would be much too small to undertake the task demanded of them. He considers that the 300 were mounted warriors who would have been accompanied by a larger number of foot soldiers, not considered worthy of mention in the poem.

Mynyddog feasted the warriors at Din Eidyn for a year, then launched the attack on Catraeth. This was probably an attempt to drive back the advance of the Angles. However, the Gododdin were opposed by a larger Anglo-Saxon army, and they suffered a catastrophic defeat at their hands. In Dumville's view, if we do take the *Gododdin* poem at face-value, and its attribution to Aneirin, it would seem to fit well with the mid-sixth century date given to Aneirin by the author of the *Historia Brittonum*. '(I)t is particularly notable that the more archaic B-text of the *Gododdin* never mentions the Bernicians, speaking always of the men of Deira as the enemies of the Votadini/Gododdin. If we envisage the situation as historical, we might think that a major defeat of the Votadini by the Deirans would have opened up the prospect of Germanic settlement in their territory, that is, in what was to become Bernicia'.[291] At some time after the battle, the Angles absorbed the Gododdin kingdom into Northumbria, possibly after the fall of their capital *Din Eidyn* in 638.

Other interpretations of events have been put forward. Dillon (1973) thinks it unlikely that by the end of the 6th century Primitive Welsh would have developed into a language 'not notably earlier than that of the ninth century'. Jackson (1969), however, sees 'no real substance' in this argument, and he points out that the poetry would have been transmitted orally for a long period before being written down, that it would have been modernised by reciters, and that there is nothing in the language used which would rule out a date around 600. In 1997, John Koch published a new study of the poem. He considered that, in view of references to Catraeth in three early poems, there is a case for identifying the attack on Catraeth with *Gweith Gwen Ystrat* 'the Battle of Gwen Ystrat'. This would date the poem to *c.* 570 rather than 600. Tim Clarkson has pointed out that the reference in the *Gweith* poem is to 'the men of Catraeth', and it does not state that the battle was fought there.

Malcolm Lambert is hesitant, and he writes, 'A presumed oral phase, the sovereign power of the bards to compose their verse, to subtract and add stories and allusions, the reality of interpolations which can be demonstrated and the justified fear of others which cannot, all militate against the drawing out from this moving, often beautiful collection of verse much reliable and datable historical information.'[292] However, most modern scholars, Jackson and Jarman, for example, accept the conclusions of Stephens and Williams. Charles-Edwards thinks that the poem is the authentic work of Aneirin.[293] The fact that the great majority of the warriors mentioned in the poem are not known from other sources has been put forward by

---

[291] Dumville, in Bassett, *Origins*, 1989, 216.
[292] M Lambert, *Christians and Pagans*, 2010, 125.
[293] T M Charles-Edwards, 'The Authenticity of the Gododdin: an historian's view' in R Bromwich, R Brinley Jones, eds, *Astudiaethau ar yr Hengerdd* (Studies in Old Welsh Poetry), 1978, 66.

several authors as an argument against the idea that the poem could be a later composition. The men commemorated in *Y Gododdin* do not appear in the pedigrees of any Welsh dynasty. Ifor Williams's theory that the core of the work of Taliesin and Aneirin was written about 600 is broadly accepted.[294]

The poem *Y Gododdin* pictures a group of lordly warriors wholly committed to the business of fighting. Of one, Ywain, it was said he was, 'Quicker to the field of blood/Than to a wedding,/Quicker to the ravens' feast/Than to a burial' (lines 23-25). Jackson translated, 'He would sooner have been food for ravens than get due burial'. If the homeland was at peace such men would travel in search of war – 'The warrior tirelessly rushed to battle/In whatever land he heard tidings of it' (lines 622-3). When these men struck a blow they would not need to strike again (line 962). In the word-picture of Gwawrddur there is an interesting aside: 'He fed black ravens on the rampart of a fortress/Though he was no Arthur' (lines 971-2). Clearly at the time this poem was woven together Arthur was already a by-word for warrior-hood.

The poet mentions shattered shields (lines 33, 179), with nothing left that a hand could get hold of (line 959), a sure sign of a warrior's prowess and hardihood. These warriors cut down 'men who did not flee' (line 36), 'slew those who withstood' (line 636). To have left enemies unslain would, afterwards, be a burden on the mind (lines 88-9). The thought here calls to mind a couplet of Taliesin's, 'And those that had not fled/Were braver than they were wise'. Three hundred went forth to Catraeth, and 'Three hundred impetuous horses' (line 875). Only three returned alive: Aeron, Cynon, and the poet, and this last went, not to fight, but to see, to understand, to make names live forever (lines 246-7). For men such as these it was everliving fame in the songs of the poets that they sought. Of Buddfan it was said that 'The poets of the world judged him to be of manly heart' (line 276), of others 'until the end of the world they shall be praised' (line 868). Again, such men hoped that valour in the field would gain them a welcome in the land of heaven (lines 238, 773).

Degsastan

Some three years after Catraeth Aedan (that is, Aedán mac Gabrán, king of Dalriada, *c.* 574-606), aroused by Æthelfrith's successes, took the field against him with a large army. The fourteenth-century Scottish historian, John Fordun, says (in his *Scottichronicon*) that the original plan was for the Britons to attack the Northumbrians from the south and Aedán from the north. One wonders if the expedition to Catraeth was undertaken in support of Aedán's advance, only for the two hosts to fail in co-ordinating their attacks. Such failure might explain the dubious reputation Aedán has in British tradition.[295]

Aedán's advance led to the battle of *Degsastan*, (Bede, *HE* I, 34) 'This name seems to mean, 'Stone of Degsa' (presumably a notable standing stone). We do not now know where this was, though Dawston Rigg, at the head of Liddesdale in Roxburghshire, has been suggested. However, the evidence for this is not strong.

---

[294] Davies, *A History of Wales*, 2007, 45.
[295] Bromwich, *Trioedd*, 2006, 273.

This was in 603 or 604. Hering, a disaffected Bernician prince (son of Hussa, Æthelfrith's predecessor) is said to have led the Scots army. The outcome was a shattering defeat for the Scots, and Bede says that after *Degsastan* no Scottish king dared to attack the Northumbrians again. Æthelfrith's brother, Theobald, was killed at the battle. His role is not clear: 'he could as easily have been the ally of Aedán as a supporter of Æthelfrith'.[296]

Chester 613/6

Bede tells us that when the British bishops would not accept the authority of Augustine and work with him in the conversion of the English, Augustine gave them this warning: if they would not accept peace with their Christian brethren they would have to accept war with their enemies (*HE* II. 2). It was by the hand of Æthelfrith that this foretelling came true. He gathered a great army to fight the Britons at Chester, and many monks came from Bangor Is-Coed to pray for the British host. Æthelfrith, viewing the battle site, asked who these were, and when he was told their purpose, he said, 'If they are praying to their God against us, then, even if they do not bear arms, they are fighting against us.' He gave orders that they should be attacked first. Some 1,200 monks were slain, only fifty escaping. The Welsh Triad 60 tells us that Gwiawn, son of Cyndrwyn and father of Cynddylan, was one of the 'Three Gate-Keepers at the Contest of Bangor Orchard'. There is a tradition that the reference is to the battle of Chester. Selyf king of Powys is reputed to have been killed in this battle.

The wedge now driven through British territory may in fact have been established some twenty years before. '(T)here are enough ancient place-names in Cumberland and Lancashire to suggest that Æthelfrith could have ridden from the Solway to the Mersey through territory in the occupation of his own people'.[297]

The Idle 616/7

As we shall see when we come to the story of Edwin of Deira, Æthelfrith finally came to defeat and death at the battle of the River Idle, in 616/7, by the hand of Rædwald of East Anglia.

One last matter: Did Æthelfrith have two wives? The mother of his sons Eanfrith, Oswald and Oswiu was Acca/Acha. But according to *Historia Brittonum* 63 he gave 'Dynguaroy' to Queen Bebba. and it was thereafter named 'Bebbanburg' (Bamburgh) after her. Twice Bede mentions that Bamburgh was named after a former queen Bebbe (*HE* III. 6, 16), but he does not say whose queen she was.[298]

Edwin

The tale of Edwin of Deira would not be out of place in a treasury of Old English heroic poetry. The historian, Frank Stenton, wrote, 'The tale is impressive in Bede's

---

[296] McClure/Collins edition of Bede's *Ecclesiastical History*, 374.
[297] Stenton, 1967, 78.
[298] Carole Hough, 'Women in place-names' in Carroll and Parsons, *Perceptions of Place*, 2013, 264-6.

Latin, but it would have been told much better in Old English verse'.[299] It is a tale of exile and loneliness, of loyalty, treachery, brushes with death, a dawn attack, shattering victory, and, at the end, 'defeated valour'.

Bede gives no dates for the reign of Ælle, the father of Edwin, but he speaks of him as being still king at the time of Augustine's arrival (*De Temporum Ratione*, cap. 66), that is, in AD 597. After Ælle's death, his oldest son, Æthelric, ruled from *c.* 599 - *c.* 604.

During the reign of his enemy, Æthelfrith of Bernicia, Edwin had to live in exile, latterly at the court of Rædwald of East Anglia. Æthelfrith sent messengers to Rædwald urging him to slay Edwin, offering gold for doing the deed, threatening war if that king refused. The first time Rædwald said 'no', but when the messengers came a second time, then a third, bringing increased offers, his resistance was weakened, either by the proffered bribes, or by the threats of war. He told the messengers he would either slay Edwin or hand him over to them. But when he told his queen what he had undertaken to do, she at once warned him that it was in no way fitting that a great king should sell his best friend for gold when that friend was in such trouble. In this he would sacrifice his own honour. Rædwald heeded his queen's advice, and as soon as the messengers of Æthelfrith had gone he acted swiftly, raising an army and not giving Æthelfrith time to gather his whole force. The two armies met on the east bank of the River Idle, and Æthelfrith was defeated and killed. The speed of Rædwald's advance, and the surprise achieved, suggest he used the Roman roads. In which case the battle was probably fought somewhere near Bawtry, where the western branch of Ermine Street crossed the River Idle.

Edwin was now able to go back to his homeland and take the kingship of Northumbria, probably with Rædwald as his overlord. After the death of the latter Edwin became Bretwalda, that is, overlord of the other English kings (Bede, *HE*, II. 12). From what Bede says of Edwin's kingly style (*HE* II. 16) it may be that he saw himself as heir to the powers of the *Dux Britanniarum*. For example, he was always preceded by a standard-bearer.[300]

Early in his reign Edwin moved against the British enclave of Elmet, east of Leeds. This small British kingdom had long been a serious hindrance to military cooperation between invaders to the north and south of it. The kingdom had got in the way of Anglo-Saxon settlement in the valleys of the Aire and Wharfe. It was conquered in the end, *c.* 620.[301] Edwin's move was sparked by the death of a kinsman, Hereric, who had sought refuge there in the days of Æthelfrith. Hereric was poisoned while the guest of a certain Cerdic, probably Ceretic of Elmet.

---

[299] Stenton, 1967, 79.

[300] Myres, 1989, 196.

[301] Yorke says that Elmet was still a separate entity at the time of the Tribal Hidage (*Kings and Kingdoms*, 1990, 84).

Edwin went on to seek a marriage alliance with the important Kentish kingdom (*c.* 624). He asked for the hand of Æthelburh, sister of king Eadbald. At first Eadbald answered that it was not lawful for a Christian maiden to be given to a heathen. Edwin then assured him that he would in no way hinder the Christian worship practised by the maiden. Indeed, he might accept this religion himself if it was judged by his wise men to be 'a holier worship and more worthy of God' (*HE* II. 9). Then the maiden was sent to Northumbria. Paulinus was consecrated bishop (625) and sent with her to watch over her spiritual welfare.

The following year, 626, an assassin named Eomer was sent by Cwichelm, king of the West Saxons. This Eomer carried a short sword, two-edged and smeared with poison. He came on Easter Day and entered the king's hall on the pretence of delivering a message from his lord. Suddenly he leapt up and made a rush at the king, but Lilla, a devoted thegn, threw himself between the king and the assassin. Lilla was killed and, such was the force of the blow, the king was wounded. Others then fell upon the assassin who fought with such fury that he killed another of the king's men, Forthhere, before he was overpowered (*HE* II. 9).

That same night the queen bore Edwin a daughter, who was named Eanflæd, and the king swore that if God would grant him his life, and victory over those who had plotted his death, then he would renounce his idols and serve Christ. As a pledge of his truth he gave his daughter to Paulinus to be baptised. In due course Edwin was healed, and he marched against the West Saxons. He either slew those who had plotted his death, or forced their surrender.

Much of Bede's tale follows Edwin's slow and winding path to Christian faith. For Edwin still hesitated, though he now made it his business to learn the faith thoroughly from Paulinus. The Pope (Boniface V) wrote to him. He also wrote to Queen Æthelburh. He bade her persist in prayers and pious teaching so that her husband, one with her in earthly marriage might, when this life is passed, be one with her in the bonds of faith (*HE* II. 10, 11).

Edwin would sit alone for long periods, pondering what he should do. And one day Paulinus came to him, placed his hand on the king's head, and asked him if he recognised the sign. Certainly he remembered! One night, many years before, he had sat thus, thinking on the nearness of death: Rædwald was about to hand him over to his enemies. And in the dead of night, unlooked-for, there came one he had never seen before, dressed in strange clothes. The man asked about his sorrow, asked him, what if he, the stranger, could persuade Rædwald not to hand him over? What if he could assure him that his foes would be destroyed and he, Edwin, would become king? And what if the one who truly foretold these things then offered Edwin counsel as to his salvation – would he accept such advice? Edwin had promised that he would. Well, said Paulinus, the time to fulfil that promise had come! (*HE* II. 12)

Edwin now called a meeting of his council and each one was asked in turn what he thought of the new doctrine of Christianity. Coifi the chief of the priests answered boldly: he had served the old gods with more zeal than any of the others present, yet those others had received more benefits and honour from the king. If the new doctrine was found to be better and more effectual then let all accept it. After this, another of the king's chief men drew a word-picture from the king's hall in winter, the king with his ealdormen and thegns feasting, warmth inside, storm and wintry tempest raging outside. Then a sparrow flies in at one door and quickly flies out through the other. For a brief moment it knows the light and warmth of the hall, and then it is gone. The counsellor ended by saying, 'So this life of man appears but for a moment; what follows or indeed what went before, we know not at all. If this new doctrine brings us more certain information, it seems right that we should accept it' (*HE* II. 13).

Others said the same, then Paulinus was invited to speak, and when he had done, Coifi responded, 'For a long time now I have realized that our religion is worthless … I advise your Majesty that we should promptly abandon and commit to the flames the temples and the altars which we have held sacred without reaping any benefit.' The king now openly accepted the gospel, and he asked the high priest who should be the first to profane the altars and shrines of the idols. 'I will,' answered Coifi, 'for through the wisdom the true God has given me no one can more suitably destroy those things which I once foolishly worshipped, and so set an example to all.' Then taking a sword and a spear and mounting the king's stallion – knowingly flouting the laws that bade a high priest ride only a mare, and not bear arms – he rode to the temple (at Goodmanham, a little way east of York). When he got there he cast the spear into it, then ordered his companions to burn it down. So it was that the next Easter Day, in the year 627 or 628, Edwin was baptised at York (*HE* II. 14). According to Welsh tradition he was baptised by Rhun son of Urien (*Historia Brittonum* 63).

Why did Edwin hesitate for so long? He may have had genuine spiritual and intellectual difficulties, but there may have been political factors as well. Rædwald of East Anglia had been his protector, and also overlord as the Bretwalda. This king had converted to the new faith, but afterwards shaken off the Christianity of his former overlord, Æthelberht of Kent, and set up altars for the pagan gods alongside the altar for the Christian God. Rædwald might not have looked kindly on his own protégé accepting Christianity. It was perhaps only when Rædwald had passed from the scene, and the balance of power had shifted, that Edwin felt he could safely ignore East Anglian power. It is interesting to note that the first thing Edwin did after his baptism was to persuade Eorpwald, son of Rædwald, to accept the Christian faith (*HE* II. 15).

Edwin's reign ended, as it had begun, on the field of battle. It seems that at some point Edwin conquered the Isle of Man, and Anglesey (*HE* II, 5), and besieged Cadwallon of Gwynedd on Priestholm, off the tip of Anglesey. Cadwallon's answer was an invasion of Northumbria, in alliance with Penda, 'a most energetic member of the royal house of Mercia' (*HE* II. 20). Edwin fell in battle against them at *Hæthfelth* 'Hatfield Chase', in 632 or 633. It has been suggested that Hatfield Chase would have been a good place for an ambush, as the road from Lindsey to York was forced by the surrounding marshes to pass through a narrow gap, where an army could be trapped against the River Don. Perhaps the allies lay in wait for Edwin there.

Oswald, Oswiu

After Edwin's death his kingdom fell apart. Deira passed to Osric, a son of Edwin's uncle Ælfric, and Bernicia to Eanfrith, a son of Æthelfrith. These two kings quickly forsook the Christian faith and, in Bede's view, were soon justly punished. In 634 Osric rashly besieged Cadwallon in a fortified town, and Cadwallon 'broke out suddenly with all his forces, took Osric by surprise, and destroyed him and all his army.' Cadwallon went on to ravage Northumbria for a whole year (633-34). After a while Eanfrith unwisely came to him with a view to making peace, bringing only twelve chosen thegns with him. Cadwallon destroyed him, too. After this 'those who compute the dates of kings' decided to wipe out the memory of this dreadful year, take it from the two apostate kings and add it to the reign of the godly Oswald (*HE* III. 1).

In 634 Æthelfrith's sons, Oswald and Oswiu, came back from exile in Scotland. Oswald 'Brightblade' (*Historia Brittonum*, 64) moved against Catwallaun / Cadwallon with an army 'small in numbers but strengthened by their faith in Christ'. On the eve of battle Oswald had a cross hastily made, and a hole dug for it. He then took hold of the cross with both hands and kept it upright while his men packed in earth and fixed it in position. When this was done he called on his men to kneel and pray that God in his mercy would defend them in their fight against a proud and fierce enemy (*HE* III. 2).

Cadwallon is said to have had with him an immense host, and he boasted that it was irresistible (*HE* III. 1). Yet he was defeated in battle at a place which Bede names Denisesburn or Heavenfield (*HE* III. 2). Where was this? Some hold that the battle site was north of Hadrian's Wall close to St Oswald's chapel, which was built where it was believed Oswald had raised that large wooden cross and led his army in prayer. It is further suggested that Oswald, having arrived unseen from the north, placed his army in an excellent defensive position between Brady's Crag to the north, and the Wall to the south, with the River Tyne to the west.[301] This meant that an attacking Welsh army could not outflank Oswald and its advantage in numbers would have been lost. According to this view Cadwallon did attack here, and was defeated at this location.

There are two things to be said in response to this account of the battle. First, Bede clearly says that it was Oswald, not Cadwallon, who made the attack, that he advanced just as dawn was breaking, so taking the Welsh host by surprise. Second, Bede goes on to say that the place, on its north side, is 'close to the wall with which the Romans once girded the whole of Britain'. This is, clearly, a reference to Hadrian's Wall and places the battlefield to the south of that Wall. Bede adds that the site was near Hexham.

Heavenfield:
how it might have been

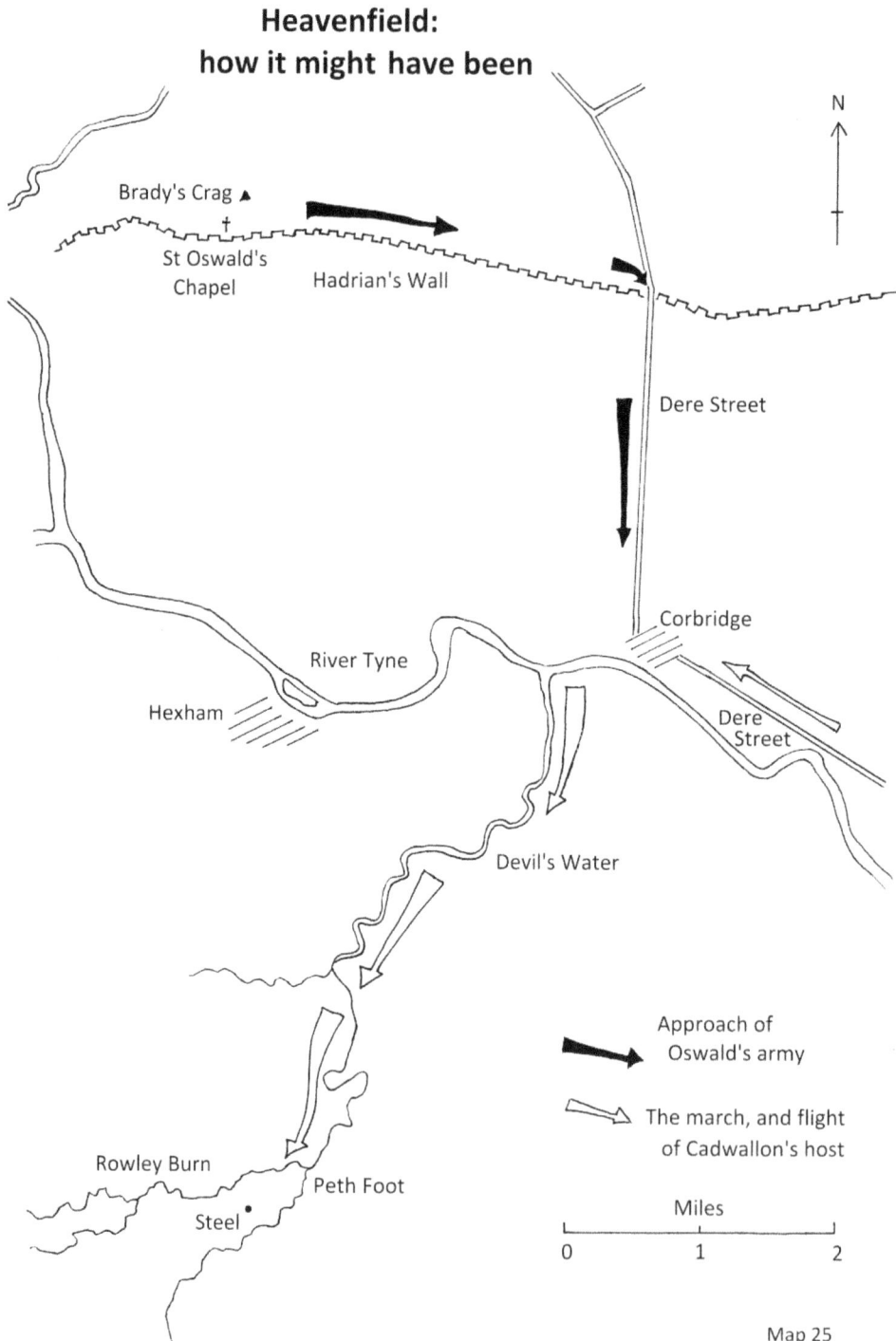

N

Brady's Crag ▲
St Oswald's
Chapel
Hadrian's Wall

Dere Street

Corbridge

River Tyne

Hexham

Dere
Street

Devil's Water

Approach of
Oswald's army

The march, and flight
of Cadwallon's host

Rowley Burn

Steel

Peth Foot

Miles

0   1   2

Map 25

F M Stenton says the battle was fought 'near Rowley Burn in the wild country south of Hexham'.[302] This fits with the view of Max Adams who, in his book on the life of Oswald, goes into the matter in some detail. He says that the location of Denisesburn was found by a nineteenth century antiquary, Canon William Greenwell, in a charter of 1233, which refers to twenty acres of land 'between Denisesburn and Divelis' (that is, Devil's Water). In a footnote Adams says that he here quotes from the late Hexham historian, Tom Corfe (1997). In Adams's reconstruction Oswald attacked Cadwallon's camp at Corbridge, at dawn, catching the Welsh unprepared. They were driven, in disorder, southwestwards up the valley of Devil's Water to the ford at Peth Foot, where the Rowley Burn meets that stream. Here, near the hamlet of Steel, the host was finally caught in what is a narrow steep-sided valley and was destroyed. Oswald thus gained an improbable victory by 'a combination of stealth and impetuosity'.[303]

By 635 Bernicia, Deira and Elmet were formally united as the kingdom of Northumbria. Bede tells us that Oswald 'held under his sway all the peoples and kingdoms of Britain, divided among the speakers of four different languages, British, Pictish, Irish, and English' (*HE* III. 6). Rheged was annexed about 635, perhaps through the marriage of Oswiu with princess Rhianfellt. (The marriage may have been contracted during the time of Oswiu's exile.) Rhianfellt was of the royal line of Rheged, being the daughter of Royth, son of Rhun, son of Urien (*Historia Brittonum* 57, 63). In 638 Oswald captured the plains of Manaw around Dinas Eidyn. During his short reign (633/4-642) Oswald actively supported Christian mission, in particular the work of Aidan, who came from Iona and became bishop and abbot of Lindisfarne.

Penda of Mercia, like enough, recognized Oswald's authority at this time, but he may nevertheless have been hostile to Northumbrian power, or at least was perceived by Oswald as a threat and a hindrance. After some eight or nine years, fighting was renewed and led to the battle of *Maserfelth* (*HE* III. 9), that is, Maserfield, or Maserfeld ('marsh or border field'). This is the 'Maes Cogwy' of Welsh poetry, or 'Cocboy' in the *Historia Brittonum*. From at least the 12th century the location of the battle has been taken to be Old Oswestry ('Oswald's Tree'), which at that time was probably still part of Powys. If the identification is correct then Oswald was in enemy territory and presumably engaged in a war of aggression, or at least in a pre-emptive strike.[304]

According to the *Historia Brittonum*, 65, and the *Annales Cambriae* (annal for 644), Penda's brother Eowa was among the dead. He also is said to have been a king of the Mercians, and it has been suggested that he may have been the dominant ruler, king of the northern Mercians, while Penda ruled the southern Mercians. Another possibility mooted is that Eowa had been subject to Oswald, and fought at

---

[302] Stenton, 1967, 81
[303] M Adams, *The King in the North*, 2013, 157-8. Stenton, 1967, 81.
[304] McClure/Collins edition of Bede's *Ecclesiastical History*, 390.

Maserfelth as his ally. Adams' reading of events is that Eowa was tributary to Oswald, and that Oswald moved in his support. The location of the campaign perhaps suggests that Penda and his ally Cynddylan of Powys were gathering a force on the Mercian border for an assault on Eowa in the Mercian heartlands, and that Oswald had come to know, or guess, what was afoot. In his counter-move Oswald would have marched either across the Pennines through Elmet to Chester, or gone south to Doncaster, then south-west to join Eowa at Lichfield, following Roman roads all the way. Oswald's purpose in heading down through the Welsh marches was likely the preventing of a link-up between his enemies, perhaps hoping to fight them separately.

Oswald suffered defeat and death at *Maserfelth*. Perhaps he underestimated his enemy's strength, or he was outwitted by strategy and local knowledge. (So, having won his kingdom by the sword, he lost it in like manner, eight years later – and this is the Oswald described by one historian as 'an insipid saint-king'!) After the battle Penda ordered that Oswald's head and hands be severed from his body and hung on stakes, an offering to the battle-god, Woden. This was a great insult to the house of Bernicia and to the *folc*. Bede tells how, 'A year afterwards, his successor Oswiu came thither with an army and took them away. He buried the head in a burial-place in the church at Lindisfarne, but the hands and arms he buried in the royal city of Bamburgh' (Bede, *HE* III. 12). Oswiu's expedition deep into Mercian territory was surely undertaken at great risk. He cannot realistically have hoped to outwit or out-fight the allied armies of Mercia and Powys. It thus seems likely that this was a commando-style raid by mounted warriors, and it suggests a certain amount of 'derring-do' on Oswiu's part.[305]

Although it is not stated in *HE* it is clear that, after the death of Oswald, Northumbria again split into two. Oswiu, became king of Bernicia, but the Deirans followed Oswine, a prince of their native dynasty. He was the son of Osric, a cousin of Edwin. King Oswine was 'a man of great piety and religion.' He was also 'tall and handsome, pleasant of speech, courteous in manner, and bountiful to nobles and commons alike.' He was generous to the poor, and humble. In Aidan's view he was too good for this world, and he feared Oswine would soon be snatched from this life – and Aidan was proved right (*HE* III. 14). Oswiu clearly wanted Oswine out of the way. The latter sought refuge from his powerful neighbour, going to the house of a certain Hunwold, believing him to be a friend. But Hunwold betrayed him and Oswiu caused him to be put to death.

We have seen that Oswiu had a British wife, Rhianfellt. Oswiu acquired a new, English, queen soon after his accession. He was king of Bernicia, 642-670, and of Deira, 655-670.

---

[305] Adams, 2013, 243.

Penda of Mercia

Penda was another of the notable heathen lords of war (after Ceawlin and Æthelfrith), and he remained stubbornly heathen to his dying day. The *Anglo-Saxon Chronicle* says that he became king of Mercia in 626, at the age of fifty, and that he reigned for thirty years. These figures are commonly discounted today. It is often suggested, for example, that fifty was his age at death, following a reign of thirty years. It has been noted that Penda's sister was not married until the 640s, and his sons Peada and Wulfhere were still young men in the 650s.[306]

Penda's first recorded battle was against the West Saxons at Cirencester in 628. After the battle the combatants made an agreement, which suggests that the fighting had been inconclusive. Cirencester, however, along with the rest of the country north of the Thames, passed to the Hwicce, which seems to imply that Penda had the best of things.

It may have been after this victory that the English made a thrust into the coastal lowlands of south-east Wales. If this move had been successful it would have given them control of both sides of the Severn mouth. However, in the battle of Pont y Saeson, in about 630, the men of Gwent, led by Tewdrig, with Meurig, gained an important victory, and held the Wye border.

As we have seen Penda more than once worked in cooperation with the Welsh, perhaps as the junior partner to begin with. On the first such occasion he allied with Cadwallon of Gwynedd against Edwin of Northumbria. Edwin's death at Hatfield Chase was followed by months of ravaging across the Northumbrian countryside. Bede was clearly appalled at this alliance between a heathen and a Christian prince – 'Christian by name and profession' but in truth a barbarian more cruel than the heathen. Cadwallon's rampage was ended when Oswald and Oswiu came back from exile, defeated him and slew him at 'Heavenfield'.

It may have been in the Maserfield campaign that Cynddylan of Powys lost his life. One stanza of the Welsh poem *Marwnad Cynddylan*, 'Lament for Cynddylan', reads:

> Grandeur in battle! So good was the destiny
> that Cynddylan, the battle leader, got
> seven hundred chosen soldiers in his retinue,
> When the son of Pyd requested, he was so ready!
> He did not go to the wedding feast; he was not married.
> O God! What different company, what black burial?
> I shall lament until I would be with the throng under the earth
> for the slaying of Cynddylan, of majestic fame.

(The 'son of Pyd' may be a reference to Penda, the son of Pybba.)

---

[306] Peers, 2017, 56.

The verse saga *Canu Llywarch Hen* celebrates Cynddylan's defence of the line of the River Tern in Shropshire, on the Powys border, and laments the destruction of his hall at Pengwern. This hall may have been on the Wrekin, near Wrockwardine, but John Davies thinks it was probably the Berth, in the marshes and mosslands to the north of Baschurch.[307]

The haunting *Canu Heledd* cycle is a lament for Cynddylan and his hall, attributed to his sister, Heledd:

> Dark is Cynddlan's hall tonight
>   With no fire, no bed.
> I weep awhile, then am silent.
>
> Dark is Cynddlan's hall tonight
>   With no fire, no candle.
> Save for God, who'll keep me sane?
>
> Dark is Cynddlan's hall tonight
>   With no fire, no light.
> Grieving for you overcomes me.
>
> Dark of roof is Cynddylan's hall
>   After that blest assembly.
> Woe who neglects the good that offers.

Margaret Gelling says that Cynddylan's English enemies could only be Mercians, and 'There is no way in which the *Canu Heledd* poems can represent genuine historical traditions of seventh-century events. Yet if Oswald was the aggressor in 642 then Cynddylan's English enemies would have been the Northumbrians. Dr Jenny Rowland suggests that *Marwnad Cynddylan* was composed very soon after Cynddylan's death, but that his death was at the battle of *Gai/Winwæd* rather than at *Cocboy/Maserfelth*.[308]

The battle of Maserfelth upset the balance of power in the Middle Severn valley. Penda was now without question the most formidable king in England. At an unknown date, but before the death of Aidan in 651, Penda campaigned deep into Bernicia and sought to take Bamburgh. Finding he could not break into the fortress either by assault or siege he thought to set it on fire. He had his men pull down all the nearby steadings and then pile beams, rafters, walls of wattle, and roofing thatch against that side of the fortress which faced the land. A favourable wind arose and the 'bonfire' was set alight. Aidan was spending time on Inner Farne, only two miles away, and he saw the flames and the smoke. Then, 'the story goes' (writes Bede) 'that he raised his eyes and hands towards heaven and said with tears, "Oh, Lord, see

---

[307] Davies, *A History of Wales*, 2007, 62.
[308] J Rowland, *Saga Englynion*, 303-7, cited in Brooks, in Bassett, *Origins*, 1989, 168.

how much evil Penda is doing." As soon as he had uttered these words, the winds veered away.' The flames were carried towards those who kindled them, putting such fear into them that they gave up the siege (*HE* III. 16).

In 654 or 655 Penda invaded East Anglian territory and slew Anna the king. A possible site for the battle is at Blytheburg near Southwold on the Suffolk coast. Penda may have established Anna's brother Æthelhere in his place, for the latter was present in Penda's army when he launched his *Winwaed* campaign against the Northumbrians. Æthelwald's Deirans provided guides for this expedition. This Æthelwald was the son of Oswald. After his uncle, Oswiu, had had Oswine of Deira killed in 651 Æthelwald became king in Deira. This may have happened by Oswiu's say-so, or, perhaps more likely, in defiance of him and as an ally of Penda. However, Bede says the Deirans refused to take part in actual combat against their fellow Northumbrians – they are said to have retired before battle was joined. Penda also made a new alliance with the Welsh leaders. According to Bede there were thirty *duces regii*, or 'royal ealdormen', in the army that Penda led against Oswiu, and it is said that there were British kings among them (*Historia Brittonum* 64, 65). Cadafael ap Cynfeddw of Gwynedd was one such, though he slipped away at the last moment, and according to *Historia Brittonum* earned the nickname 'battle-shirker'.

So great was Penda's army that Oswiu offered much treasure in exchange for peace, but the offer was refused. With no other option before him Oswiu committed his cause to God (*HE* III. 24) then led out his small army. He reduced the odds against him by deploying in a strong position on high ground, forcing Penda's army to advance through a flooded river valley. The river *Winwaed* has not been identified, but it is assumed to be one of the tributaries of the Humber. Stenton and others place the Winwaed east of Leeds. If this is the right general area it is not far from the later battle sites of Towton and Marston Moor, and it has been said that the narrow stretch of land between the Trent/Humber wetlands and the Pennines was the 'cockpit' of Anglo-Saxon England, a corridor that Mercians would use when aiming for York, and Northumbrians when striking southwards towards the Trent.[309]

Penda's army was linguistically and religiously diverse, and having thirty leaders was surely a complication. Perhaps Penda crossed the Winwaed and was attacked by Oswiu before he could reform, so that he ended up fighting with a river at his back. Bede says that more men died by drowning in the river afterwards, than in the fighting itself. Oswiu gained a devastating victory. Penda was slain, along with most of the royal ealdormen who had gone with him to the battle.

Elmet

Elmet/Elfed (or Elmedsætna) is perhaps the 'elm-forest'.[310] Its general location is indicated by the villages of Barwick in Elmet and Sherburn in Elmet, to the east of Leeds, and a reference by Bede suggests that the whole region of Leeds lay within

---

[309] Peers, 2017, 76; Stafford, 1985, 96.
[310] C Thomas, *Celtic Britain*, 1997, 50.

the province. It thus seems to have occupied the area north-west of the Nottinghamshire county boundary and south-west of the Vale of York up to the Pennine watershed.[311] Tadcaster was in Elmet.[312]

The Elmet folk seem to have been a hardy lot, true survivors. A sixth-century tombstone in Gwynedd describes the dead man as 'Elmetiaco', that is, 'an Elmetian'. Charles Thomas comments, 'Here, surely, lies the prototype Yorkshireman, in exile; insisting that, even in death, he be distinguished from feebler folk raised elsewhere'.[313]

Elmet was absorbed into the kingdom of Northumbria in the 620s.

Craven

There may have been a small British kingdom of Craven in the north-west corner of the West Riding of Yorkshire. Its existence has been suggested by later administrative evidence.[314]

The making of Northumbria

Northumbria came into being through the union of Deira and Bernicia, and the absorption of small Celtic kingdoms such as Elmet. This happened shortly before Bede's lifetime, and it may have been he who coined the name 'Northumbria', and popularised it through his *Ecclesiastical History*.

---

[311] Bruce Eagles, in Bassett, *Origins*, 1989, 212; Alcock, 1975, 138.
[312] Rivet and Smith, *The Place-names of Roman Britain*, 1981, 289.
[313] Thomas, *Celtic Britain*, 1997, 51.
[314] Yorke, *Kings and Kingdoms*, 1990, 83.

Chapter 11   British kingdoms of the south-west

In the early seventh century, under Ceolwulf, Wessex consisted of Oxfordshire, Berkshire, the north and centre of Hampshire (with the Jutes of the south probably recognising West Saxon overlordship), Wiltshire, South Gloucestershire, and the extreme north of Somerset, while the rest of Somerset, and Dorset remained in British hands.

The Durotriges

Devon, Somerset and Dorset may be based on Late Roman or sub-Roman divisions, perhaps districts dependent on Exeter, Ilchester and Dorchester respectively. The Dorset/Somerset border may once have been the boundary between the North and South Durotriges.[315] It has been further suggested that the Somerset Avon had formerly separated the Durotriges of Dorset from the Dobunni of Gloucestershire. In the sixth century the woodland of Selwood (Old Welsh *Coit Maur*), the Wiltshire Avon, and the Bokerly Dyke, may have been the Durotrigan boundaries facing the west-thrusting Anglo-Saxons. [316] The West Wansdyke, probably of fifth- or sixth-century British construction, was perhaps built to shield the Somerset area.

The Saxons' westward advance is hard to track because most of the fighting happened in places which cannot now be identified. 'Beandune', where Cynegils and Cwichelm fought with the Britons in 614, is one example. Dorset was probably conquered in the seventh century rather than the sixth. The former *civitas* of the Durotriges then became the land of the West Saxon 'Dornsætan' – the name perhaps derived from Romano-British *Durnovaria*, 'Dorchester'.

East Somerset was still in British hands in 650, but the county was probably conquered following Cenwalh's victory over the Britons at the battle of *Peonnum*, near Penselwood on the Somerset/Wiltshire border, in 658. After the battle the Britons fled as far as the River Parrett, perhaps the old boundary of the Durotriges with Dumnonia.[317]

Dumnonia

It is hard to see who but the traditional native leadership can have formed the fifth-century British dynasty which arose in Dumnonia. Tintagel seems to have been the court of a king, perhaps the king of all Dumnonia.[318]

Exeter was in Saxon hands by 680-90, but the British kingdom of Dumnonia was still in existence in 710 when its king, Gereint, was attacked by king Ine of Wessex and his kinsman, Nunna (Nothhelm) king of Sussex. The Saxon conquest of Devon was followed by a speedy and thorough settlement of the newly-won lands.

---

[315] Yorke, *Wessex in the Early Middle Ages*, 1995, 86-7.
[316] Yorke, 1995, 85.
[317] Dark, 1994, 126.
[318] Dark, 1994, 91-2.

Chapter 12   Drawing the threads together

It has been suggested above that the Anglo-Saxon settlements began with the bringing in of Germanic warrior-farmers and their womenfolk. They were placed on empty lands as *laeti*, and in return for land the newcomers were to contribute troops to the defence forces in Britain. As the grip of the Romano-Britons slackened in the fifth century, the leaders of these settlers were well placed to take over 'going concerns'. This may have happened all down the eastern seaboard from Bernicia in the north, where the Votadini may have planted Germanic troops, to Deira and Lindsey, East Anglia, Essex, Kent, and then along the south coast from Sussex as far as Southampton Water. The only personal names we have are those of Soemil, who may have taken over Deira, the brothers Hengest and Horsa in Kent, Ælle of Sussex, and possibly Cerdic in the Hampshire coastlands. This Cerdic may have been of mixed Saxon-British stock, the offspring of a Saxon warrior who had forged good connections through marriage into a British noble family. It may be that the western end of the Saxon Shore was entrusted to him by the sub-Roman authority. He was then well-placed to take power into his own hands as that authority waned.

With these bridge-heads established, and with the weakness of the Romano-British leadership exposed, we can understand how readily many Angles, Saxons, Jutes and others would have left their north German and Danish coastlands, abandoning the struggle against the encroaching sea. Once across the North Sea they would have been able to press inland, making use of the Humber and its tributaries, and the rivers draining into the Wash, 'the great front door' of eastern Britain. Some of those who crossed to East Anglia probably went straight on from there, to join with others who had pushed up the Trent valley, and so found what would become the kingdom of Mercia. Other groups settled in the Fenlands. Others again may have pressed up the Wash rivers to the Middle Thames, to join Saxon settlers in the area around Dorchester, Abingdon, and Oxford. This would seem to have been the first homeland of the West Saxons, the result, perhaps, of an earlier planting of *laeti* in a sensitive border area.

At this point the steady Germanic advance seems to have stirred a British fight-back, led first by Ambrosius Aurelianus, then by 'Arthur'. In the account we have given Arthur has been taken to be a historical figure – not a king, but the leader of a mobile force of cavalry and light infantry. The leaders of the sub-Roman British kingdoms perhaps ceded command of their forces to him, and he spearheaded attacks on the young Saxon states, up and down the land. It was suggested that the key areas in this war were the Humber/Lincoln region, and a Romano-British petty-state centred on London, as the Britons sought to drive wedges between Saxon-occupied lands.

It was then suggested that in the face of so potent a threat the Anglo-Saxons came together under the leadership of the Bretwalda, Ælle of Sussex. He summoned the war-bands of the Anglo-Saxon states of the south-east to a gathering place in the Wallingford area. The combined force then pressed south-westwards into British territory, only to be cornered and destroyed at Badon Hill (perhaps Liddington Castle).

The British now had the upper hand, and as late as the year 600, though the English held much of the eastern side of Britain, their grip was still uncertain. England was a patchwork of small and vulnerable statelets. The better-known ones, such as Bernicia, Deira, Mercia, East Anglia, Kent, and Wessex were still small enough. And there were many others, including the small polities of the Middle Angles named in the Tribal Hidage.

The Britons were undone by their own infighting, and by the rise of a number of able 'lords of war'. The first of these warriors was Ceawlin of Wessex, who, in the second half of the sixth century overran much of the southern midlands, from the Bedford area in the east to Cirencester and Gloucester in the west.

As the seventh century unfolded the smaller, weaker Anglo-Saxon kingdoms were side-lined by the stronger ones, then swallowed up. It has been suggested that a kind of 'knock-out competition' took place. Thus an ambitious and forceful leader would bring weaker neighbours under his control, helped perhaps by some inter-marriage. Then he would go on to the next 'round' and add others to his kingdom. In the north Bernicia and Deira were rivals, and first one, then the other, had the upper hand. At the last inter-marriage produced heirs acceptable to both, and the kingdom of Northumbria was then able to absorb the small British states of Elmet and Rheged. The Mercians added Lindsey to their kingdom, and then took over the small polities of Middle Anglia. The North Folk and the South Folk were brought together as the kingdom of East Anglia. The West Saxons absorbed the Jutes of Hampshire and Wight.

In the north there was now (in the first half of the seventh century) a three-cornered contest between the Welsh of Gwynedd, allied with Penda of Mercia, pitted against the Northumbrian lords of war: Æthelfrith, then Edwin, then Oswald and Oswiu. The decisive encounters were at Denisesburn (Heavenfield) in 634, where Oswald destroyed the war-host of Cadwallon of Gwynedd, and at the Winwaed in 654, where Oswiu overthrew Penda and his Welsh allies. The author of the later Welsh chronicle known as the *Brut* acknowledged, with anguish, that the Britons had lost the crown of the kingdom.

Why did the Britons lose the war?

Although the population of Britain fell markedly in the later Roman period (from a high of about five million to perhaps 2-4 million in the third/fourth centuries[319]) yet its people still greatly outnumbered the Anglo-Saxon incomers. Moreover they

---

[319] C Thomas, *Celtic Britain*, 1997, 34; B Cunliffe, *Wessex to AD 1000*, 1993, 263-4.

inherited considerable military 'hardware' from the departing Romans: a chain of shore forts, coastal signal towers, a network of good roads, perhaps some scout-ships. How was it, then, that they lost the war? A number of suggested answers have been put forward.

First, the bids made for imperial power (by Magnus Maximus, 383-8, and Constantine III, 407-11) surely drained the country of much trained manpower. It would not have been easy to replace these soldiers. Furthermore, John Davies holds that because the south-east of Roman Britain had been long demilitarised, traditions of political and military self-help had withered.[320]

Second, the Britons had to fight on two fronts at once. The Picts and the Scots had been raiding Britain, from the north and west, since the fourth century. In Gildas's story the Britons invited the Saxons in to fight these enemies, only to find that they had brought a hawk into the dovecote.

Third, although the territories occupied by the Anglo-Saxons by 550 were not extensive, they included the most fertile land.

Fourth, it has been suggested that the lower classes may not have regretted the fall of the old aristocracy. The lords of the Anglo-Saxon incomers may have seemed less oppressive than the *civitates*, which were led by men who wished to carry on in the Roman way.

Fifth, perhaps after 550 the Britons were weakened by the plague. This spread across southern Europe in the 540s, reaching Britain by about 547-9, when it carried off Maelgwyn Fawr of Gwynedd. The English may have escaped because they lacked Mediterranean contacts. Perhaps one reason why they shunned the old Roman towns was a fear of the plague.[321]

Sixth, it has been said that the Britons failed against the Anglo-Saxons because they were forever fighting among themselves. 'Arthur' (if he was a historical figure) was killed in battle against fellow Britons. We have seen how the brothers Gwrgi and Peredur sought to defend a strong British kingdom in the York/Catraeth area against the Angles, but they also had to tackle the renegade warlord Gwenddolau. One of Taliesin's poems commemorates the battle of Argoed Llwyfain fought between Urien of Rheged and a certain Flamddwyn. This same Urien was later murdered by an assassin sent by an 'ally' turned jealous rival. It is true that the Anglo-Saxons also fought among themselves, but perhaps in the crucial early days, under Bretwaldas such as Ælle of Sussex and Ceawlin of Wessex, they did act together.

---

[320] Davies, *A History of Wales*, 2007, 46, 66.
[321] Davies, *A History of Wales*, 2007, 46, 66-7.

Providence at work

Early medieval writers saw the hand of Providence behind events in this world, a view they drew from the Bible. They saw God as the Lord of all history, the great assayer and repayer, the one who confirms the folly of sinful men and women so that they bring about their own downfall. When he steps into the story the outcome he brings about is many-sided, in the biblical story of the Exodus, for example. This was: 1) a judgment on the gods of Egypt, 2) the overthrow of Pharaoh's pride, 3) deliverance for Israel, 4) a manifestation of God's power and name through all the earth, 5) a foreshadowing of the Redemption (the slain lambs of Passover night pointing forward to the Lamb of Calvary).

God uses the great of the earth (Nebuchadnezzar of Babylon, Cyrus of Persia, and others), but it is the lowly of this world who are the real movers of history. God does more through younger sons (like David), women, strangers, and through 'trivial' events – a 'chance' meeting, a king's sleepless night (Genesis 24, Ruth 2, Esther 6:1). History is only incidentally about the rise and fall of nations, and the march of 'progress'. In essence it is the record of God's formation of eternal souls.[322]

War is one feature of a fallen world, and even here, in the suffering, God is at work. Victory in war is no proof of God's favour, and the winner should remember that God may be doing more in the story of the defeated nation. 'Historical disasters may be as richly productive as historical triumphs, and often more so'.[323] The disasters sent upon Israel were always meant to drive them back to God. The characteristic divine 'tactic' is to bring good out of evil.[324] In the end God is undefeatable, as he steps in to rescue both his weak and faltering servants and his threatened plans. Every 'defeat' turns out to be a step towards victory.

How would men with this Biblical grounding, looking back from, say, AD 700, 'read' the events of the years 350-650? They might see Satan, the great Enemy, at work, using war and chaos to sow fear and unbelief, then using peace and security to foster a love of comfort, and laxity over sin. They might see him stirring up rivalry among the British leaders, goading the latter to false deeds and words. They may also have seen in this God's 'strange work', as he allowed the Enemy such leeway that the disasters he wrought were also God's judgment on a corrupt society. (Both a Gildas and a Bede could see eye to eye on this!) Yet God was also at work in mercy – his judgments were always meant to drive men and women back to him.

It was by his 'strange work' that God brought the Saxons into the Romano-Christian world, where they could be more easily reached with the gospel. The author of the *Exodus* poem (tenth/early eleventh century) saw the English as a 'new Israel', Germanic warriors crossing the sea on the way to their own promised land.

---

[322] J Daniélou, *The Lord of History*, 1968, 102.
[323] J Daniélou, 1968, 101.
[324] D Bebbington, *Patterns in History*, 1979, 184.

What was the approach taken by Bede, our most notable early medieval historian? Merrills notes that he does not give the Anglo-Saxons an origin myth like the tales other Germanic peoples passed down. Merrills suspects that Bede saw the beginnings of the English race not in some tale of bold venturing from beyond the seas, or in wars of conquest, but in the story of their conversion to Christianity. Like the tales of the origins of the Britons, the Goths, and others, this story begins in a far-off place, in this case Rome. Gregory is the founding hero, who sets the great journey in train, and he plays a key role in the later succession of power within the group. The first book of the *Historia Ecclesiastica* had told how 'they' (the Angles, Saxons and Jutes) had settled in Britain. With the coming of the gospel (*HE* I.23ff) we move on to the real history, the story of 'our' people. Merrills concludes that for Bede the English were a people whose very being as a nation was dependent upon their conversion.

For the most part the Britons could not reconcile themselves to the Anglo-Saxons. They grieved over the broken faith, the ruin of Britannia, and the taking of so much British land. About the year 610 the Welsh monk Beuno heard the English language, the 'language of paganism', spoken by English colonists on the further bank of the Severn, and this led him to migrate to Gwynedd. The British writer of the *Historia Brittonum* (once attributed to Nennius, but now seen as a case of 'author unknown') engagingly acknowledges that he has gathered up all he could find and 'made a heap' of it. Yet there is a central theme, concerned with the fates of two peoples, the Britons and the English. The outworking of the history is seen in the tale of the relationship between the Gallo-Roman saint Germanus, the British king Gwrtheyrn/Vortigern (who is presented as if he were a pagan) and the English *dux* Hengest. The treatment of the encounter between Germanus and Gwrtheyrn recalls the encounter between Patrick and Lóegaire,[325] and that between Elijah and Ahab in 1 Kings 17-22.[326]

The writer of the *Historia Brittonum* wanted to make sense of the past, and perhaps his main concern was to encourage the Britons to come to terms with defeat and loss of territory. He does understand their longings to see the English driven back into the German Ocean, 'Yet what concerns him more is the role of the Britons in the providential history not just of their own island but also of Ireland ... The victories of a Gwrthefy (Vortimer), or an Arthur, might be glorious, but they had no future.

---

[325] In a seventh century life of Patrick it is told that Lóegaire, High King of Ireland, after making attempts on Patrick's life, was warned by the saint that he must accept the Christian faith or die. Having taken the counsel of his people, he gave in and was baptised. But according to another early life of Patrick, by Tírechán, Lóegaire held to his paganism in spite of Patrick's miracles. He said that his father Niall would not have allowed him to convert, and after death he must be buried in the earthworks of Tara.

[326] Ahab was ruler of the northern kingdom of Israel in the ninth century BC. He crowned a life of wickedness with the judicial murder of Naboth and the taking over of the dead man's family vineyard. When he went to see his ill-gotten gains he found that fearless prophet, Elijah, waiting for him. The prophet told him that God was going to bring destruction on his head. Three years later Ahab fell in battle against his Syrian enemies.

The triumphs of a Patrick and of a Rhun ab Urien would bring whole peoples to salvation.' (Patrick, of course, was the apostle of Ireland. Rhun, son of Urien of Rheged shared with Paulinus in the baptising of the Angles of Northumbria.) When writing of the failure of the first (Roman) mission to Ireland, under Palladius, the writer comments that 'no one can acquire anything on earth, unless it be given to him from heaven above' (*Historia Brittonum* 50). This truth held good in Britain, too. The Saxon settlement led by Hengest succeeded not 'because of their strength, but because it was the will of God' (*Historia Brittonum* 45). This did not mean that the English were a chosen race, only that God had a particular purpose for them (their conversion) at this particular time. Nor did it mean that he was done with the Welsh, that he had written them off. As we saw above God is often doing more in the story of a defeated nation than he is doing among the victors.

Appendices

Place-name evidence

Is it possible to draw up any sort of chronology of places-names? A number of points can be made on this subject:

A place-name may appear old, but if the settlement in question is a successful one there may be no archaeological confirmation, early remains being greatly disturbed through centuries of human activity, and early structures buried under later buildings.

'-ing' names (from OE -ingas) were once thought to be the oldest layer. Amongst such names are: Reading, '(the place of) Reada's folk', and Hastings, 'the place of the Hastingas' (that is, the people of [the chieftain] Hæsta). The Essex Rodingas (from whence the Roding village names) may have been descended from the continental Rodingas of the *Widsith* poem, and ultimately from the Reudigni of Tacitus.[327] More recent writers see '-ing' names as belonging to the settlements of first-generation pioneers moving out from the original coastal settlements.

The -ham names are now seen as probably the oldest layer, but they do not necessarily tell us when a settlement was founded. Place-names can and do change. The name 'Durham', for example, has come about through the Norman scribes of Domesday Book mistaking an English name which would otherwise have come down to us as 'Dunholm'.[328]

Topographical names such as 'ford' are, in general, older than habitative names.

Place-names such as Wallington, Surrey and Walton, Sussex (incorporating the Old English *walh*, 'Welshman'), point to British survival.

One last point: the change of language from British to Anglo-Saxon, seen in the place-names, means that the migrations were substantial, and not merely the movement of a warrior élite. (The Norman conquest, an aristocratic settlement by a mere few thousand overlords, can here be used as a sort of 'controlled experiment'. Its impact on English place-names was minimal.)

Bretwaldaship

The 'Bretwalda' was the 'Britain-wielder (ruler)'. The title first came into use, perhaps, in the early days of the Anglo-Saxon settlements, when the position of the newcomers was insecure, and a British revival was a real possibility. It was the title of the head of a military confederacy. Furthermore, the concept of 'Britain', the belief found among the Welsh that the self-contained island of Britain should

---

[327] Myres, 1989, 42n.
[328] M Gelling, *Signposts to the Past, Place-Names and the History of England*, 1988, 25.

have a supreme ruler, assuredly exercised a powerful influence on the imagination of the Anglo-Saxons.[329]

In practice the Bretwaldas were kings who held overlordship in the south. Bede names the following: Ælle of Sussex, Ceawlin of Wessex, Æthelberht of Kent, Rædwald of East Anglia, and Edwin, Oswald and Oswiu, all of Northumbria. He names none after Oswiu, and the Parker *Anglo-Saxon Chronicle* probably simply followed Bede when, under 829, it referred to Ecgberht of Wessex as eighth Bretwalda. In fact three Mercian kings – Wulfhere, Æthelbald and Offa were overlords in the south in the late seventh/eighth centuries.

Charles-Edwards notes that war-leadership, with one over-king heading the contingents of a number of kings, was an essential element of the position of the Bretwalda. Moreover, 'The scope and character of the authority assigned to 'Arthur' in the *Historia Brittonum* is also closely comparable.'[330]

Oral tradition

From time to time unfortunate remarks are made (by otherwise able historians) belittling the worth of oral tradition. J N L Myres has been quoted, writing of the 'Confusing effects of oral transmission in illiterate societies'. This is surely a twentieth century perspective on a past with a very different culture from ours. For us, paper and ink, and the computer, are everything. But for earlier ages it was trustworthy oral witness that counted. After quoting Myres, Margaret Gelling comments 'Illiteracy is of course particularly conducive to accurate oral transmission'.[331]

Barbara Yorke asks, How far back might we trust the Anglo-Saxon genealogies? and she suggests that the second half of the sixth century might be the limit of oral tradition at the time when it came to writing these things down.[332] But this may be an underestimate. Stenton notes that, 'It is easy to underestimate the length of time covered by two good memories'.[333] Thus, if, about 650, a seventy-year-old was telling what he had heard as a boy from a grandfather, also living to seventy, this would be enough to span the period from 520-650.

Patrick Geary writes of the relationship between land, and oral and written witness. He notes that, 'Land not only formed the basis of a family's wealth and power: land was the means by which a family knew itself in historical perspective'.[334] This meant that assured property bounds were important and if there was a dispute, it was

---

[329] Kirby, 2000, 18.

[330] Charles-Edwards, 'The Arthur of History', in Bromwich, Jarman and Roberts, eds, *The Arthur of the Welsh*, 1991/1999, 24.

[331] Gelling, in Hooke, editor, *Anglo-Saxon Settlements*, 1988, 61-2.

[332] Yorke, *Kings and Kingdoms*, 1990, 4.

[333] F M Stenton, 'The Foundations of English History', in D M Stenton, ed, *Preparatory to Anglo-Saxon England*, 1970, 121.

[334] Patrick J Geary, 'Land, Language, and Memory in Europe 700-1100', *Transactions of the Royal Historical Society,* Sixth Series, IX, 1999, 171.

through oral witness that the written evidence was filled out. There had to be a beating of the bounds, led by a group of knowledgeable and trustworthy men, who would show where the boundaries were, and speak forth their witness. Their sworn statement had to be heard and recorded first in the memory of witnesses who would then confirm it in writing, and the written document could later be used as a help to memory of the events.[335] Stafford agrees: 'The rituals accompanying the transfer of land, and the presence of responsible witnesses at these rituals, were still equally if not more important than the written record.'[336]

Limitations of archaeology

Great strides have been made in archaeological work in a couple of generations, yet many 'ifs' and 'buts' remain:

An important general problem is that archaeological findings are often based on conclusions which have been reached by historians. But the latter may have sought support from archaeological theories, so there is a danger of arguing in circles.

Another problem which limits the archaeological record is that not all materials survive. Wood and textiles disappear in most soil conditions, leaving only slight traces; iron rusts away and may leave no more than a stain in the soil; clay pots, and fragments thereof, and jewellery, survive much more readily.

A third issue concerns the scope, or lack of it, for excavation. It has been noted that it is rarely possible to excavate a successful settlement. Early traces of human activity will be buried under later layers of occupation. And blanks on an archaeological map may simply mean that no excavations have taken place.

Dating is crucial for archaeology. Archaeologists use stratification as a major dating method, that is, they date finds in relation to other finds, coins for example. If there is no such material at a site then typology becomes crucial. Here subjective questions enter in: how do styles develop? Is it correct to suggest (as is commonly done) that the simplest must be the oldest, and the most complex the most recent? Are different styles an indication of different dates, or of different styles used at the same date by different groups? Are there backwaters where 'old' styles lingered? How old were the goods when lost or deposited? What part have fashion and social status played?

And after these difficulties have been faced there remains the matter of interpretation. J N L Myres, writing not so long ago, declared, 'That Saxon settlement did occur on a considerable scale in the fourth century is certain'. He says, for example, that Germanic cremation urns of no later than the mid-fourth century have been found at Venta Icenorum (Caistor-by-Norwich), pointing perhaps to a settlement of *laeti*.[337]

---

[335] Geary, 1999, 178.
[336] Stafford, 1985, 66-7.
[337] Myres, 1989, 84-5, 87.

Such conclusions have been 're-assessed' in recent years. It is urged that the decorative motifs on what had been classified as 'Romano-Saxon' ware can be paralleled on other pottery – and on glassware and metalwork – of Roman manufacture and fourth-century date. It should therefore be seen as standard late Roman provincial, with no ethnic overtones. And of the metalwork it is now said that it was the fourth-century Roman styles that influenced the fifth-century Germanic. Further, it is held that the belts were in fact standard insignia of office not only for military personnel, but for late Roman civilian officials as well.

As we observe these changing interpretations of what is basically the same evidence, we may wonder how far scholarly fashion, and peer pressure in the academic world, have influenced the archaeological scene. In another context J R R Tolkien speaks of an 'anxiety to be original'.[338] John Davies has commented wryly, 'the years 400-600 have become a tournament for scholars, with each successive contributor to the debate eager to unhorse his predecessor'.[339]

Dark Age warfare

Armies were small. The Roman field army *c*. 400 was probably no more than about 6,000 strong, and the post-Roman successor kingdoms probably had armies of only about 1,000 each.[340] For the kings and nobility of both sides war was a normal state of affairs. Among the reasons for war-making were: to win a reputation, to gain the prestige of overlordship over neighbouring rulers, material gain (for example, cattle), exacting tribute, exterminating/ expelling/ subjugating a people in order to take their territory. 'The bearing of long-lasting grudges after military defeat was an essential ingredient of politics'.[341]

Mobile warfare

Although hard evidence is scarce, it seems that Dark Age armies were highly mobile. For example, seventh century kings such as Oswald and Ecgfrith of Northumbria campaigned far from home. From the striking correlation of Dark Age battle sites with Roman roads and major ancient tracks like the Ridgeway, it is evident that the armies made good use of roads, and that roads, bridges, and fords must have been kept in good repair. To maintain speed an army would travel as light as possible. Little use was made of strongholds and prepared positions. There may, however, have been fortified points along the roads, where supplies and gear could be stored, freeing mounted forces to advance quickly, unencumbered by baggage carts and packhorses.

How did Dark Age armies find one another? With both sides using the roads, the area of search would have been limited. And we must suppose that commanders made use of scouting parties on horseback, and they presumably enlisted local people as guides (though recorded instances are hard to find).

---

[338] J R R Tolkien, *Tree and Leaf*, 1975, 58.
[339] J Davies, *A History of Wales*, 2007, 44.
[340] Alcock, 1975, 336.
[341] Gelling, in Bassett, *Origins*, 1989, 191.

Weapons

As late as the 10th century the possession of weapons was the mark and proof of freedom, of the right to take part in the local courts.

The weapon of the common foot-soldier was the spear, and it was the lords and the warriors of the hearth-troops who used the sword. (Swords – and helmets, and chain mail – were costly and prestigious, and few would have had them.) A sword would have a value in gold, but its worth as a 'maððum' (treasure) counted for far more. In the first place there was the making of the sword. (The smith – a skilled craftsman such as Wayland – was a figure of power and mystery in Germanic culture.[342]) In the ongoing 'life' of the sword every warrior who used it, every battle, every oath sworn upon its naked edge, every feud it had caused or settled, contributed to the tale of that sword, its 'worth'.[343] Warriors were sometimes bidden to swear mighty oaths on their swords, the implication being that if the warrior afterwards broke faith the sword would fail in time of need, or even turn against him. The warrior might also swear loyalty to his lord with his hand on the hilt of his lord's sword.[344] The incidence of blood-poisoning resulting from wounds from weapons that were not surgically clean must have been quite high. This may have led to the idea of the venomous blade.[345]

The other key piece of war-gear was the shield. In the poetry it was the 'linden board' (lime wood) which featured, but alder, willow and poplar were the woods most commonly used. These three, with lime, are all light, fibrous, and tough. In the defensive wall the shield would be braced on the left shoulder and knee to withstand a charge. The long, spiked metal apex of the boss made a formidable weapon for parrying or thrusting.

Some say that the bow was not the first choice weapon of the English. It was not prestigious and was perhaps the weapon of the lower orders, for bows were cheap, and men would have them anyway (for hunting). Others say the Anglo-Saxons *did* make some use of longbows made of ash,[346] with arrowheads of bone or iron. The shafts were generally notched or marked in some way, as a sign of ownership, so that they could be re-claimed after a fight.

Battle

Battle was a high-risk strategy. On the one hand it brought matters to a decision and could save the country from the horrors of rampaging armies. On the other hand, to lose a battle was perhaps to lose everything, so that a commander might seek to avoid battle unless he was confident of winning. Battles tended to happen when a commander thought he had enough troops to outmatch the other, or when he had run out of other options. One tactic that was sometimes used was the dawn

---

[342] Pollington, *The English Warrior*, 1996, 109.
[343] Pollington, 1996, 35.
[344] Pollington, 1996, 44.
[345] Pollington, 1996, 152n.
[346] Nicolle and McBride, 1994, 16; Alcock, 1975, 281.

attack. Most warfare took place in the summer, so a dawn attack made use of the cool of the morning.

Once battle had become inevitable, Dark Age commanders would choose their ground carefully. Against Penda in 655 Oswiu reduced the odds by deploying in a strong position on high ground, and forcing Penda to advance through a flooded river valley. Finding a short line with secure flanks enabled a smaller army to counter an enemy's superior numbers. Another consideration was to have somewhere such as woodland to which a mauled army could retreat. In later wars the Vikings often massed, and launched their attacks from, dense woodland, making it hard to gauge their numbers and movements.[347]

Hearth troops

Large armies were made up of sub-units, serving under different lords, each having his own hearth-troop of professional warriors. (Some troops would have included warriors from distant tribes in search of glory, as we see in the *Gododdin* poem.) Such men married late, if at all, and spent the best years of their lives in the service of their lord. When not fighting they would be hunting or hawking, or in hall feasting and drinking. Here the warrior would be enveloped in the world (doubtless idealized) of the sagas and praise poetry, hearing how their fellows and forebears repaid the mead drunk, and the gifts received, by absolute loyalty to their lord. To fall in battle, fighting for him, was considered an honourable death. Did the Dark Age warrior not fear death in battle? It has been suggested that he was a fatalist, accepted that what will be, will be, and that it was better to die gloriously than to live dishonourably. Some warriors, especially the Welsh, thought that to die in bed was a disgrace. Yet we know from the poem, *The Battle of Maldon,* that there were good and bad apples in every barrel. Some did indeed live and die according to their oaths. Others, it is clear, did not.

Battle tactics

The standard formation was the shield-wall or board-wall (or the war-hedge in the *Maldon* poem). The line of warriors would stand to receive a charge behind overlapping shields with a thicket of spearpoints thrust forward. The advancing enemy would see a line of wood and metal, eyes glinting between leather cap and shield, the only vulnerable points being the head and the lower legs. Breaking through this human wall would be akin to breaching the walls of a fort, and one source did indeed compare the Battle of Hastings to a siege.

Since everyone, whether Angle, Saxon, Briton or Viking, adopted shield-wall tactics in battle, the challenge was how to break through. If the commander had chosen his ground well, it would be impossible to outflank him. Sometimes, perhaps, the opposing shield-walls simply advanced towards one another and fought it out. However, there is evidence that Roman tactics were familiar to Dark Age commanders through tracts such as that of Vegetius, written down in the early

---

[347] S Pollington, 1996, 183.

fifth century. As a means of breaking through, Vegetius recommended the 'wedge'. Well-trained troops would mass in front of the shield-wall in wedge formation some ten lines deep. The wedge would then charge forward, keeping formation in order to penetrate the line with great force at a narrow point. Once the wall was broken more men would flood in and the enemy would be outflanked or even attacked from behind.

The right way to prevent this, according to Vegetius, was to 'swallow the charge' by receiving it in a curved formation known as the 'forceps'. It was easier to do this in a dense formation, but of course required training and a cool commander. Both the wedge and its countermeasures depended on firmness under fire and on fighting together as a well-drilled unit. How well drilled, in fact, were Dark Age armies? No drill manuals have come down to us. On the other hand, re-enactment experience suggests that formations can be taught basic proficiency in spear-and-shield warfare very quickly. In a battle men could disengage, as if by common consent, to retrieve arrows and spears, to clear the dead and wounded, to make running repairs, and to re-form.[348]

Victory or defeat in a Dark Age battle depended not only on physical strength and skill, but on morale, and this called for able and strong leadership and a sense of comradeship. The breaking point of a battle might come through the death of a leader, the capture of a banner, the fall of a prominent warrior. There are many instances of a Dark Age army disintegrating under pressure. In the last stand of the hearth-troop around their fallen lord, the band were held together not so much by respect for their leader as by loyalty to each other. The Northern poets loved the soul-rending situations from which a man could not emerge with both honour and life. The poets loved the sad and desperate inevitability of failure.

---

[348] Pollington, 1996, 184.

Early Sources

Gildas (c 500-c 570)

Gildas wrote a book called *De Excidio Britanniae* (DEB), 'On the Ruin of Britain'. There is historical information in the book, though the work is not really a history book. Yet, as one writer has put it, scholars have 'picked over every word'. Why? Because there is no other near-contemporary source of any length for the history of these islands in the late fifth and early sixth centuries.

There are two medieval Lives of Gildas, but today these works are seen as of little historical value. So we have no sure knowledge of the man's roots, his dates, and where he lived and worked. Even his name is a puzzle. It is not recognizably British, nor has anyone traced it in any other language. It has even been suggested that it is a false name, hiding the identity of a wanted man. (He attacked the morals of the British political leaders of his day, and we may suppose that they might not have taken that lightly.)

We can be almost certain that Gildas was a native Romano-Briton, and, like enough, he spoke a Brittonic dialect. The time-scale of Gildas's life is very hard to work out, even though he tells us the year of his birth. This is in *DEB* 26.1 where he writes of the siege of Badon Hill, and says, 'That was the year of my birth; as I know, one month of the forty-fourth year since then has already passed.' If only we knew when Badon Hill was fought! It was probably somewhere between 490 and 516.

Some suggest that Gildas wrote about the year 540 (so giving a date for Badon, and a birth date for Gildas, of about 500). This dating depends on Maglocunus, or Maelgwyn, king of Gwynedd from about 534 to 549, one of the five kings attacked by Gildas. Maelgwyn died in a great plague, dated 547 in the *Annales Cambriae*, 549 in the *Annals of Ulster*. This is thought to be the plague referred to by Byzantine and western writers, which started in Persia about 541/2, spread to the Eastern Empire, thence to southern Gaul by about 544, probably reaching Britain about 547/9

Where was Gildas's home area? Some have argued that it was in the north, because it is the Picts and Scots who feature as the enemies of the Britons, and Gildas refers to mountains and mountain-pastures. Those who say that Gildas lived in the south (and there are strong arguments for this view – see below) hold that the Picts and Scots did not confine their raiding to the north, and the mountains might be part of Gildas's 'rhetorical topography', whose function was rarely geographical.

As to the evidence for a southern homeland we may note, first, that Gildas was well aware of the key importance of the Kent-Gaul channel crossings. He refers to the 'noble' Thames perhaps suggesting some familiarity with it, and his general outlook is town-based, pointing to a home area 'south of the Mersey and east of the Long Mynd'. He says that British pilgrims could no longer go to the shrines of the martyrs, that is,

Alban of Verulam and Aaron and Julius of Caerleon (*DEB*, 10.2). For someone living in the north this should not have been a problem, but it may be that the middle Thames Saxons barred the way for southern pilgrims. Higham concludes that Gildas was a thoroughly southern lowlander, and he thinks that we can narrow this down further. He says that Gildas has more specific information about Constantine of Dumnonia than of the other kings, and he says this suggests he was writing from 'next door', (for reasons of personal safety) in the *civitas* of the Durotriges – roughly modern Dorset.

There are different traditions about where Gildas received his education. The earlier Life of Gildas, written in Brittany, says that his parents entrusted him to the monk Illtyd, to learn the scriptures and the liberal arts, at the monastery of St Illtyd at Llanilltyd Fawr. This is thought to be unlikely, but it may be that Gildas did spend part of his life in a monastic environment, for he shows some sympathy for asceticism and the monastic movement.

If Gildas did not study in a monastery, where did he gain his classical education? What can be learned about this from a study of his Latin? His written Latin is utterly correct by Late Latin standards. He consistently used technical words (such as foederati, annona) accurately, and he is thoroughly familiar with Vergil. Michael Lapidge notes that *De Excidio* is a well-planned piece of literature.

It seems safe to say that Gildas was trained in rhetoric, but by private tutors, not in one of the rhetorical schools (which must surely have collapsed by the early years of the sixth century). This would mean that some form of Roman government was still in place, offering career openings to a man like Gildas, and that there was an audience of cultured, Christian, aristocratic, Romanised Britons for whom Gildas wrote. He shows knowledge of key Latin works, but relied more on oral tradition (he could have gained information from his parents' and grandparents' generations), and he gives 'an impressionistic version of events'. Yet his sketch of British society in the west in the sixth century is broadly in keeping with what can be learned from later charters, saints' Lives and annals from Wales.

Lapidge sums up with the following hypothesis: that Gildas trained for a government administrative career, that he was afterwards ordained, that he was perhaps converted to the monastic way and renounced his earlier secular training, and that he then took up a career in the British Church as an outspoken critic of corruption in Church and State. It would seem that through his preaching against ecclesiastical corruption he became the leading reformer of the sixth century Church in these islands.

Drawing on the Bible Gildas wrote for a 'besieged Britannia'. He presented a providential view of history, and he was interested in the past only as it revealed the pattern of history and explained the present. He believed that the present was the continuation of biblical history, and he saw the Britons as a chosen people, their life a continuation of the history of Israel. As God had made his covenant with Israel, so was there a 'contract' or treaty between God and his people, the Britons. By their sins the Britons had broken the treaty. For this the inevitable outcome was the withdrawal of God's protection. They had also broken faith with the Romans, so that Roman protection had failed, too. The victories of the Saxons, then, were less a political and military matter, much more a matter of breach of faith on the part of the Britons. The Saxons were instruments of God's wrath. Gildas identified with the biblical prophet, Jeremiah, who contended with the apostate seventh-century kings of Judah. The thrust of his work has been summed up as follows: 'Kings Britain has, but usurpers; judges has she, but ungodly' and 'priests Britain has, but foolish ones' (*DEB* 27, 66).

There are a few further points to be made about Gildas. He was very sparing of names, and chronology was not a high priority for him. He collected anecdotes not for historical purposes, but as illustrations to support his understanding of historical cause and effect. His description of the geography of the land presented an idealised, Eden-like Britain. And he also presented an idealised Christian past with Christianity reaching Britain in the time of Tiberius (*DEB* 8), that is, within four years (at most) of the crucifixion.

We must acknowledge that Gildas never meant to give us formal history. Yet 'picking over' his work is not a wholly foolish enterprise. When he was dealing with events of only one or two generations back he would have needed to be sure of his facts, otherwise he would have lost credibility. The letter to Aëtius, the siege of Badon Hill, and the long period of peace which followed, would have been public knowledge, and Gildas's credit as a preacher would surely have been lost if he was wildly out. But we cannot be sure how far back this argument is valid.

Bede

As well as his Christian writings Bede (who lived from about AD 673 to 735) penned two important and influential works on chronology and computation, *De temporibus* and *De temporum ratione*. Bede had a longstanding interest in chronological scholarship, and he set everything into the *annus Domini* ('year of our Lord') frame. This form of dating seems to have been first used by Dionysius Exiguus (died about 527), but it was Bede's use of it in his *Historia Ecclesiastica gentis Anglorum* ('History of the English Church and People') which led to its coming into general use.

Bede names his sources in the Preface to the *Historia*. We learn that his principal authority and adviser was Abbot Albinus of St Peter's and St Paul's (later St Augustine's), Canterbury. This was the most important centre of intellectual life in England at this time. Bede tells us that Albinus took his facts 'from written records or from the old traditions'. Some version of the Kentish origin story is likely to have been known in Kent in Bede's day, and some information on the East and West Saxons.

Another informant was Daniel, bishop of the West Saxons, who sent Bede, 'in writing', something of the history of the church among the West and South

Saxons, and on the Isle of Wight. The monks of Lastingham monastery gave Bede some account of the conversion of Mercia. Bede gained information on the church of the East Angles 'partly from the writings or the traditions of men of the past, and partly from the account of the esteemed Abbot Esi'. He got information on Lindsey either from the letters of Bishop Cynebert, 'or from the lips of other trustworthy men'. And he could also draw on the resources of the Wearmouth-Jarrow monastery library. Bede's letters, and his account of his sources, show that he was in touch with ecclesiastics over much of England and beyond. Clearly Bede belonged to a quite extensive world of information. For the history of the church in Northumbria Bede drew material from 'the faithful testimony of innumerable witnesses' who knew the facts, apart from what he knew himself. For most of his knowledge of the history of the English churches in the seventh century Bede had to turn to oral witness by men of his own day, and some of this was influenced by the conventions of both Germanic and Christian story-telling. He did, however, weigh the reliability of witnesses.

When Bede set his work in the *annus Domini* framework, this was not simply a way of organising historical facts. It brought the history of the world into relationship with redemption. Bede saw the incarnation of the Word as the decisive turning-point in world history. And in the history of the world since the redemption it was not the empires of this world that were central, but the church. The story of the growth of the church begins in the book of Acts, and now Bede saw himself as writing the latest, perhaps even the last, chapter in that ongoing story.

For Bede Britain was set almost at the outermost edge of the world, and island retreats such as Iona, Lindisfarne, and Farne seemed to border the otherworldly. As for Hibernia (Ireland) Bede pictured it as a land of milk, honey and vines, another Canaan. The two islands (Britain and Ireland) were seen in 'spiritual interdependence', coming to their fullest potential only through contact with each other. Furthermore, had not the Lord said that the gospel must be preached to all nations and then the end would come (Matthew 24:14)? Thus the story of the English and their conversion was set not only near the edge of the world, but also, perhaps, near the end of time.

So Bede's work is both parochial and universal. He gave the Anglo-Saxons a new history by incorporating them into the history of the island of Britannia and the history of the church of Rome. He had a wide knowledge of the Bible, and often called to mind some words of Paul about Israel in the wilderness, their grumbles and complaints, and the judgments of God upon them. The apostle remarked, 'these things happened to them as a warning, but they were written down for our instruction' (1 Corinthians 10:11). So Bede peopled his history with Christian champions (and a few villains to shun). The kings, bishops, missionaries and others of his story are compared to biblical archetypes, so that the players of Bede's drama become embodiments of the familiar characters on the great Christian stage. When one discovered a meaning in the past, something that we may learn from, then it was found that the past was not wholly past and gone, and the time-gap was bridged. So we may say that when Bede was choosing material to use in the *Historia* he was influenced by his search for moral examples from the past, examples that would help the society of his own day in making moral choices. Yet he knew that the picture of the past that he presented must be as accurate as possible, so that the pattern of God's relationship with man would emerge clearly.

We have seen that Bede did not have much to say about the secular origin stories of the Germanic inhabitants of Britain, or of their migration traditions. He did not, in truth, find the origins of the English nation in a shared military past, though he did see the Anglo-Saxon migration as a necessary step towards Pope Gregory sending missionaries to convert them. He found the origins of the English rather in the account of Gregory and the English boys in a Roman slave market (*HE* II.1). It was the conversion of the English to Christianity that, for him, made them a nation.

How shall we assess Bede as a witness? It has been noted that he was hard on the Britons because, in his view, they failed to reach out to their English neighbours with the gospel, and because they stubbornly held to the Celtic dating for Easter against that of Rome. The hostility and mistrust was mutual. Davies comments wryly, 'If they [the Welsh] had to have enemies, it was preferable for those enemies to be pagans; they would not then reach heaven as well as Pengwern.'[349]

He has also been accused of bias in not including any Mercian kings in his list of those who held the 'Bretwaldaship', or overlordship of all Britain (*HE* II.5). (Note that the concept of the 'Bretenanwealda' – usually shortened to Bretwalda, 'Britain-ruler' – perhaps continued a British understanding that Britain had had, and should have, one high overlord.) In answer it must be said that Bede lived before the time of Mercia's greatness in the later eighth century. The only early Mercian candidate for the Bretwaldaship would be Penda. Perhaps Bede could not bring himself to acknowledge the might of that militant pagan. Yet it could be that Penda, for all his deeds in war against Northumbria, never gained general acceptance as overlord of the English.

Certainly there are flaws in Bede's writing. He might lack a key date, or be misled by mistakes in the material he drew upon. He made some mistakes of his own, such as errors in transcription or arithmetic, or faulty deductions. Then there are supposed 'mistakes' which arise, as Harrison notes, 'when it is assumed that considerations which apply to modern history should be applicable to pre-Conquest England'.

And what of Bede's dependence on oral witness for much of his information? For many scholars today it seems that oral witness is taken as a negative. Yet F M Stenton has remarked that Ceolwulf, the king of Northumbria to whom Bede addressed his *Historia*, was well known for his interest in the history of the English people. He was acquainted with much heroic verse which has since disappeared. The fact that he read and approved a first copy of the *Historia* should be given due

---

[349] Davies, *A History of Wales*, 2007, 75.

weight. And Bede himself declares (in the Preface to his *Historia*), 'I have laboured honestly to examine whatever I could ascertain from common report for the instruction of posterity.' And we may also note that when Bede was less than sure about the truth of his information he would write *perhibentur* ('it is said'). And 'he had a scholar's dislike of the indefinite, and traditions of events to which no date or circumstances could be assigned fell outside his conception of history.'[350]

It is dangerous to reject anything Bede offers as historical fact. On the whole, Bede's careful work is acknowledged even by critical scholars. Certainly Bede had his own standpoint. But if he was to convince and persuade he had to record events as accurately as possible. Bede's achievements are very great.

The Anglo-Saxon Chronicle

On the face of it the *Anglo-Saxon Chronicle* is a very late source for the period of the Anglo-Saxon settlement, with the first 'edition' known to us being completed in 892. Might there have been earlier editions? Perhaps the historical work of Bede was a spur to the writing of annals in Wessex as well as in Northumbria. F M Stenton argued that soon after King Alfred's accession in 871 the Chronicle which we have today was updated as far as 858 (and later carried as far as 891). He thought that the chronicler of 858 probably had before him an older set of annals, running from about 750. In another paper Stenton argued that traces of archaic grammatical construction in the pre-750 annals, the employment of methods of computation so ancient that their meaning cannot now be recovered, and the frequent reference to obscure place-names, led to 'an almost overwhelming presumption' that part at least of these annals go back to the seventh century. He noted the 'remarkable precision' of some of the annals. Examples are: the record that Cuthred was the godson of Birinus (*Chronicle* 639) – a detail which few would remember for long; the reference to an eclipse of the sun and a great pestilence in 664, and the record of 'the great mortality of birds' in 671. G H Wheeler argued that it was hard to see why the annal of 674, with its genealogy for the short-lived king Æscwine, should have been composed in 892, more than 200 years after his death. Wheeler further argued, from a study of the genealogies embedded in the annals, that the section from 648-750 incorporated a contemporary record of events.

If there was an eighth century source whose annals went back to 648, there might be implications for annal-keeping before that date. Stenton saw the entry for 648 as the first annal which contains within itself an indication of contemporary writing, but he thought that it would hardly do as the beginning of a West Saxon Chronicle. He thought it likely that the writer would have carried the record back at least to the start of the mission of Birinus in 634 and the baptism of the West Saxon king Cynegils in 635. The Easter Tables of the Dorchester-on-Thames scriptorium could have provided a framework for the setting down of contemporary annals.

---

[350] Stenton, 1967, 8

What of the sixth century annals? Stenton thought that a mid-seventh century chronicler might have written down oral traditions about Cerdic, Cynric, and Ceawlin. He notes that an annalist writing in the mid-seventh century could have gained information from old men who, in their youth, had taken part in the wars of Ceawlin. And he goes further: 'It would have been possible for an aged annalist writing at the middle of the seventh century to have set down, even at that late date, information received in youth from men who were living in the time of Cerdic himself.'[351] He notes, as marks of antiquity, the integrity seen in the refraining from smoothing away inconsistencies, the triviality of some entries, the enigmatical character of others, and 'laconic allusions' in the manner of heroic poetry. The *Chronicle*'s reference, under 584, to Ceawlin's victory and anger might be an example of such allusion. Stenton noted indications that, in part at least, the tale of Hengest and Horsa had been handed down in alliterative verse. Likewise Leslie Alcock thought that the names of battles and warriors could have been drawn from battle poems about the heroic deeds of the dynasties of Hengest of Kent, Ælle of Sussex, and Cerdic of Wessex. He further suggests that the 'fire and slaughter' imagery of accounts of the English settlement comes from Anglo-Saxon heroic poetry.

Kenneth Harrison also suggests that the materials for the *Chronicle* annals for 450-660 may have been collected together soon after the latter date. Malmesbury (founded about 640) or Sherborne might have been the place of compilation. He says of the early *Chronicle* entries 'there is no padding or embroidery, no attempt to link the earliest entries together or breathe life into a fossil record'. Harrison further suggests that there may have been early written annals from Kent to draw on. Queen Bertha and her bishop-chaplain, Liudhard, were literate. The queen's Merovingian kin were very aware of heredity, and Æthelberht may have learned from them. However, Harrison ends by saying that record-keeping in sixth century Kent is possible rather than probable.

It almost goes without saying that others dissent from theories of early record-keeping. Barbara Yorke, for example, allows the possibility of near contemporary mid-seventh century annals, but doubts that the hypothetical compiler(s) also wrote up the fifth and sixth centuries. She thinks, rather, that the early annals 'read as a seamless whole in the form in which they were cast in the ninth century and it is impossible to detect now any earlier stages in their compilation'.

Can a study of the wording and turns of phrase of an Old English prose text tell us about authorship and dating? In theory it can. F M Stenton argues that an occasional archaic case-ending, or pre-Alfredian form of a proper name, show that truly old material has been brought in. In her study of the vocabulary of the *Chronicle* Janet Bately notes that for the most part the book is marked by a plain style, and generally unemotional language. She says that the annals for 449-584 are marked off from the rest of the *Chronicle* by their regular use of the formula 'the place called'.

---

[351] D M Stenton, ed, *Preparatory*, 1970, 121.

The Historia Brittonum

The Historia Brittonum was long thought of as the work of Nennius, who lived around 770-810. Today this theory is largely discounted, and the suggested date for the book is now about 829-30. The Preface to the *Historia* is marked by a 'curious mixture of boast and modesty'. The writer engagingly acknowledges that he has gathered up all he could find and 'made a heap' of it, and he asks his readers to forgive him as he goes on like a chattering bird. (David Dumville argues that the Preface was no part of the original text.)

A key question is, what sort of historical writing is the *Historia Brittonum*? Dumville sees it as 'synthetic' history, meaning that it is 'an expression of a sense of national unity projected back into a legendary past'. Charles-Edwards acknowledges that there is synthetic history in the *Historia* (for example, the accounts of the origins of the Irish and the British). But if an interest in origin tales is to be enough to brand a whole text as synthetic (and therefore worthless as evidence), then we would have to write off Paul the Deacon's *Historia Langobardorum*, and Bede's *Historia Ecclesiastica*.

Charles-Edwards sees the *Historia Brittonum* as more synchronistic history, where the concern is to establish a chronological relationship between the histories of different peoples. The writer of the *Historia* weaves the histories of the Romans, the Irish and the English into his account of the Britons. (The model for such works was Eusebius's fourth-century Chronicle of history.)

The 'heap' begins with the Six Ages of the World, then goes on to accounts of British and Irish origins, a sketch of the Roman period, chapters about St Germanus and St Patrick, the tale of Ambrosius or Emrys, an account of the campaigns of Arthur, and the 'Northern British History'. This last is thought to be a hybrid Anglian-British document, focused on the Ida dynasty. It has been suggested that Rhun, the son of Urien Rheged, may have put some of this material together. Lastly, there is a record of the Wonders of the British Isles.

Annales Cambriae

Annales Cambriae 'The Annals of Wales' is the name given to a chronicle written in Latin, and derived from various sources. The earliest is a 12th-century manuscript presumed to be a copy of a mid-10th century original; later editions were compiled in the 13th century. As well as events in Wales the *Annales* record happenings in Cornwall, England, Scotland, and sometimes further afield.

The principal versions of *Annales Cambriae* are found in four manuscripts:

Manuscript A is written in a hand of about AD 1100-1130, and it was placed within a manuscript of the *Historia Brittonum*, followed by a pedigree for Owain ap Hywel (died 988). The Annals seem to run from about AD 445 to the second half of the 10th century, making it likely that the original text belongs to that century.

MS B was probably written at the Cistercian abbey of Neath, at the end of the 13th century.

MS C is part of a book written at St David's, also of the late 13th century.

MSS D and E are found in a manuscript written at the Cistercian abbey of Whitland in south-west Wales in the later 13th century.

The *Annales Cambriae* contain two entries that refer to Arthur. These have been advanced as proof of the historicity of Arthur, as they were believed to have been derived from contemporary records. That view is no longer widely held, but all the others named in the chronicle are historical figures, and so it could be argued that Arthur and Medraut are, also.

The entries read:

> Year 72 (*c.* 516) The Battle of Badon, in which Arthur carried the cross of our Lord Jesus Christ on his shoulders for three days and three nights and the Britons were victors.

> Year 93 (*c.* 537) The strife of Camlann in which Arthur and Medraut (Mordred) fell, and there was death in Britain and in Ireland.

Concerning Arthur's cross at Badon, it is mirrored by a passage in the *Historia Brittonum* where Arthur was said to have borne the image of the Virgin Mary 'on his shoulders' during a battle at a castle called Guinnion. In Old Welsh the words for 'shoulder' (*scuit) and 'shield' (*scuid) might easily be confused. Geoffrey of Monmouth played upon this dual tradition, and wrote of Arthur bearing 'on his shoulders a shield' emblazoned with the Virgin.

Continental sources

An entry in the *Gallic Chronicle* of 452 tells us that, 'The Britains at this time have been handed over across a wide area through various catastrophes and events to the rule of the Saxons'. The annal has been taken as referring either to 445/6 or to 441/2. The second *Gallic Chronicle* (511) has a like entry, dated 440: 'The Britains, lost by the Romans, fell under the control of the Saxons'. The two annals may have a common source. It is not at all clear how these annals might be reconciled with Gildas's record of an appeal to Aëtius in 446.

Bibliography

Adams, Max, *The King in the North: the life and times of Oswald of Northumbria* (London: Head of Zeus, 2013)

Alcock, L, *Arthur's Britain* (Harmondsworth: Penguin Books, 1975)

Alexander, M, *The Earliest English Poems* (Harmondsworth: Penguin Books, 1977)

Anon, *Historia Brittonum*, edition edited by John Morris under the title 'Nennius: British History and The Welsh Annals' (London, Chichester: Phillimore, 1980)

Ashe, Geoffrey, *Caesar to Arthur* (London: Collins, 1960)

Ashley, M, *The Mammoth Book of British Kings & Queens* (London: Robinson, 1998)

  - *A brief history of King Arthur* (London: Robinson, 2010)

Ashton, M, and Lewis, C, *The Medieval Landscape of Wessex* (Oxford: Oxbow Books, 1995)

Asser, *Life of King Alfred*, translated by S Keynes and M Lapidge (Harmondsworth: Penguin Books, 1983)

Bassett, Steven, Editor, *The Origins of Anglo-Saxon Kingdoms* (London and New York: Leicester University Press, 1989)

Bebbington, D W, *Patterns in History* (Leicester: IVP, 1979)

Bede, *The Ecclesiastical History of the English People*, Judith McClure, Roger Collins, eds, (Oxford: OUP, 2008)

Bidwell, Paul, *Roman Forts in Britain* (Stroud: The History Press, 2007)

Blair, P H, *Roman Britain and Early England* (Thomas Nelson, 1963)

Blake, Steve, and Lloyd, Scott, *Pendragon: The definitive account of the origins of Arthur* (London: Rider, 2002)

Bliss, A, ed, J R R Tolkien, *Finn and Hengest: The Fragment and the Episode* (London: HarperCollins, 1982/1998)

Bromwich, R, and Brinley Jones, R, eds, *The Authenticity of the Gododdin: an historian's view* (Cardiff: University of Wales Press, 1978)

  - and, Brinley Jones, R, eds, *Astudiaethau ar yr Hengerdd* (Studies in Old Welsh Poetry), Gwasg Prifysgol Cymru, 1978

Bromwich, Rachel, and Jarman, A O H, and Roberts, Brynley, F, editors, *The Arthur of the Welsh* (Cardiff: University of Wales Press, 1991)

  - ed, *Trioedd Ynys Prydein* (Cardiff: University of Wales Press, 2006)

Brooks, Nicholas, *The Early History of the Church of Canterbury* (Leicester: Leicester University Press, 1984)

  - *Anglo-Saxon Myths, State and Church 400-1066* (London: Hambledon Press, 2000)

Bruce-Mitford, R L S, *The Sutton Hoo ship Burial, A handbook* (London: British Museum, 1968)

Carroll, Jayne, & Parsons, David N, *Perceptions of Place* (Nottingham: English Place-Name Society, 2013)

Carver, Martin, *The Sutton Hoo Story* (Woodbridge: The Boydell Press, 2017)

Chadwick, H M, *The Origin of the English Nation* (Cambridge: CUP, 1907)

Chambers, R W, *Widsith: A study in Old English Heroic Legend* (Cambridge: CUP, 1912)

Cleary, A S Esmonde, *The Ending of Roman Britain* (London: Batsford, 1989)

Cook, S A, and Adcock, F E, and Charlesworth, M P, eds, *The Cambridge Ancient History*, Volume XI, 'The Imperial Peace A.D. 70-192' (Cambridge: CUP, 1936) Chapter II, The Peoples of Northern Europe, The Getae and Dacians, by G Ekholm and A Alföldi

  - F E, and Charlesworth, M P, and Bayne, N H, eds, *The Cambridge Ancient History*, Volume XII, 'The Imperial Crisis and Recovery A.D. 193-324' (Cambridge: CUP, 1939) Chapter V, The invasions of people from the Rhine to the Black Sea, by A Alföldi

Copley, G J, *The Conquest of Wessex in the 6th century* (London: Phoenix, 1954)

Cunliffe, Barry, *Wessex to AD 1000* (London: Routledge, 1993)

Daniélou, Jean, *The Lord of History* (Cleveland and New York: Meridian Books, 1968)

Dark, K R, *Civitas to Kingdom: British Political Continuity 300-800* (Leicester: Leicester University Press, 1994)

Davies, J, *A History of Wales* (Harmondsworth: Penguin Books, 2007)

Davies, W, *Wales in the Early Middle Ages* (London: Leicester University Press, 1996)

Drewett, Peter, and Rudling, David, and Gardiner, Mark, *The South-east to AD 1000* (Harlow: Longman, 1988)

Eilert Ekwall, Eilert, *The Concise Oxford Dictionary of English Place-names* (Oxford: OUP, 1960)

  - *English River Names* (Oxford: OUP, 1968)

Ellis, P B, *Celt and Saxon* (London: Constable, 1993)

Ellis, Peter, editor, *Roman Wiltshire and after* (Devizes: Wiltshire Archaeological and Natural History Society, 2001)

Evans, Angela Care, *The Sutton Hoo Ship Burial* (London: British Museum Press, 1989/1994)

Evans, Stephen S, *Lords of Battle* (Martlesham, Suffolk: Boydell and Brewer, 2000)

Everitt, A, *Continuity and Colonization: the evolution of Kentish settlement* (Leicester: Leicester University Press, 1986)

Foord, Edward, *The Last Age of Roman Britain* (Edinburgh: Harrap, 1912)

Frere, Sheppard, *Britannia: A History of Roman Britain* (London: Routledge & Kegan Paul, 1967)

Gelling, M, *Signposts to the Past* (Chichester: Phillimore, 1978, 1988)

- *The West Midlands in the Early Middle Ages* (Leicester: Leicester University Press, 1992)

Geoffrey of Monmouth, *Historia Regum Britanniae* (London: J M Dent & Sons, 1912, reprinted 1944)

Gildas, *De Excidio et Conquestu Britanniae*, edited by M Winterbottom (London, Chichester: Phillimore, 1978)

Grant, M, *The Fall of the Roman Empire* (London: Phoenix, 1975)

Green, D H, *Language and history in the Early Germanic world* (Cambridge: Cambridge University Press, 1998)

Grinsell, L V, *The archaeology of Wessex* (York: Methuen, 1958)

Guest, Lady Charlotte, trans, *The Mabinogion* (London: Voyager/HarperCollins, 2002)

Harrison, K, *The Framework of Anglo-Saxon history to A.D. 900* (Cambridge: Cambridge University Press, 1976, 2010)

Haywood, John, *Dark Age Naval Power* (Hockwold-cum-Wilton, Norfolk: Anglo-Saxon Books, 1999)

Herbert, Kathleen, *Looking for the Lost Gods of England* (Hockwold-cum-Wilton, Norfolk: Anglo-Saxon Books, 1994)

Higham, N J, *The English Conquest* (Manchester: Manchester University Press, 1994)

- *An English Empire* (Manchester: Manchester University Press, 1995)

Hills, Catherine, *Origins of the English* (London: Duckworth, 2003, 2006)

Holmes, M, *King Arthur: A military history* (London: Octopus Publishing, 1998)

Hooke, Della, ed, *Anglo-Saxon Settlements* (Oxford: Basil Blackwell, 1988)

- *The Landscape of Anglo-Saxon England* (London: Leicester University Press, 1998)
- *The Anglo-Saxon Landscape of North Gloucestershire* (Friends of Deerhurst Church, 1990)

Jarman, A O H, *Aneirin: Y Gododdin* (Llandysul, Dyfed: Gomer Press, 1990)

Johnson, Stephen, *Later Roman Britain* (London: Book Club Associates, 1980)

Kirby, D P, *The Earliest English Kings* (London: Routledge, 1991, 2000)

Laing, Lloyd, *Celtic Britain* (London: Scribner, 1979)

Lambert, Malcolm, *Christians and Pagans* (New Haven: Yale University Press, 2010)

Laycock, Stuart, *Britannia - The Failed State: Tribal Conflict and the End of Roman Britain* (The History Press, 2008)

 - *Warlords, The Struggle for Power in Post-Roman Britain* (Brimscombe Port, Stroud: The History Press, 2009)

Leahy, Kevin, *The Anglo-Saxon kingdom of Lindsey* (Stroud: The History Press, 2010)

Lindsay, J, *Arthur and his times* (London: Frederick Muller, 1958)

Lowe, Chris, *Angels, Fools and Tyrants* (Edinburgh: Canongate Books, 1999)

Lyle, M, *Canterbury: 2000 years of history* (Stroud: The History Press, 2002)

Mallory, J P, *In Search of the Indo-Europeans* (London: Thames and Hudson, 1989)

Mayr-Harting, H, *The Coming of Christianity* (London: Batsford, 1972)

Merrills, A H, *History and Geography in Late Antiquity* (Cambridge: Cambridge University Press, 2005)

Morris, J, *Age of Arthur*, 1 (Chichester: Phillimore, 1977)

 - *Arthurian Period Sources* 3, (Chichester: Phillimore, 1995)

Myres, J N L, *The English Settlements* (Oxford: OUP, 1989)

Nicolle, D, and McBride, A, *Arthur and the Anglo-Saxon Wars* (London: Osprey, 1984/1994)

Peers, Chris, *Offa and the Mercian Wars* (Barnsley: Pen & Sword Books, 2012/2017)

Pollington, S, *The English Warrior* (Hockwold-cum-Wilton: Anglo-Saxon Books, 1996)

Putnam, W, *Roman Dorset* (Wimborne, Dorset: Dovecote Press, 1984)

Reed, T Dayrell, *The Rise of Wessex: A further essay in Dark Age History* (York): Methuen, 1947)

Rivet, A L F, and Smith, Collin, *The Place-names of Roman Britain* (London: Book Club Associates, 1981)

Rowland, John, *Saga Englynion*

 - and others, editors, *Welsh Family History* (The Association of Family History Societies of Wales, 1993)

Rowley, Trevor, Editor, *Anglo-Saxon Settlement and Landscape*, British Archaeological Reports 6, 1974

Salway, P, *Roman Britain* (Oxford: OUP, 1981)

Sawyer, P H, *From Roman Britain to Norman England* (London: Methuen, 1978)

Sisam, Kenneth, 'Anglo-Saxon royal genealogies', in *Proceedings of the British Academy*, 39, 1953, 287-346, recently reprinted in the collection '*British Academy Papers on Anglo-Saxon England*', Oxford University Press, 1990

Snyder, Christopher A, *An Age of Tyrants* (Stroud: Sutton Publishing, 1998)

Stafford, Pauline, *The East Midlands in the Early Middle Ages* (Leicester: Leicester University Press, 1985)

Stenton, D M, ed, *Preparatory to Anglo-Saxon England* (Oxford: OUP, 1970)

Stenton, F M, *Anglo-Saxon England*, Oxford History of England (OUP: Oxford, Second edition 1947/1967)

Tacitus, *The History Germania & Agricola* Volume 2 of 'The Historical Works of Tacitus, translated by Arthur Murphy, edited by E H Blakeney (London: J M Dent & Sons, 1908/1939)

Thomas, C, *Britain and Ireland in Early Christian Times AD 400-800* (London: Thames and Hudson, 1971)

  - *Christianity in Roman Britain to AD 500* (London: Batsford, 1983)
  - *Celtic Britain* (London: Thames & Hudson, 1997)

Todd, Malcolm, *The Northern Barbarians 100 BC - AD 300* (London: Hutchinson University Library, 1975)

Tolkien, J R R, *Tree and Leaf, Smith of Wootton Major, The Homecoming of Beorhtnoth Beorhthelm's Son* (London: Unwin Books, 1975)

Wacher, John, *The Towns of Roman Britain* (London: Book Club Associates, 1974)

Wallace, Hume, *The Underwater Book: The Search for Roman Selsey*, 1968

Wallenberg, J K, *Kentish Place-Names*, 1931

Webster, Leslie, and Backhouse, Janet, *The Making of England: Anglo-Saxon Art and Culture AD 600-900* (London: British Museum Press, 1992)

Welch, M G, *Early Anglo-Saxon Sussex*, BAR no.112

White, R, and Barker, P, *Wroxeter, Life and Death of a Roman City* (Stroud: Tempus, 1998)

Yorke, Barbara, *Kings and Kingdoms of early Anglo-Saxon England* (London: Routledge, 1990).

  - *Wessex in the Early Middle Ages* (London: Leicester University Press, 1995)

Journals

Anlezark, D, 'Sceaf, Japheth and the origins of the Anglo-Saxons', *Anglo-Saxon England*, Volume 31, December 2002.

Bonney, D J, 'Pagan Saxon burials and boundaries in Wiltshire', *Wiltshire Archaeological and Natural History Magazine*, 61, 1966.

Coates, R, '*Wippedesfleot* in the Anglo-Saxon Chronicle', *Journal of the English Place-Name Society* 49, 2017.

Dornier, A, ed, *Mercian Studies*, 1977.

Dumville, D N, 'The West Saxon Genealogical Regnal List and the chronology of Wessex', *Peritia*, Volume 4, 1985.

Evison and Myres in *The Antiquaries Journal*, 1968.

Filmer-Sankey, William, and Tim Pestel, *Snape Anglo-Saxon Cemetery: Excavations and Surveys 1824–1992*, East Anglian Archaeology, 95, 2001.

Geary, Patrick J, 'Land, Language, and Memory in Europe 700-1100', *Transactions of the Royal Historical Society,* Sixth Series, IX, 1999.

Goodier, A, *Medieval Archaeology*, 28, 1984.

Hart, Cyril, 'The Tribal Hidage', in *Transactions of the Royal Historical Society*, Fifth Series, 21, 1971.

James, D J, 'Sorviodunum – A Review of the Archaeological Evidence', *Wiltshire Archaeological and Natural History Magazine*, 95, 2002.

Musty, J, and J E D Stratton, 'A Saxon cemetery at Winterbourne Gunner, near Salisbury', *WANHM*, 59, 1964.

O'Loughlin, J L N, 1964, 'Sutton Hoo – the evidence of the documents', *Medieval Archaeology* 8, 1964.

Tyler, Susan, 'Anglo-Saxon settlement in the Darent valley and environs' in *Archæologia Cantiana*, Volume CX, 71-81 (Stroud: Alan Sutton Publishing, for the Kent Archæological Society, 1993).

Yorke, Barbara A E, 'Joint kingship in Kent c. 560 to 785', *Archaeologia Cantiana*, volume 99, 1983.

Yorke, B, 'Fact or Fiction?' *Anglo-Saxon Studies in Archaeology and History* 6, 1993.

Index

Eormenric of Kent, 90, 91
Eormenric the Ostrogoth, 11, 12, 27, 28, 33, 36, 90, 105, 106
Eorpwald, 148
Eowa, 151
Episford, 82, 84
Ermine Street, 68, 125, 146
Esla, 37, 39, 110
Esmonde Cleary, A S, 84
Essex, 12, 13, 26, 43, 54, 55, 74, 76, 77, 89, 103, 111, 114, 125, 127, 159, 165
Everitt, A, 86
Exeter, 16, 157
Faversham, 87
Feddersen Wierde, 41
Fens, 60
Fethan leag, 132
Fifeldor, 33, 36
Finn Folcwalding, 11, 28, 79, 80
Finno-Ugric, languages, 17
Finnsburg Fragment, 28, 39, 77, 79, 85
Flavia Caesariensis, 51, 68
Florence of Worcester, 98, 136
foederati, 9, 12, 44, 55, 74, 142, 174
foedus, 9, 12, 44
Fonaby, 71
Fowler, P, 116
Franks, 12, 30, 41, 67, 96, 113
Fraomar, 45
Frealaf, 37, 39, 72
Freawaru, 11
Freawine of the Waernas, (see also Frowinus), 35, 36, 37, 39, 110
Frey, 24
Freya of the sagas, 24
Fridla, 12, 105, 106
Frisians, 12, 28, 30, 41, 44, 80, 81, 113
Frithela, 105
Frithuwold, 103
Frithuwulf, 37, 39, 81
Frowinus, 34, 35
Fullofaudes, 45
Fyn, 31, 73
Garulf, 79, 80
Gaul, 43, 46, 50, 51, 55, 77, 81, 85, 96, 173
Gaute/Gauti, 38, 39
Geat, 37, 38, 39, 40
Gefwulf, 80, 81

Gelling, M, 53, 127, 154, 166
Geoffrey of Monmouth, 67, 82, 83, 181
Gereint, 16, 157
Germani, 18, 21, 22, 23, 24, 27, 28, 44
Germania, 18, 21, 22, 23, 24, 25, 26, 27, 28, 29, 30, 31
Germanus of Auxerre, 50
Gesta Danorum, 34
Gesta regum Anglorum, 37
Gewisse, 39, 98, 101, 105, 106
Gifford, E&J, 58, 60
Gildas, 13, 51, 53, 73, 77, 78, 93, 98, 113, 117, 118, 121, 122, 161, 162, 173, 174, 175, 181
Gioti, 31
Giwis, 39, 106, 110
Gloucester, 13, 43, 114, 121, 132, 160
Gododdin, 15, 119, 142, 143, 170
Godwulf, 37, 39
Goodmanham, 148
Goscelin, 135, 136
Goths, 18, 33, 163
Gotland, 31
Grainthorpe, 69
Gratianus, 46
Great Chesterford, 45, 74
Gregory of Tours, 91
Gregory, Pope, 163, 177
Grendel, 11, 28, 79
grubenhäus - sunken-featured building, 9, 45
Guthhere, 79
Guthlaf, 79, 80
Guthulf, 80, 81
Gwallawg of Elmet, 140
Gwawrddur, 144
Gwen Ystrat, 143
Gwenhwyfar, 120
Gwiawn, son of Cyndrwyn, 145
Gwoloph, the battle, 53
Gwrgi and Peredur, 139, 161
Gwynedd, 12, 15, 117, 122, 140, 142, 148, 153, 155, 156, 160, 161, 163, 173
Gwyrangon, 82
Gyrwe, 14, 93, 125, 127
Hadrian's Wall, 44, 45, 120, 149
Hæstingas, 97, 125
Haithebi, 37
Harpstedt culture, 18

Harrison, K, 177, 179
Harrow, 65, 76
Harrow Pightle, 65
Hatfield Chase, 148, 153
Haywood, J, 58, 64
Heavenfield or Denisesburn, 15, 149,
    153, 160
Hecana, 14, 136
Hedeby, 37
Heledd, 154
Helmingas, 67
Hengest, 2, 28, 42, 44, 55, 77, 78, 79, 80,
    81, 82, 83, 84, 85, 90, 91, 101, 105,
    106, 114, 159, 163, 164, 179
Hengist, 31, 78
Henry of Huntingdon, 128
Heopwinesfleot, 78, 83
Heorot, 11
Heptarchy, 54
Herbert, K, 38
Hereford, 14, 133
Heremod, 37, 38
Hereric, 146
Hering, 145
Herminones, 21
Heruli, 31
Hibaldstow, 69
Hickes, G, 80
High Down, Sussex, 96, 97
Higham, N J, 117, 174
Hildeburgh / Hildeburh, 79, 80, 81
Historia Brittonum, 14, 31, 39, 53, 67, 73,
    77, 78, 81, 82, 83, 88, 90, 91, 93, 106,
    114, 118, 122, 139, 140, 143, 145, 148,
    149, 151, 155, 163, 166, 180, 181
Historia Ecclesiastica, 27, 78, 101, 163,
    175, 180
Historia Francorum, 91
Hnæf / Hnæf Half-Dane, 11, 28, 79, 80,
    81, 85
Holstein, 30, 31, 41, 55
Holyhead, 43
Honorius, 49, 119
Hooke, 53, 133
Horncastle, 68, 69, 72
Horningas, 125
Horsa, 77, 78, 82, 85, 90, 91, 101, 159,
    179
Housesteads, 44

Hrothgar, 11, 28, 67, 79
Hrothwyn / Rhonwen, 82, 85
Humber, 12, 13, 16, 42, 68, 69, 72, 155,
    159
Huns, 11, 12, 33, 41, 77
Hunwold, 152
Husmerae, 133
Hwala, 37, 38
Hwicce, 14, 54, 101, 133, 136, 153
Hwiccena, 136
Hygd, 28, 33
Icel, 91, 127, 129
Icknield Way, 14, 116, 118, 129
Iclingas, 91
Ida, 93, 139, 180
Iddawc, Agitator of Britain, 120
Idle, 15, 68, 145, 146
Ilchester, 115, 157
Illtyd, 122, 174
Indo-Europeans, 17
Ine of Wessex, 157
Ingævones, 21
Ingeld, 11
Ingoberga, 91
Ipswich, 60, 62
Isle of Wight, 98, 99, 101
Istævones, 21
Italy, 41, 45, 55, 106
Jackson, K, 115, 137, 143, 144
Japheth, 37
Jarman, 118, 143
Jastorf culture, 18
Jeremiah, 175
Jutes, 12, 16, 31, 41, 44, 54, 55, 77, 78,
    79, 80, 81, 82, 84, 85, 98, 99, 108, 117,
    118, 157, 159, 160, 163
Jutland, 12, 30, 31, 41, 57, 58, 85
Kenchester, 130, 133
Kent, 12, 13, 39, 43, 54, 55, 64, 67, 76,
    77, 78, 81, 82, 84, 85, 86, 87, 88, 89,
    90, 91, 92, 97, 99, 101, 103, 106, 107,
    110, 113, 114, 118, 125, 131, 148, 159,
    160, 166, 173, 175, 179
Keto, 34
Kirby, D P, 109
Kirmington, 69, 71
Koch, J, 143
Kurgan, 17

laeti, 10, 12, 13, 44, 45, 55, 69, 71, 72, 73, 74, 75, 104, 105, 107, 159, 167
Lambert, Michael, 143
Lament for Cynddylan, 153
Lancaster, 43
Langobardi / Lombards, 11, 29, 31, 35, 41
Laycock, S, 53
Leicester, 45, 68, 125
Leintwardine, 130
Lichfield, 129, 152
Liddington Castle, 14, 117, 160
Lilla, 147
Lincoln, 13, 45, 51, 68, 69, 71, 72, 83, 114, 115, 159
Lincoln Cliff or Edge, 68
Lincolnshire Wolds, 68
Lindenses, 115
Lindinienses, 115
Lindinis, 115
Lindisfarne, 51, 93, 129, 140, 143, 151, 152, 176
Lindiswara, 54
Lindsey, 13, 55, 68, 69, 71, 72, 93, 101, 103, 130, 148, 159, 160, 176
Linnuis, 114, 115
Litus Saxonicum, 10, 78, 99, 108
Llwyfenyd (Lyvennet in Cumbria, 142
Lombards / Langobardi, 11, 29, 31, 35, 41
London, 13, 45, 51, 62, 67, 68, 74, 75, 76, 77, 82, 89, 114, 118, 159, 185
Loughor, 43
Loveden Hill, 71
Lowbury Hill, 108
Lucius Artorius Castus, 119
Lyminge, 87, 88
Lympne, 42, 43, 88, 97
Maelgwyn / Maglocunus, 117, 121, 123, 140, 161, 173
Maelgwyn Fawr, (see also Maglocunus), 161
Maes Cogwy or Cocboy, (see Maserfelth), 151
Maethhild, (see also Magnhild), 38
Magana, 130, 133, 135, 136
Maglocunus / Maelgwyn, 117, 121, 122, 123, 140, 161, 173
Magnentius, 45

Magnhild, 39
Magnis (Kenchester), 133
Magnus Maximus, 45, 121, 161
Magonsætan / Magonsæte, 14, 15, 101, 130, 133, 135, 136, 137
Main, 29
Mainz, 44
Mälaren, 66
Malone, K, 38
Malton, 42, 45
Manau / Manaw, (see Gododdin), 15, 151
Marcus, 46
Marinus of Tyre, 20
Marius, 31
Marwnad Cynddylan, Welsh poem, 153, 154
Maserfeld, 151
Maserfelth, 15, 135, 136, 151, 152, 154
Maserfield, 151, 153
Matthew Paris, 128
Mearcrædesburna, 95, 96, 118
Medrawd, 120
Medway, 84, 86, 87, 89
Men of the North, 140, 142
Meonware, 54, 98
Mercia, 11, 15, 33, 54, 60, 72, 76, 77, 91, 97, 98, 101, 103, 125, 127, 128, 129, 130, 148, 151, 152, 153, 159, 160, 176, 177
Merewalh, 135, 136
Merlin, 139
Merovingians, 90
Meton, 109
Middle Saxon shuffle, 74
Middlesex, 13, 76, 103, 114
Mildburg, 135, 136
Milton Regis, 87
Modthryth, 33
Mons Badonicus or Badon Hill, 13, 98, 117
Morcant, 140
Mote of Mark, 66
Mucking, 74
Mynddog Mwynfaw, king of the Gododdin, 142, 143
Myrddin - Merlin, 139
Myres, 31, 45, 50, 105, 108, 117, 118, 130, 132, 166, 167, 186
Myrgings, 11, 28, 33, 34, 35, 36

Some of our other titles

Please see www.asbooks.co.uk for latest availability and prices

Plain English – A Wealth of Words
Bryan Evans

The message here is not that we should strive in a narrow-minded way to scorn and drive out all borrowed words – it is that, if we stop and think, we can probably find a plain English word for what we want to say. We will thus keep plain English alive and help it thrive. We have been given a great gift, let us wherever possible use it and keep it safe.

This wordbook outlines the story of English then it offers 'A hundred words to start you off' (*shorten* rather than *abbreviate, speed up* instead of *accelerate, drive home* rather than *emphasize*, and so on). In the main part of the book will be found over 10,000 English words that are still alive and well, then a list of some 3,600 borrowed words, with suggestions about English words we might use instead. It is hoped that this book will help readers think about the words they use, and in doing so speak and write more clearly.

£9.95   328 pages

The Life and Times of Hengest
Bryan Evans

Here is the tale of Hengest set against the end of Roman rule in Britain and the beginning of the Anglo-Saxon conquest. This is an excellent account of the Anglo-Saxon migration.

The book begins with an overview of the wider European stage. Then, events in Britain are looked at through the words of Gildas, Bede, the *Anglo-Saxon Chronicle* and *Historia Brittonum*. What information can be gleaned from them and how reliable are they? What impact have modern genetic studies had on our understanding of the age of migration? The main arguments concerning the extent of Anglo-Saxon migration are conveniently summarised.

Part two provides a cultural setting for Hengest and includes information about warcraft and beliefs. An account of early English poetry outlines of some of the tales that formed part of the matter of the poet: the tales of Offa of Angeln, Heoden and Hild, Welund, Waldere.

Part three includes the *Finnsburg Fragment*, the Anglo-Saxon poem that tells of Hengest. Using clues from this and other sources the author has wrought two 'Anglo-Saxon' poems, telling the tale of Hengest.

£14.95   black & white maps and drawings, 280 pages

First Steps in Old English
An easy to follow language course for the beginner
Stephen Pollington

A complete and easy to use Old English language course that contains all the exercises and texts needed to learn Old English. This course has been designed to be of help to a wide range of students, from those who are teaching themselves at home, to undergraduates who are learning Old English as part of their English degree course. The author has adopted a step-by-step approach that enables students of differing abilities to advance at their own pace. The course includes practice and translation exercises, a glossary of the words used in the course, and many Old English texts, including the *Battle of Brunanburh* and *Battle of Maldon*.

£16·95   272 pages

Old English Poems, Prose & Lessons   2 CDs
read by Stephen Pollington

These CDs contain lessons and texts from *First Steps in Old English*. They are also a useful companion to *Learn Old English with Leofwin*.

Tracks include: 1. Deor. 2. Beowulf – The Funeral of Scyld Scefing. 3. Engla Tocyme (The Arrival of the English). 4. Ines Domas. Two Extracts from the Laws of King Ine. 5. Deniga Hergung (The Danes' Harrying) Anglo-Saxon Chronicle Entry AD997. 6. Durham 7. The Ordeal (Be ðon ðe ordales weddigaþ) 8. Wið Dweorh (Against a Dwarf) 9. Wið Wennum (Against Wens) 10. Wið Wæterælfadle (Against Waterelf Sickness) 11. The Nine Herbs Charm 12. Læcedomas (Leechdoms) 13. Beowulf's Greeting 14. The Battle of Brunanburh 15. A Guide to Pronunciation.
And more than 30 other lessons and extracts of Old English verse and prose.

£12   2 CDs - Free Old English transcript from www.asbooks.co.uk.

Wordcraft: Concise English/Old English Dictionary and Thesaurus
Stephen Pollington

This book provides Old English equivalents to the commoner modern words in both dictionary and thesaurus formats. The Thesaurus presents vocabulary relevant to a wide range of individual topics in alphabetical lists, thus making it easily accessible to those with specific areas of interest. Each thematic listing is encoded for cross-reference from the Dictionary. The two sections will be of invaluable assistance to students of the language, as well as to those with either a general or a specific interest in the Anglo-Saxon period.

£9.95   256 pages

An Introduction to the Old English Language and its Literature
Stephen Pollington

The purpose of this general introduction to Old English is not to deal with the teaching of Old English but to dispel some misconceptions about the language and to give an outline of its structure and its literature. Some basic knowledge of these is essential to an understanding of the early period of English history and the present form of the language.

£5.95   48 pages

Learn Old English with Leofwin – part 1 - beginners
Matt Love

This is a new approach to learning old English – as a *living language*. Leofwin and his family are your guides through six lively, entertaining, topic-based units. New vocabulary and grammar are presented in context, step by step, so that younger readers and non-language specialists can feel engaged rather than intimidated. The author has complemented the text with a wealth of illustrations. There are listening, speaking, reading and writing exercises throughout. Free soundtracks are freely available on the Anglo-Saxon Books website.

£16.95 160 pages

Learn Old English with Leofwin – part 2 - improvers
Matt Love

This second part of the course resumes the good work of the first. It continues the story of Leofwin and his family and has the same approach to learning Old English and the same style of quirky illustrations drawn by the author. The words and drawings are evidence of Matt's great love of Old English and his gentle sense of humour, which shines through and helps make this a course like no other. As before, there are listening, speaking, reading and writing exercises throughout. The answers are freely available as soundtracks on the Anglo-Saxon Books website.

Matt was a modern language teacher and he has used that experience to make learning Old English as easy as possible. Instead of using heroic verse, and the like, he uses everyday language and an approach that is similar to childhood learning.

£16.95 208 pages

The Sword in Anglo-Saxon England
From the 5th to 7th century
Paul Mortimer & Matt Bunker editors and contributors

The contributors to this book bring their practical and academic knowledge to an exploration of new ideas and information about the making and use of swords in the early Anglo-Saxon period. They provide an insight to the symbolism of swords, their decoration and place in society. Other items carried and worn by warriors are similarly treated.

This is an extensive survey of writings about swords from the Early Middle Ages, together with discussions on the way swords may have been used and worn. There is a chapter about the language of the sword and runic associations. Several modern sword-smiths have provided knowledge gained from forging weapons. In addition to those who have contributed essays, there are many scholars, smiths, craftspeople, re-enactors and others who have added to the ideas, theories and discussions presented in this book.

Illustrations - 180 colour; 76 B&W. £45 480 pages

Runes: Literacy in the Germanic Iron Age
Stephen Pollington
The fuþark or runic alphabet has been studied for several centuries. Scholarly opinion about the origins and purposes of the writing ranges from the purely pragmatic to the highly symbolic, with a great deal of speculative fringe literature.

This new survey takes into account recent finds from Britain, Scandinavia and the Continent together with new interpretations of old finds. It investigates the reasons for the creation of the script. The culture which devised the runes must have been familiar with one or more existing alphabet. What combination of factors impelled the script's creation? How was it transmitted from generation to generation? Who used it, when and how? The author divides the thousand-year history from inception to widespread adoption into phases, each with its own characteristic usages. The study traces the runes' transition from 'hieratic' to 'demotic', from the secret of a closed social class to the common property of entire societies.

£35 428 pages

The Battle of Maldon: Text and Translation
Translated and edited by Bill Griffiths
The Battle of Maldon was fought between the men of Essex and the Vikings in AD 991. The action was captured in an Anglo-Saxon poem whose vividness and heroic spirit has fascinated readers and scholars for generations. *The Battle of Maldon* includes the source text; edited text; parallel literal translation; verse translation; a review of 103 books and articles.

This edition has a helpful guide to Old English verse.

£5.95   96 pages

Beowulf: Text and Translation
Translated by John Porter
The verse in which the story unfolds is, by common consent, the finest writing surviving in Old English, a text that all students of the language and many general readers will want to tackle in the original form. To aid understanding of the Old English, a literal word-by-word translation is printed opposite the edited text and provides a practical key to this Anglo-Saxon masterpiece.

£6.95   192 pages

An Introduction to Early English Law
Bill Griffiths
Much of Anglo-Saxon life followed a traditional pattern, of custom, and of dependence on kin-groups for land, support and security. The Viking incursions of the ninth century and the reconquest of the north that followed both disturbed this pattern and led to a new emphasis on centralized power and law, with royal and ecclesiastical officials prominent as arbitrators and settlers of disputes. The diversity and development of early English law is sampled here by selecting several law-codes to be read in translation - that of Æthelbert of Kent, being the first to be issued in England, Alfred the Great's, the most clearly thought-out of all, and short codes from the reigns of Edmund and Æthelred the Unready.

£5.95 96 pages

Tastes of Anglo-Saxon England

Mary Savelli

These easy to follow recipes will enable you to enjoy a mix of ingredients and flavours that were widely known in Anglo-Saxon England but are rarely experienced today. In addition to the 46 recipes, there is background information about households and cooking techniques.

£5.95   80 pages

Anglo-Saxon Runes

John. M. Kemble

Kemble's essay *On Anglo-Saxon Runes* first appeared in the journal *Archaeologia* for 1840; it draws on the work of Wilhelm Grimm, but breaks new ground for Anglo-Saxon studies in his survey of the Ruthwell Cross and the Cynewulf poems. It is an expression both of his own indomitable spirit and of the fascination and mystery of the Runes themselves, making one of the most attractive introductions to the topic. For this edition new notes have been supplied, which include translations of Latin and Old English material quoted in the text, to make this key work in the study of runes more accessible to the general reader.

£5.95   80 pages

Rudiments of Runelore

Stephen Pollington

This book provides both a comprehensive introduction for those coming to the subject for the first time, and a handy and inexpensive reference work for those with some knowledge of the subject. The *Abecedarium Nordmannicum* and the English, Norwegian and Icelandic rune poems are included in their original and translated form. Also included is work on the three Brandon runic inscriptions and the Norfolk 'Tiw' runes.

£5.95   88 pages

English Heroic Legends

Kathleen Herbert

The author has taken the skeletons of ancient Germanic legends about great kings, queens and heroes, and put flesh on them. Kathleen Herbert's extensive knowledge of the period is reflected in the wealth of detail she brings to these tales of adventure, passion, bloodshed and magic.

The book is in two parts. First are the stories that originate deep in the past, yet because they have not been hackneyed, they are still strange and enchanting. After that there is a selection of the source material, with information about where it can be found and some discussion about how it can be used.

£9-95   268 pages

Peace-Weavers and Shield-Maidens: Women in Early English Society
Kathleen Herbert

The recorded history of the English people did not start in 1066 as popularly believed but one-thousand years earlier. The Roman historian Cornelius Tacitus noted in *Germania*, published in the year 98, that the English (Latin *Anglii*), who lived in the southern part of the Jutland peninsula, were members of an alliance of Goddess-worshippers. The author has taken that as an appropriate opening to an account of the earliest Englishwomen, the part they played in the making of England, what they did in peace and war, the impressions they left in Britain and on the continent, how they were recorded in the chronicles, how they come alive in heroic verse and riddles.

£5.95 64 pages

Looking for the Lost Gods of England
Kathleen Herbert

Kathleen Herbert sifts through the royal genealogies, charms, verse and other sources to find clues to the names and attributes of the Gods and Goddesses of the early English. The earliest account of English heathen practices reveals that they worshipped the Earth Mother and called her Nerthus. The tales, beliefs and traditions of that time are still with us in, for example, Sand able to stir our minds and imaginations.

£5.95 64 pages

Anglo-Saxon FAQs
Stephen Pollington

125 questions and answers on a wide range of topics.
Are there any Anglo-Saxon jokes? Who was the Venerable Bede? Did the women wear make-up? What musical instruments did they have? How was food preserved? Did they have shops? Did their ships have sails? Why was Ethelred called 'Unready'? Did they have clocks? Did they celebrate Christmas? What are runes? What weapons and tactics did they use? Were there female warriors? What was the Synod of Whitby?

£9.95 128pages

Anglo-Saxon Tools
Dennis Riley

The tools used in Anglo-Saxon England where much like those found elsewhere in Europe at that time. Most are surprisingly like those in use today.
Many excavated tools are chunks of rust which provide little visual information, so the pictures used here are of reconstructions that draw on archaeological evidence. Some are accurate reproductions of specific tools and others are 'generic reproductions' in which the general style of the tool is captured. The author looks at the design and construction of the tools and their social importance.
The reconstructions show the tools as they may have originally looked. Because of their likeness to the originals, the reconstructions can be put to practical use and insights gained into their efficiency, durability and ease of use. This elevates the artefacts from rusty museum exhibits into functional tools that allow the user to experience the problems and pleasures of Anglo-Saxons craftsmen.
The tools included here were used for working with wood, leather, bone, horn, metals, pottery and textiles. They were used in farming, digging and building..

£16.95 80 colour & 5 black & white illustrations 160 pages

Dark Age Naval Power

A Reassessment of Frankish and Anglo-Saxon Seafaring Activity

John Haywood

In the first edition of this work, published in 1991, John Haywood argued that the capabilities of the pre-Viking Germanic seafarers had been greatly underestimated. Since that time, his reassessment of Frankish and Anglo-Saxon shipbuilding and seafaring has been widely praised and accepted.

In this second edition, some sections of the book have been revised and updated to include information gained from excavations and sea trials with sailing replicas of early ships. The new evidence supports the author's argument that early Germanic shipbuilding and seafaring skills were far more advanced than previously thought. It also supports the view that Viking ships and seaborne activities were not as revolutionary as is commonly believed.

> 'The book remains a historical study of the first order. It is required reading for our seminar on medieval seafaring at Texas A & M University and is essential reading for anyone interested in the subject.'
>
> F. H. Van Doorninck, *The American Neptune*

£16.95 hardback 224 pages

English Martial Arts

Terry Brown

Little is known about the very early history of English martial arts but it is likely that methods, techniques and principles were passed on from one generation to the next for centuries. By the sixteenth century English martial artists had their own governing body which controlled its members in much the same way as do modern-day martial arts organisations. It is apparent from contemporary evidence that the Company of Maisters taught and practised a fighting system that ranks as high in terms of effectiveness and pedigree as any in the world.

In the first part of the book the author investigates the weapons, history and development of the English fighting system and looks at some of the attitudes, beliefs and social pressures that helped mould it.

Part two deals with English fighting techniques drawn from books and manuscripts that recorded the system at various stages in its history. All of the methods and techniques shown in this book are authentic and have not been created by the author. The theories that underlie the system are explained in a chapter on *The Principles of True Fighting*. All of the techniques covered are illustrated with photographs and accompanied by instructions. Techniques included are for bare-fist fighting, broadsword, quarterstaff, bill, sword and buckler, sword and dagger.

Experienced martial artists, irrespective of the style they practice, will recognise that the techniques and methods of this system are based on principles that are as valid as those underlying the system that they practice.

£14.95 220 photos 240 pages

A Guide to Late Anglo-Saxon England
From Alfred to Eadgar II 871–1074
Donald Henson

This guide has been prepared with the aim of providing the general readers with both an overview of the period and a wealth of background information. Facts and figures are presented in a way that makes this a useful reference handbook.

Contents include: The Origins of England; Physical Geography; Human Geography; English Society; Government and Politics; The Church; Language and Literature; Personal Names; Effects of the Norman Conquest. All of the kings from Alfred to Eadgar II are dealt with separately and there is a chronicle of events for each of their reigns. There are also maps, family trees and extensive appendices.

£9.95   maps, 3 family trees, 208 pages

The English Elite in 1066 - Gone but not forgotten
Donald Henson

The people listed in this book formed the topmost section of the ruling elite in 1066. It includes all those who held office between the death of Eadward III (January 1066) and the abdication of Eadgar II (December 1066). There are 455 individuals in the main entries and these have been divided according to their office or position.

The following information is listed where available:

What is known of their life;

Their landed wealth;

The early sources in which information about the individual can be found

Modern references that give details about his or her life.

In addition to the biographical details, there is a wealth of background information about English society and government.

A series of appendices provide detailed information about particular topics or groups of people.

£14.95   272 pages

Tolkien's *Mythology for England*
A Guide to Middle-Earth
Edmund Wainwright

Tolkien set out to create a mythology for England and the English but the popularity of his books and the recent films has spread across the English-speaking world and beyond.

You will find here an outline of Tolkien's life and work. The main part of the book consists of an alphabetical subject entry which will help you gain a greater understanding of Tolkien's Middle-Earth, the creatures that inhabit it, and the languages they spoke. It will also give an insight into a culture and way-of-life that extolled values which are as valid today as they were over 1,000 years ago.

This book focuses on *The Lord of the Rings* and shows how Tolkien's knowledge of Anglo-Saxon and Norse literature and history helped shape its plot and characters.

£9-95 hardback 128 pages

The Origins of the Anglo-Saxons
Donald Henson
This book has three great strengths.

First, it pulls together and summarises the whole range of evidence bearing on the subject, offering an up-to-date assessment: the book is, in other words, a highly efficient introduction to the subject. Second – perhaps reflecting Henson's position as a leading practitioner of public archaeology (he is currently Education and Outreach Co-ordinator for the Council for British Archaeology) – the book is refreshingly jargon free and accessible. Third, Henson is not afraid to offer strong, controversial interpretations. The Origins of the Anglo-Saxons can therefore be strongly recommended to those who want a detailed road-map of the evidence and debates for the migration period.

Current Archaeology

£14.95 296 pages

The Elder Gods – The Otherworld of Early England
Stephen Pollington
The purpose of the work is to bring together a range of evidence for pre-Christian beliefs and attitudes to the Otherworld drawn from archaeology, linguistics, literary studies and comparative mythology. The rich and varied English tradition influenced the worldview of the later mediaeval and Norse societies. Aspects of this tradition are with us still in the 21st century.

£29   70 illustrations 528 pages

Anglo-Saxon Riddles
Translated by John Porter
Here you will find ingenious characters who speak their names in riddles, and meet a one-eyed garlic seller, a bookworm, an iceberg, an oyster, the sun and moon and a host of others from the everyday life and imagination of the Anglo-Saxons. Their sense of the awesome power of creation goes hand in hand with a frank delight in obscenity, a fascination with disguise and with the mysterious processes by which the natural world is turned to human use.   This edition contains **all 95 riddles of the Exeter Book in both Old English and Modern English.**

£5.95 144 page

English Sea Power 871-1100 AD
John Pullen-Appleby
This work examines the largely untold story of English sea power during the period 871 to 1100. It was an age when English kings deployed warships first against Scandinavian invaders and later in support of Continental allies.

The author has gathered together information about the appearance of warships and how they were financed, crewed, and deployed.

£9.95 hardback 114 pages

Anglo-Saxon Burial Mounds
Princely Burials in the 6th & 7th centuries
Stephen Pollington

This is the first book-length treatment of Anglo-Saxon Barrows in English. It brings together some of the evidence from Sutton Hoo and elsewhere in England for these magnificent burials and sets them in their historical, religious and social context.

The first section comprises the physical construction and symbolic meaning of these monuments. The second offers a comprehensive listing of known Anglo-Saxon barrows with notes on their contents and the circumstances of their
discovery. The five appendices deal with literary and place-name evidence.

£18.95   272 pages

Leechcraft: Early English Charms, Plantlore and Healing
Stephen Pollington

An unequalled examination of every aspect of early English healing, including the use of plants, amulets, charms, and prayer. Other topics covered include Anglo-Saxon witchcraft; tree-lore; gods, elves and dwarves.

The author has brought together a wide range of evidence for the English healing tradition, and presented it in a clear and readable manner. The extensive 2,000-entry index makes it possible for the reader to quickly find specific information.

The three key Old English texts are reproduced in full, accompanied by new translations.

Bald's Third Leechbook; *Lacnunga*; *Old English Herbarium*.

£25   28 illustrations   536 pages

Anglo-Saxon Attitudes – A short introduction to Anglo-Saxonism
J.A. Hilton

This is not a book about the Anglo-Saxons, but a book about books about Anglo-Saxons. It describes the academic discipline of Anglo-Saxonism; the methods of study used; the underlying assumptions; and the uses to which it has been put.

Methods and motives have changed over time but right from the start there have been constant themes: English patriotism and English freedom.

£5.95   hardback   64 pages

The Rebirth of England and English: The Vision of William Barnes
Fr. Andrew Phillips

English history is patterned with spirits so bright that they broke through convention and saw another England. Such was the case of the Dorset poet, William Barnes (1801–86), priest, poet, teacher, self-taught polymath, linguist extraordinary and that rare thing – a man of vision. In this work the author looks at that vision, a vision at once of Religion, Nature, Art, Marriage, Society, Economics, Politics and Language. He writes: 'In search of authentic English roots and values, our post-industrial society may well have much to learn from Barnes'.

£9.95   160 pages

Monasteriales Indicia
The Anglo-Saxon Monastic Sign Language
Edited with notes and translation by Debby Banham

The *Monasteriales Indicia* is one of very few texts which let us see how evryday life was lived in monasteries in the early Middle Ages. Written in Old English and preserved in a manuscript of the mid-eleventh century, it consists of 127 signs used by Anglo-Saxon monks during the times when the Benedictine Rule forbade them to speak. These indicate the foods the monks ate, the clothes they wore, and the books they used in church and chapter, as well as the tools they used in their daily life, and persons they might meet both in the monastery and outside. The text is printed here with a parallel translation. The introduction gives a summary of the background, both historical and textual, as well as a brief look at the later evidence for monastic sign language in England.

£5.95   96 pages

Anglo-Saxon Food & Drink
Production, Processing, Distribution, and Consumption
Ann Hagen

Food production for home consumption was the basis of economic activity throughout the Anglo-Saxon period. Used as payment and a medium of trade, food was the basis of the Anglo-Saxons' system of finance and administration.

Information from various sources has been brought together in order to build up a picture of how food was grown, conserved, distributed, prepared and eaten during the period from the beginning of the 5th century to the 11th century. Many people will find it fascinating for the views it gives of an important aspect of Anglo-Saxon life and culture. In addition to Anglo-Saxon England the Celtic west of Britain is also covered.

This edition combines earlier titles – *A Handbook of Anglo-Saxon Food* and *A Second Handbook of Anglo-Saxon Food & Drink*.

Extensive index.

£25   512 pages

The Cædmon Poems
A Verse Translation of Anglo-Saxon Christian Poetry
Damian Love

Cædmon lived in the 7th century and retold parts of the Old Testament in English. Over the next four hundred years a series of anonymous poets followed in his footsteps. Their poems have collectively become known as the Cædmon poems, which the author has skilfully rendered into Modern English.

High among their achievements are the works of those who followed Cædmon's example and rewrote the stories of the Old Testament for their own time, combining Germanic tradition with the Christianity of the Mediterranean world to create vivid new renditions of the great bible narratives. In Exodus, Genesis B, and Judith they produce masterpieces that rank beside Beowulf as monuments of their era.

This book is the first to represent the Old Testament genre comprehensively in modern English verse translation, making it available to students and non-specialist readers in a form that captures much of the vigour and rhythmic texture of the original poems.

There is an extensive Introduction and Explanatory Notes.

£9.95   A5   304 pages

Organisations

Þa Engliscan Gesiðas (The English Companions)

Þa Engliscan Gesiðas is a historical and cultural society exclusively devoted to Anglo-Saxon history. The Fellowship publishes a quarterly journal, *Wiðowinde,* and has a website with regularly updated information and discussions. Local groups arrange their own meetings and attend lectures, exhibitions and events. Members are able to share their interest with like-minded people and learn more about the origins and growth of English culture, including language, literature, archaeology, anthropology, architecture, art, religion, mythology, folklore and material culture.

For further details see www.tha-engliscan-gesithas.org.uk

Regia Anglorum

Regia Anglorum is an active group of enthusiasts who attempt to portray as accurately as possible the life and times of the people who lived in the British Isles around a thousand years ago. We investigate a wide range of crafts and have a Living History Exhibit that frequently erects some thirty tented period structures.

We have a thriving membership and 40 branches in the British Isles and United States - so there might be one near you. We especially welcome families with children.

www.regia.org

The Sutton Hoo Society

Our aims and objectives focus on promoting research and education relating to the Anglo Saxon Royal cemetery at Sutton Hoo, Suffolk in the UK. The Society publishes a newsletter SAXON twice a year, which keeps members up to date with society activities, carries resumes of lectures and visits, and reports progress on research and publication associated with the site. If you would like to join the Society please see website: www.suttonhoo.org

Wuffing Education

Wuffing Education provides those interested in the history, archaeology, literature and culture of the Anglo-Saxons with the chance to meet experts and fellow enthusiasts for a whole day of in-depth seminars and discussions. Day Schools take place at the historic Tranmer House overlooking the burial mounds of Sutton Hoo in Suffolk.

For details see – www.wuffingeducation.co.uk & www.wuffings.co.uk

Places to visit

Bede's World at Jarrow

Bede's world tells the remarkable story of the life and times of the Venerable Bede, 673–735 AD. Visitors can explore the origins of early medieval Northumbria and Bede's life and achievements through his own writings and the excavations of the monasteries at Jarrow and other sites.

Location – 10 miles from Newcastle upon Tyne, off the A19 near the southern entrance to the River Tyne tunnel. Bus services 526 & 527

Bede's World, Church Bank, Jarrow, Tyne and Wear, NE32 3DY

www.bedesworld.co.uk

Sutton Hoo near Woodbridge, Suffolk, IP12 3DJ

Sutton Hoo is a group of low burial mounds overlooking the River Deben in south-east Suffolk. Excavations in 1939 brought to light the richest burial ever discovered in Britain – an Anglo-Saxon ship containing a magnificent treasure which has become one of the principal attractions of the British Museum. The mound from which the treasure was dug is thought to be the grave of Rædwald, an early English king who died in 624/5 AD.

This National Trust site has an excellent visitor centre, which includes a reconstruction of the burial chamber and its grave goods. Some original objects as well as replicas of the treasure are on display.

2 miles east of Woodbridge on B1083   Tel. 01394 389700

West Stow Anglo-Saxon Village

An early Anglo-Saxon Settlement reconstructed on the site where it was excavated consisting of timber and thatch hall, houses and workshop. There is also a museum containing objects found during the excavation of the site. Open all year 10am (except Christmas) Last entrance summer 4pm; winter 3-30pm. Special provision for school parties. A teachers' resource pack is available. Costumed events are held on some weekends, especially Easter Sunday and August Bank Holiday Monday. Craft courses are organised.

For further details see www.weststow.org or contact:

The Visitor Centre, West Stow Country Park, Icklingham Road, West Stow,
Bury St Edmunds, Suffolk IP28 6HG   Tel. 01284 728718

Lightning Source UK Ltd.
Milton Keynes UK
UKHW032044090822
407057UK00005B/138